MW00635676

God Bless You Joe Stalin

God Bless You Joe Stalin:

The Man Who Saved Capitalism

Lewis E. Kaplan

Algora Publishing
New York

www.algora.com

ISBN: 0-87586-464-3 (softcover)
ISBN: 0-87586-465-1 (hardcover)
ISBN: 0-87586-466-X (ebook)

Library of Congress Cataloging-in-Publication Data —

Kaplan, Lewis E.
God bless you Joe Stalin: the man who saved capitalism / by Lewis E. Kaplan.
p. cm.
Includes bibliographical references and index.
ISBN 0-87586-465-1 (hardcover: alk. paper)—ISBN 0-87586-464-3 (trade paper: alk. paper)—ISBN 0-87586-466-X (ebook)
1. Cold War. 2. Stalin, Joseph, 1879-1953. 3. Capitalism—United States. I. Title.
D843.K336 2006
940.55—dc22

2006010962

Front Cover: Yalta 60th Anniversary: Grandsons of Stalin, Roosevelt and Churchill. —Jevgeni Dzjoegasjvili,Curtis Roosevelt and Winston Churchill, the grandsons of World War II leaders Stalin, Roosevelt and Churchill meet in Maastricht, Netherlands, for a conference to commemorate the Yalta agreement signed by their grandfathers 60 years ago as a foundation mark for modern Europe.
Image: © Olaf Kraak/epa/Corbis
Photographer: Olaf Kraak Date Photographed: October 1, 2005
Location Information: Maastricht, Netherlands

Printed in the United States

To my wife Carolyn, without whose insights and scrupulous editing this book would not have been possible.

Table of Contents

Introduction

At the turn of the twentieth century, capitalism produced its first miracle, the billion-dollar corporation, United States Steel. Thanks to the efforts of the American banker, J. P. Morgan, and the necessary support of Andrew Carnegie, the steel magnate, America now stood as the foremost capitalist nation in the world. United States Steel's volume represented more capital than the total deficit of the United States government in 1900. A little more than 100 years later, $1 billion is a mere bagatelle. Bill Gates, one of the founders of Microsoft, remains Number One, with a net worth of close to $50 billion. However, there are more than 300 US billionaires today, representing a combined net worth of $1 trillion, according to *Forbes* magazine. As for millionaires, the research firm of TNS estimates that more than eight million households have a net worth of more than $1 million, excluding the value of private residences. And, these statistics refer only to the US. When you add to these figures the personal wealth of Western Europeans, the incredible fortunes amassed by the oil-rich sheiks along the Persian Gulf, and the holdings of the Russian oligarchs who benefited from the "privatization" of the assets of the Soviet Union, the total amount is staggering. Whence came all this wealth, amounting to tens of trillions of dollars? Did some new genie appear with a different version of Aladdin's lamp? Or, strange as it might seem, could the efforts of one man, inadvertently, have produced this unbelievable largesse?

For those who might assume that the title chosen for this book, *God Bless You Joe Stalin*, was meant to be ironic, sarcastic, satiric, or just clever and eye-catching, be disabused. This work deals with the man who altered forever the shape and form of capitalism, which in turn led to the greatest prosperity this country and the rest of the world has ever experienced.

To accept this premise would seem to defy collective wisdom. But, then again, collective wisdom only stands up until it has been knocked down. History, after all, is a series of events, some serendipitous, others less so, which scholars subsequently attempt to place in some sort of logical order, to better understand what actually occurred. Tracing the course of past events is no problem, once the historian has access to the physical data. It is in the interpretation of this raw material where historians often err. Finally, objectivity is generally lost because it is the victor who puts down his sword and takes up the pen.

Today, Joseph Stalin is depicted as a dictator who ruled the Soviet Union with an iron fist in order to achieve his objective — a Socialist state under the total control of, or at least in the interests of, the proletariat. In reality, this was an effort by a ruling clique, led by Stalin, to create a new society, in which the phrase "economic justice" would supersede in importance that of the conventional Western concept of morality.

That is the fundamental tenet of Marxism. In place of the few enjoying the fruits of labor of the many, there would be an equitable distribution of the nation's wealth. It was an effort by Karl Marx and others to highjack the European Romantic Movement of the late eighteenth and early nineteenth centuries and endow it with a philosophical base. It was the battle cry of the French Revolution, with its *liberté, égalité, fraternité*, now dressed up in German determinist philosophy. It was sufficiently romantic and absurd to appeal to a small segment of the intelligentsia who immediately embraced Marx's messianic call for social and economic justice. It terrified some of the bourgeoisie because this modern Old Testament prophet predicted the inevitability of such a shift.

This is not a book about Marx, who even today, in some academic circles, is considered to be one of the most important savants of modern times. But this book does attempt to deal with Stalin, the man, and his views on the Soviet Union and the capitalistic world that surrounded his experiment with a state Socialist society. The text makes no effort to criticize or justify his actions, but does attempt to place his actions in some perspective. By viewing Stalin in this fashion, it is possible to understand that even after his death more than a half century ago, his indelible mark on today's civilization is such that all of us are beholden to him. Through his effort to lead the children of Russia into the Promised Land, he set in motion forces that affected every nation on this globe. Unlike Marx, who was nothing more than a theoretician, viewing the world simplistically, Stalin was a hands-on pragmatist. He created something that had never existed before — a viable Socialist state.

Where Marx preached that the rise to political power of the proletariat was historically inevitable, Stalin understood that only force could produce the desired results. This brutally honest and cynical view was perceived by the outside world as unwarranted barbarism. From Stalin's point of view, it was a necessity if a Socialist economy was to be successful. He had neither the time nor the patience to wait for the proletariat's consciousness of their destiny to emerge. As he would remark to the writer, John Gunther, "A million deaths is a statistic; a single death a tragedy."

To his critics in the West, and to those who managed to survive the Soviet system he established, he was both immoral and amoral at the same time. They could not comprehend that his goal was to create a new breed of selfless men and women who gradually would learn to subordinate their own desires and egos to the greater good of society in general. This is what Marx had outlined in his writings, and what Stalin was determined to implement.

He saw himself, following Lenin's death, as the only remaining Bolshevik capable of bringing order out of chaos. The Russian empire, which the Bolsheviks now controlled, encompassed many diverse peoples, cultures, religions, languages and customs. He believed that only he, who had studied the problems that this diversity presented, would be capable of addressing the enormously complicated situation. If the great experiment of creating a Socialist state out of the residue of a corrupt and venal tsarist regime was to succeed, then the first problem that had to be addressed was incorporating these disparate nationalities into a greater Russia, while still allowing them to maintain elements of their national identity. Unlike Lenin or Trotsky, Stalin was a native Georgian and understood the centrifugal forces that could destroy the Soviet Union before it had established a firm and solid base.

Great men do not wait for power to be served to them on a silver platter. Make no mistake, when history is written a hundred years from today, Stalin will be considered the most influential man of the twentieth century. At the present time, when a Socialist state has been confined to the dustbins of history, Stalin is measured mostly by the excesses of his cruelty towards the citizens of the USSR and its satellite states. His achievements are buried in lost history: over a period of just 15 years, starting almost from square one, a major industrial state would be created; free education would reach even the remotest parts of the vast country; universal health care would become available for all of its citizens; access to advanced education would be based on a merit system; every person capable of working would be given employment. In a mere decade and a half, the most backward country in Europe would take on the trappings of becoming a modern state. The Moscow subway, opened in 1936, was the most modern in the world. Dams and hydroelectric power plants would bring electricity to millions. To accomplish such a Herculean task in a brief period of time required intense discipline. Those who rebelled against the system were quashed. As he would say, "You don't make a revolution with silk gloves." Thus occurred the death of millions of *kulaks* in the Ukraine who fought the government when it set out to "collectivize" their private farms. Under a Soviet state, all power resided in the government. Marx, in his romantic take on socialism, would refer to the ruling class as the dictatorship of the proletariat. In the Soviet Union, it was Stalin and those who managed to survive his purges.

That is the Achilles heel of any revered or feared leader. As long as he is alive, his power is so absolute that he can alter his stance without coming under question. On the negative side, by not tolerating any opposition to his policies, when he passes from the scene he leaves a vacuum that is impossible to fill. By crushing all and any opposition to his reign, Stalin left only followers, not leaders, incapable of any independent thinking. The Politburo had been a one-man show.

It is difficult for the Western mind to understand his legacy. He was not a man but a man-God. Literally out of nothing he had forged the creation of a modern state. He had accomplished it through the use of terror and fear. Through the force of his leadership, the Soviet Union emerged from the Second World War as the second leading power in the world. In the Politburo, every step taken by his successors was measured against what Stalin would have done under similar circumstances. He was a living ghost. Khrushchev was dismissed from power by the members of the Politburo because they believed he had practiced adventurism in challenging the United States during the Cuban missile crisis. It mattered little to them that the United States had been forced to withdraw its missiles from Turkey as part of the *quid pro quo*. Stalin never had challenged the United States directly in its own hemisphere; Stalin always used surrogates when he wished to confront the American colossus. The approach to the Cold War that Stalin had initiated was frozen in a time capsule of the early 1950s. Unlike China's Deng Xiaoping, who recognized the limitations of a Socialist economy, Stalin's successors stayed the course until the regime disappeared.

The adage *the enemy of my enemy is my friend* explains the unholy alliance of the Soviet Union, the United States and Britain that took place during the Second World War. For the moment, it was time to put ideology aside. In those dark days of 1943 when the fate of Europe seemed to hang on the success or failure of the Soviet army to halt the seemingly unbeatable German army, the image of Stalin as a ruthless dictator was put in the closet. Hollywood and the press took on the task of his rehabilitation. Overnight, he became good old Uncle Joe, with an ever-present pipe in his mouth, a defender of freedom and democracy. Stalin must have been amused by such a description. He was well aware that prior to the Nazi invasion of the Soviet Union, his portrait in the West was hung side by side with that of Adolf Hitler.

Following the signing of the Nazi-Soviet peace pact and the combined invasion and partition of Poland in 1939, Winston Churchill would tell his radio audience that he could not describe Russia, saying, "It is a riddle wrapped in a mystery inside an enigma." Churchill was a brilliant wordsmith, but despite that catchy phrase of his there was nothing mysterious about the Soviet Union. It was the only Socialist nation in the world. It had abolished private property and, worse yet, reneged on all the debts that the tsarist regime had contracted. At the time of the Munich crisis, it had been excluded from the *pourparler* that sold Czechoslovakia down the river. It was Hitler, afraid of a two-front war as in 1914, who had initiated the Soviet-German non-aggression pact in 1939. Stalin had accepted it because he felt the Soviet Union required time to re-arm before the Nazi war machine unleashed its forces on Russia. Of course, neither Stalin nor Churchill had expected that the French army would collapse after just six weeks of war.

Hypocrisy is as old as mankind. At Yalta, President Franklin Roosevelt, British Prime Minister Churchill and Stalin would drink toasts to everlasting friendship. The three men then would assent to the creation of a United Nations, and within it, a Security Council of the five leading powers that would be responsible for maintaining the peace of the world. Having agreed to such a formidable formula, the Big Three had their glasses refilled so as to toast one another again. Next on the agenda was the status of Germany and Austria, once there was an unconditional surrender on the part of Germany. While agreeing on a joint four-power occupation of their common enemy, Germany, Free French divisions now having joined the American and British effort, the actual zones of occupation would be determined by the territory occupied by the Allied and Soviet armies. This was a setback for the Soviet Union, since the center of German heavy industry lay within the zones that would be occupied by Allied troops. The one commitment Roosevelt was given by Stalin was that once the war in Europe was over, the Soviet Union would declare war on Japan and invade Japanese-held Manchuria. In recompense for this act of fealty to the wartime alliance, Roosevelt agreed that the Soviet Union could annex the Kuril Islands and Sakhalin to the Soviet eastern empire. Russian blood would not be spilled in vain. Whether this called for another toast on the part of the three heads of state was not recorded. Left in abeyance was the final disposition of Polish territory, now occupied by Soviet troops. While Roosevelt and Churchill attempted to get a commitment from Stalin on free Polish elections, Stalin kept stalling. In February 1945, the military situation in Europe was still fluid. It would remain so until Hitler's suicide in his Berlin bunker, and the agreement by the German generals to an unconditional surrender.

Stalin never had any intention of allowing free elections in Poland. He was well aware of the animosity of the Polish people towards Russia, which dated back centuries, not to mention the bitterness caused by the more recent occupation of eastern Poland following the Nazi-Soviet invasions of 1939. Under free elections the pre-war Polish government, exiled in Britain, would easily defeat any Communist candidate that the Soviet Union would back. More important to Stalin, and unbeknownst to his two newly acquired friends, he was well aware that the United States was close to developing an atomic bomb. Soviet agents had penetrated Los Alamos, New Mexico, where the bomb was being assembled, and were sending reports back to the Kremlin. He also knew that Roosevelt and Churchill had deliberately withheld this information from him.

There could be only one reason. They hoped to prevent Russia from getting a head-start in producing a comparable weapon.

So Uncle Joe sat there, somewhat bemused by these two members of their respective upper class establishments, expatiating on the importance of freedom and democracy in all of these newly liberated nations. There was Churchill, who remarked early on during the war: "I did not become the King's First Minister in order to preside over the liquidation of his empire." And there was the United States, finally liberating the Philippines after almost a half-century of exploitation and defending dictators in Central and South American countries to protect US corporate interests. To Stalin, their language was hollow and meaningless. Prior to the outbreak of the war, freedom and democracy in Poland had been nonexistent. The same applied to the other Eastern European nations, all of which had allied their regimes with Hitler's Germany.

History is replete with ironies but none quite equals that which followed in the wake of Stalin's death. In his effort to extend the Soviet system into Western Europe, he would set in motion fundamental and drastic changes never before envisioned by capitalism. Each time Stalin acted in order to achieve his goal, the United States would react. Today, these initial actions and reactions are referred to as the start of the Cold War. That is the way the course of events is related in US history books. The Soviet Union was the provocateur, and the United States, a naïve and innocent victim. In fact, it was America's visceral opposition to any possible rival, Communist or otherwise, that set in motion the steps that led to the Cold War. Anyway, as far as the United States was concerned, it wasn't always *cold*. During the Korean conflict, approximately 33,000 Americans would die; in Vietnam, which lasted longer, about 58,000 Americans would be killed. Even more bizarre is the fact that the United State never was officially at war with either country. Such was the nature of the Cold War. The United States found itself fighting a shadow, the specter of communism. The nation and its political leaders became so obsessed with the subject that at times it seemed to border on hysteria.

This was Stalin's legacy to the West. In the minds of the West, he had initiated this conflict between the United States and the Soviet Union. But he framed it in such a fashion that both countries remained on similar treadmills from which there was no escape until the Soviet Union collapsed. It was as though he had written the scenario for the next half century, and succeeding governments in both the US and Russia played out the parts he had assigned to them. In early January 1946, six months after Japan had surrendered, in a major address to the Central Committee of the Communist party Stalin informed its broad membership that over the next years the Soviet Union would have to tighten its economic belt in order to be prepared for a forthcoming war with the United States.

In making such an ominous pronouncement to an audience that had yet to recover from four years of the bloodiest warfare that had ever taken place in human history, Stalin was reading from the Gospels according to Marx. Stalin's reasoning proceeded as follows. With the entire non-Communist world in a state of near bankruptcy, the capitalist American economy would have no markets that it could exploit. Since waging the war had preempted the production of civilian goods, in the first four post-war years the US economy would be successful in filling up the empty pipelines on the domestic front. However, once the empty shelves were filled, as had happened prior to the Great Depression, its only salvation would be military aggression. Therefore, the Soviet Union had to be ready to meet such a challenge. Instead of much needed civilian goods, the Soviet people would have to make do until such time as the Soviet state was militarily strong enough to thwart any designs by the United States. In other words, the economy of the Soviet Union would have to remain on a wartime footing to insure against, or prevent, any adventurism on the part of the United States. The top priority for the Soviet Union was the development of an atomic bomb in order to have military parity with the US. Following Stalin's death, and for the next 40-odd years, his successors adhered to that line. It was only when President Ronald Reagan, despite all the advice from the intellectual nay-sayers, launched his Strategic Defense Initiative, mocked as Star Wars, that the Soviet Union finally found itself in a position where it could no longer afford to maintain military parity with the United States without the economy collapsing. The result was the attempted coup against Gorbachev, which failed, and the installation of Yeltsin to attempt to pick up the pieces.

If Stalin seemed to be suffering from paranoia with regard to America's future intentions, it was not without good reason. Thanks to Stalin's faulty judgment, Lenin's great dream of a vibrant, Communist nation had come within a hairsbreadth of being obliterated. It was one thing for Stalin to dismiss Churchill's warning of an imminent German invasion — Churchill had a vested interest in provoking a war between

Germany and the Soviet Union. But it was quite another thing for Stalin to reject the same alert from his own spy in Tokyo, Richard Sorge. The result was a catastrophe beyond belief. Two-thirds of the Soviet Air Force was destroyed on the ground; none of the Soviet armed divisions were on alert, so they were totally unprepared for the onslaught. Most of the industrialized economy, which the Soviet Union had taken 15 years to build, was destroyed in the early days of the war. Stalin wasn't suffering from paranoia in 1946; he was fixated on how close the Soviet Union had come to losing the war.

Was the Cold War inevitable, as Stalin had prognosticated in early 1946? In a certain sense, it was. The two major military powers left standing, the USSR and the USA, viewed the post-war world through different lenses. The wartime alliance had been nothing more than a marriage of convenience as far as both sides were concerned. The acceptance of the Charter of the United Nations, with each member on the Security Council having the power of the veto, was but another example of this feigned romance. Above all, Stalin had no illusions. Capitalist nations were intrinsically hostile to the concept of socialism for a number of reasons. First and foremost, its economic structure represented an alternative to capitalism. During the Great Depression, prior to the outbreak of the Second World War, when there was massive unemployment in the leading capitalist nations, in the Soviet Union there was full employment. The second reason was Stalin's religious belief that a Socialist state was inevitable for every capitalist nation. Ergo, the leaders within the capitalist nations would fight to defend their own vested interests in their system. Stalin hypothesized that as the internal wealth of the USSR continued to grow, the disparity between the living conditions in its socialistic society, and those in capitalistic societies, would be diminished and serve only to accentuate the threat that socialism posed to capitalist exploitation.

On the other side of the coin, the United States viewed the expansion of communism as a threat to its own economic security. Each nation that came under the orbit of communism no longer was a potential customer for US exports. For capitalism to succeed, it depended upon continuous growth. This fact became apparent during the Depression when the United States and other capitalist nations employed high discriminatory tariffs to protect their own industries. The Bretton Woods agreements, devised to break down trade barriers by having the dollar replace gold as the means of exchange, had never been implemented by the Soviet Union and its satellite states. Should communism spread further into Western Europe, that movement would narrow further the potential for US-made merchandise. The American post-war policy of containment was concerned less with political liberties than with economic opportunities for US business.

Until October 4, 1957, the United States, with its large arsenal of atomic weapons, and the planes capable of delivering them, felt reasonably secure behind its air defenses. But on that day, when the first Sputnik roared into space, and began circling the earth every 98 minutes, the United States knew it now was vulnerable. To scientists, Sputnik ushered in the Space Age; to the military and defense experts, Sputnik opened the door to their worst fears, the inter-continental ballistic missile. In the closing years of the Second World War, Hitler had launched V-1 and V-2 rockets against Great Britain. These were relatively primitive, and while they could not be directed against specific targets and often failed to explode, when they did, they terrified the civilian population. The worst aspect of these German rockets was that there was no defense against them. Now with Sputnik, the potential existed for rockets armed with atomic war heads to cross oceans and drop their payload on unsuspecting targets. The vast oceans, which had once protected the United States, now had become the size of a bathtub. Naturally the converse applied. Moscow and Leningrad were as open to destruction as New York and Washington.

The result was an arms race between these two nations that defied all logic. As each nation developed a potentially more sophisticated weapon to deliver death and destruction, the other would do the same. Even though it was obvious that both sides had reached overkill early on, nothing could deter them. In the United States, innovations in military technology would find their way into the civilian economy; in the Soviet Union, where each facet of the national economy was compartmentalized, there was little chance of innovation being transferred to usage in the civilian sector. Except for defense, the general Soviet economy remained static throughout the period of the Cold War. Little wonder then that when Vladimir Putin succeeded Yeltsin as President of Russia, he announced that the Russian economy was no better than that of a Third World country.

And finally, America possessed a lethal weapon unavailable to the Soviet Union, the Almighty Dollar. Thanks to Bretton Woods, the dollar was used as the official currency for the exchange of commerce throughout the world. All other currencies would be measured against it. The value of the dollar could go up or down with respect to other national currencies, but it remained the accepted standard of monetary exchange. Given this unique role in world commerce, the quantity of dollars either in actual circulation or on deposit is inestimable. This has enabled the United States to run up huge deficits with its trading partners while at the same time they support the interest payments on a national deficit that has exceeded $8 trillion. It is because of this unique situation that over the years the US has been able to appropriate huge sums for its defense, while at the same time its citizens have enjoyed the highest standard of living in the world.

When the Soviet Union divided itself into separate nations, the international debt load accumulated over decades placed Russia, the largest of those nation-states, in a desperate financial position. The failure of its gross domestic product to grow over the preceding years left its currency, the ruble, in a precarious position. Now, when it was attempting to make the transition to a capitalist economy, it had to play by the same rules accorded to other capitalist nations. It had to service its debt with a currency whose value would be pegged to the dollar. There is an old German adage that states: *Geld Macht die Welt*. The Soviet Union had waged the Cold War at a terrible disadvantage. Because of its closed and isolated economy, it lacked the financial resources to deliver the proverbial guns and butter. Unlike the Almighty Dollar, which could be stretched to meet any contingency, the value of the ruble only contracted over the half century of the Cold War. The old German adage is right. Money does make the world go round.

Chapter 1. Evolution of the Almighty Dollar

"Every day I get down on my knees and thank God for the Almighty Dollar in my pocketbook.." — My late mother.

Pity the poor dollar. It has been washed, stretched, shrunk, devalued, revalued, counterfeited, challenged by the euro, and never really supplanted King Midas's gold, in the eyes of many. Yet, despite more than 60 years of wear and tear, and losing more than 90% of its original pegged value, it still remains the standard currency against which all other currencies are measured. The prices of the world's commodities, from barrels of oil to pork bellies, are quoted in dollars; the largest stock exchange in the world trades only in dollars; it is the coin of the realm for drug lords and armament dealers; it still is the official currency of the Mafia; it was worshipped by Russian Communists as well as by today's capitalists; it has remained the symbol of everything that's considered good and bad about the United States, because it is as almighty as America.

Those who perceive economics as a dismal science are not far from the truth. In order to keep economists plugging away, every year a Nobel Prize is awarded to one or more of them as compensation for their frustration. Charts and tables of figures are amassed by governments, revealing economic patterns of the past, but there is no possibility of projecting the future course of a nation's economy with certainty. A prime example was the prediction of the economists at the Congressional Budget Office, made in early 2000, projecting a 10-year surplus in the government's budget, which would drastically reduce the nation's deficit. A year later, the same economists at the CBO were projecting an annual deficit far into the future. Osama bin Laden...Who factored him into the US economy? Certainly, he was not on the economists' radar screens. Or the Yom Kippur War, which resulted in the escalation of the world's price for crude oil, causing worldwide inflation? Or try Deng Xiaoping, who set in motion the movement towards a free market economy for the Peoples Republic of China? By his actions, he revolutionized Mao Tse-tung's revolution, thereby setting Communist China on a new course that is altering the overall economy of the world. The number of external events that can alter drastically a nation's or a world's economy are infinite, which is what makes economic projections so frustrating and inaccurate. In fact, economists ought to be pitied rather than scorned.

In 1942 — when Allied fortunes were at their lowest; when German troops appeared about to take Moscow and Leningrad; when the Japanese had seized all of east Asia and had destroyed a large part of the US naval fleet at Pearl Harbor; when General Erwin Rommel's Afrika Korps seemed destined to capture Cairo — a most unusual meeting took place in Washington DC between John Maynard Keynes, the world's leading economist, and Harry Dexter White,[1] the Under Secretary of the United States Treasury. Its purpose was to determine what currency would replace gold in international trade, once Germany and Japan had been defeated. On the surface, the meeting would have appeared rather premature, but only if one doubted the final outcome of the war. Since neither President Franklin Roosevelt nor Prime Minister Winston Churchill did, the purpose for the meeting was high on the agenda of both the United States and Great Britain.

Just a year prior to the outbreak of the Second World War, the economies of Britain and the United States were still submerged in the worldwide Depression that had followed the crash of the New York

---

1. White, as it later turned out, was an agent in the employ of the Soviet Union. It was he who drafted the plan for the future of Germany, presented to Roosevelt by his boss, Secretary of the Treasury Henry J. Morgenthau, which would have stripped all of Germany of its industry and reduced its economy to that of agriculture. It was he, over Keynes' objection, who insisted that the Soviet Union be a participant in the Bretton Woods Conference in 1944 which established the ground rules for the future world economy. Called before the House Un-American Activities Committee in 1948, he denied ever having served as an agent for the Soviet Union. Two days later, he ostensibly died of a heart attack. When Whittaker Chambers opened up his famous Pumpkin Papers, which led to the conviction of Alger Hiss, there among the files was the name of Harry Dexter White. The Venona files, opened in 1995, also would confirm Chambers' allegations.

Stock Exchange in 1929. Only the war had reestablished full employment, and what was coming off the assembly lines hardly could be considered productive. Nor could the mobilization of an entire generation of young men into the armed forces be viewed as resolving the unemployment problem. If some sort of plan for a post-war economic future wasn't undertaken now, then once the war was won, the economic Depression that had fostered the rise of fascism might lead to something equally unpalatable — communism.

Both Keynes and White were in fundamental agreement about the cause for the Great Depression. The gold standard, established in 1870, which had opened the doors to free trade among the major industrial nations of the world, had been obliterated by the four years of the First World War. None of the combatants had contemplated a war of such long duration. Nor were they in a financial position to undertake such a long, costly and fruitless enterprise. As a result, the paper currency printed to remain in the military contest had wiped out the true value of their gold reserves. The job Keynes and White had set out for themselves was to find a new currency that could replace gold.

What was the gold standard? It was an unofficial, arbitrary measure agreed to by the major industrial nations, which pegged the value of their currency to that of the British pound sterling. In turn, the pound sterling was represented by a certain weight of gold. Assuming that it took five US dollars to equal one pound sterling, at any moment in time that currency could be redeemed for its equivalent value in gold. Since Britain, by far, was the wealthiest nation in the world at that time, and possessed the largest gold reserves, it was natural that its currency should be the base from which every other country's currency would be measured. Basically, a nation or a bank within a nation was expected to possess a certain percentage of gold reserves for the amount of currency it issued. Gold never actually changed hands in either domestic or international trade; it was merely the security blanket that established the financial credibility of a bank's or a nation's credit.

Following the defeat and surrender of France in 1870, the victorious Germans, in addition to annexing Alsace and parts of Lorraine, imposed an indemnity of five billion gold francs on the French government. Until this indemnity was paid, an occupying force of German troops would remain on French soil. Borrowing from Great Britain, within a brief period of time France paid off the indemnity. For the German economy, it was a windfall. Germany could now move its economy from one based on silver to one based on gold, and join the exclusive club of nations whose free trade was based on gold, namely Britain, France and the United States. There were mini-depressions in the 1890s and in the first decade of the twentieth century, but in each instance they were of short duration, and the economies of the major industrial nations snapped back.

But this was not the situation when the First World War came to an end. The victorious Allies naïvely assumed that defeated Germany would reimburse their treasuries with German gold. This expectation was absurd. The German gold reserves were in a worse position than those of the Allies. After making the first payment, Germany defaulted. Under the terms of the treaty signed by the new Weimar Republic, French and Belgian troops occupied the major industrial sector of the German economy, the Saar Basin and the Ruhr Valley. With the income from its wealthiest region cut off, the German economy went into a tailspin. Unable to export or to satisfy its own internal needs, the German treasury resorted to printing currency. The more it printed to pay government salaries, the more it needed. The inflation became so dire that people were paying for their groceries with wheel barrels filled with worthless German marks. Terrified that the country might turn to a socialist government to extricate itself from the financial disaster, a consortium of bankers from the United States, Britain and France stepped in to save the Weimar Republic. Led by the American Charles Dawes, gold reserves from these countries were used to stabilize the German mark. Reparation payments were reduced and their due-dates were extended until the German economy could recover. It was Band-Aid economics, and in 1929, the Dawes Plan was replaced by the Young Plan, reducing reparations even further, in a desperate effort to salvage the German economy.

During that post-World War I period, the victorious Allies would pretend that their own economies could ignore the drain on their gold reserves resulting from the four-year war. England, France and Italy owed money to the United States; America, although actively engaged in the conflict for only a year and a half, had amassed a debt of $22 billion. The US Treasury was waiting to be repaid; the French, British and Italian treasuries were waiting on German reparations to resolve their internal and external debts. So, during that post-war decade, the band played on.

It was the Roaring Twenties — in America, the age of the flapper, Prohibition and the bootlegger. London, Paris, Vienna and Berlin had never been so gay and frivolous. By 1927, when Britain pretended to return to the pre-war gold standard, and the United States and France followed suit, the price of shares on the New York Stock Exchange began to escalate. As the prices on the New York Stock Exchange continued to climb, this escalation fueled the appetite not only of US investors but of foreign investors as well. Financial barons were joined by the common man and woman, sharing a fantasy trip that would take them to the moon. In 1929, the fragile, magic bubble burst, ushering in a worldwide Depression.

Britain was the first country to remove itself from the gold standard, in 1931, and was followed two years later by the United States, and in 1935 by France. International trade, which had been the bastion of the capitalist system, all but dried up. Britain restricted trade to members of its Commonwealth. In 1931, Congress enacted the Hawley-Smoot tariff legislation, which effectively isolated US industry from cheaper imports. Without free trade, the economies of every nation shriveled up. Investments disappeared, and manufacturers pulled in their belts by laying off workers. All the glamour and the glitter of the Roaring Twenties had turned out to be tinsel. Without a gold standard, and with exports out of the question, nations now relied on their own currencies to stimulate their economies. All the participants in the Second World War would pay for military expenditures with paper currency. At the end of the conflict, every nation that had been engaged in the war, with the exception of the United States, was bankrupt.

But that was not the problem facing Keynes and White. Their meeting was to determine what could replace gold in the post-war world. Gold! Could anything replace gold? From the Golden Calf in the Old Testament to King Midas in mythology, it has been viewed as the quintessential metal by all humanity. From time immemorial, it has been the solid gold wedding band that binds a woman's heart to the man she marries. To artificially produce gold was the dream of every alchemist. It is coveted and accepted in every nation. With the exception of platinum, too rare to be generally circulated, it has been the metal against which all other metals used for currency have been measured. Now these two men undertook the job of finding a currency that would be accepted throughout the world as a replacement for gold.

One thing was apparent as the two men examined the broken pieces of what had once been a flourishing world commerce: there was no way to put Humpty Dumpty together again. Both Keynes and White were determined to find a formula that would enable the capitalist world to return to its halcyon days prior to 1914. The key to that solution was reconstructing a post-war system that would allow for international commerce once again. Starting from that premise, the two men addressed the important question of what currencies would be valid once the conflict had ended. Assuming that Germany and Japan would be defeated, their currencies would be worthless. All of Europe, with the exception of the four remaining neutrals — Sweden, Switzerland, Spain and Portugal — now were in German hands. Their currencies as well would be worth next to nothing. As for Great Britain and its commonwealth partners, the cost of fighting a long war would leave them in a desperate financial state. The Soviet Union had isolated itself from the West between the two wars, but judging from the damage that had already occurred to its economy, it too, if it survived, would emerge from the conflict a financial cripple.

The only economy that remained unscathed by the war was that of the United States. Not only had it become the arsenal of the Allies, but given its natural wealth in resources and population, and despite the deficits it would incur, it would emerge from the war as the only viable economy left in the world. Given this fact, White concluded that the dollar should become the world's standard for international currency, much as the pound sterling had been prior to the First World War. The value of all other currencies would be measured against the dollar. Keynes, on the other hand, fearful of the economic power that it would give to the United States in the post-war world, demurred. His concept was to create a Central World Bank into which all the participating nations would contribute a percentage of gold, depending upon their pre-war economy. This bank would issue an international currency, which he named the Bancor, a combination of the French words for bank and gold. Keynes may have had in his baggage worldwide prestige, and White no such credentials, but the bare facts were that without the support of the United States, no post-war financial system was feasible. The dollar was anointed the official currency in the post-war world to be, and the currency value of every other nation would be pegged to that of the dollar.

There still remained a stumbling block. What was the actual value of the dollar? It had to be measured against something tangible if it was to be accepted as the world's official trading currency. When the pound sterling reigned supreme, prior to the First World War, its value had been pegged to a certain weight of gold. The old value of gold may have disappeared in the ashes of that conflict, but it still maintained its symbolic worth. After much haggling, it was finally agreed that the value of the dollar would be set at $35 to one ounce of gold. In other words, while the dollar would be the standard against which the value of every other currency would be set, in the final analysis, an excess of dollars could be traded in for gold at the official rate that had been decided. King Midas would still sit on his throne.

While establishing the dollar to replace the pound sterling was one step in the right direction, the more difficult problem was how to reconstitute free trade between industrial nations in the post-war world. Neither of the men had any idea of the scope of damages that the Allied invasion of Europe would wreak on the infrastructures of France, Belgium, Holland and Germany. Nor were they able to take into account how much the Nazis had stripped from the infrastructure of the nations they conquered. Working from a blank piece of paper, they were reduced to making assumptions about conditions in the post-war world. In their minds, two things were mandatory if free trade between nations was to be reinstituted. There had to be a World Bank to which nations could apply for loans to get their economies back on their feet. In addition, there had to be put in place an International Monetary Fund (IMF) that could step in and help stabilize a nation's currency, a necessary ingredient for free trade. Each of these newly created organizations had a different function; therefore each would possess a separate Board of Governors to oversee its operations.

The concept of a World Bank and an International Monetary Fund that would lend money to nations for reconstruction and facilitate trade by sustaining weak currencies was brilliant, a noble-seeming gesture that actually bound debtor nations to the lenders. But the capitalization for these two new entities was unrealistic. Both the World Bank and the IMF were supposed to be capitalized at $10 billion each. When the money from all the nations finally participating in the venture was deposited, in didn't quite attain either goal. With all the details of this post-war financial plan finally worked out, representatives from 44 nations would gather in July 1944 at a former resort in Bretton Woods, New Hampshire, to discuss and to agree to a plan for economic and financial reconstruction following the end of the war in Europe and Asia. Upon the insistence of White, the Soviet Union sent representatives to this conference of nations. As the plans for the World Bank and the IMF were unfolded by Keynes and White, the only objection voiced by the delegates in attendance was the sum of money each nation would have to contribute in order to reach the proposed goals for capitalization. None of the delegates was concerned with the composition of each organization's Board of Governors, its Executive Director or its President. Nor could those charged with smaller contributions to the two funds complain that those countries that contributed the bulk of the proposed funds would have the principal voice in their distribution.

How much each nation was assessed to contribute to either fund would be determined by their pre-war gross domestic product. Twenty-five percent of their assessment would be contributed in gold or dollars, and the balance in their local currency, as measured in dollars. If they didn't possess sufficient gold reserves, then 10% in gold and the balance in dollars. After much haggling over the quantity of gold assigned to each nation, agreement was reached by the representatives of the participating nations. The largest share was assumed by the United States and was followed in descending order by Great Britain, the Soviet Union, China and France, or the five members who would make up the Security Council in the United Nations. (See Appendix, Tables 1 and 2.) These gold reserves would be stored in Fort Knox, Kentucky, and could be drawn upon when a nation had an excess of dollars in its balance of payments with the United States. Meanwhile, the value of each country's currency would be pegged to that of the dollar. Since the dollar would remain the only currency for international exchange, the value a government ascribed to its currency would not necessarily represent its true value in the international marketplace.

For example in post-war France, the official rate for the French franc was set at 349.49 francs to the dollar. In the international money markets, where a nation's currency was based on what it could purchase in terms of goods and services, the actual value of the French franc was 500 to the dollar. However, within France itself a dollar cashed in at a French bank would pay out only the official rate established by the government. At its best, it was an imperfect system, nor could it have been expected to be otherwise. Both Keynes and White assumed that as the world's economies grew in the post-war era, adjustments would have to be made. Unfortunately, neither of the two men was around to make the adjustments. In 1946, Keynes would die. In 1948, two days after testifying in front of the House Un-American Activities Committee, denying he was a Communist, White would die of a heart attack. Neither man expected the reaction of the Soviet Union and its satellite nations. After having agreed to its quota, neither the Soviet Union nor Poland, now under Soviet control, nor Czechoslovakia, soon to fall under the Iron Curtain, joined either of the organizations. At that moment in time, it should have been apparent to Washington that the Soviet Union had no interest in collaborating with the capitalist nations either in terms of loans for reconstruction or in international trade. It could be said that the Cold War actually commenced in 1944 at Bretton Woods. Stalin viewed the World Bank and the IMF as capitalist organizations designed to infiltrate and destroy its rivals. From his perspective, the capitalist system was bound to fail, and there was no need to become involved in the financial failures of a doomed system.

The fundamental weakness in the original concept of the World Bank and the IMF was that it did not take into account the extent of damage suffered by the European economies as a result of five years of war. From the Atlantic coastline to the Ural Mountains, the continent lay in shambles. Not only had its pre-war infrastructure been destroyed, but millions of people had been displaced from their homes. That a worldwide epidemic did not ensue, as was the case following the end of the First World War, was a miracle. Between the Red army and the German army, Eastern Europe lay prostrate. Unlike in 1918, this time the German people had the war brought directly to their front door. Allied bombings had left major German cities in ruins. Its capital, Berlin, fiercely defended by Hitler's Waffen-SS, in house-to-house combat with the Russians, was gutted. Nor was the situation much better in those countries that the Allied forces had liberated from German occupation. Throughout France, Allied bombings had left their mark on the country. While Paris remained relatively unscathed, the ancient city of Strasbourg had suffered devastating damage.

The concept of a World Bank, designed to extend loans to revive the economies of war stricken countries, made sense on paper. But on the actual ground, it was ludicrous. Loans are extended to a going business, not to one that needs a blood transfusion merely to survive. Finally, Keynes and White were unaware that the Soviet Union, then a wartime ally, viewed the distraught European economies as an opportunity for local Communist parties to take legitimate control of their post-war governments. Keynes and White had devised a game plan with an old deck of cards, circa 1918, when only Belgium and the northern sector of France had been under German occupation. In 1945, not only had all of France been under attack by the Allied armies and the German defenders, but the major ports along the Atlantic coast had undergone major damage to their facilities.

In pre-war Europe, the Soviet Union had been isolated, in part by design, in part because the capitalist economies of the world were in a state of collapse. In the immediate post-war years, it would become an active player on the European scene. Since the Soviet Union and its newly acquired satellite states remained outside the US dollar trading area, its basic interest ran counter to the goals sought from the institutions of the World Bank and the IMF. Stalin viewed the almost total collapse of the pre-war western economies as a golden opportunity to further the spread of communism to the West. Although the Comintern had been dissolved during the war years, since the Soviet Union and the Allies were engaged in a war against a common enemy, once the conflict was over it was reinstituted under a new name, the Cominform. Communist parties once again took their orders and actions directly from Moscow. Stalin viewed the economic crisis that afflicted post-war Western Europe as the precursor to an eventual Communist takeover. The role of the local Communist parties was to obstruct, as much as possible, the economic recovery of Western Europe. If Stalin had remained neutral, the European capitalist system might have collapsed from its own dead weight without the infusion of American capital. But Stalin had no patience. Given the parlous state of their economies, he assumed it would take only a few years before the local Socialists rose to power and seized the governments without resorting to force. But instead, once the values of Western European currencies were tied to the dollar, they were wed to each other in a long-term marriage. That was one of the great legacies of Bretton Woods. Acknowledging the dollar as the only major, valid currency left in the world, Europeans — whether Socialist, centrist or to the right — had to recognize the basic role of the dollar, if their economies were to be revived.

In one of the strangest ironies in the history of mankind, socialism, the system that was supposed to supplant capitalism with its inherent failings, instead unwittingly galvanized it towards a new and unpredictable direction. In order to contain the spread of communism as much as possible, the United States was prepared to jettison one of capitalism's basic principles — balancing the budget. The justification for this action was that the United States was at war. It was a war like none other in the history of mankind. It lasted almost a half a century, with neither of the adversaries ever engaging in actual combat with each other. Whether it was the Berlin Blockade, or the Korean and Vietnamese wars, the United States was fighting surrogate nations of the Soviet Union. As for Stalin, like Keynes and White, he was playing with an old deck of cards. He assumed, along with liberal US economists, that capitalism would function according to Hoyle. Once the civilian pipelines were filled in the immediate post-war period, supply would exceed demand. According to Marxist theory, the boom would be followed by the bust. With no exterior markets capable of absorbing the US's excess production, there would be massive layoffs in the US workforce. According to mid-nineteenth century Marxist thinking, those were the rules of laissez faire capitalism. Had Stalin acted differently in the immediate post-war period, he might have been right. But then again, he was a prisoner of Marxist doctrines and blinded to reality.

Some Americans in the immediate aftermath of the Second World War were prepared to give the benefit of doubt to the Soviets. This was going to be a brave new world. The Soviet Union, our wartime ally, had suffered such casualties during the conflict that the possibility of another war was out of the question. Moreover, it had agreed to join the United Nations and, as a member of the Security Council, was determined to maintain the post-war peace. Americans tend to be trusting, which is often looked upon as naïveté. Some missed the point that the Soviet Union was more than just another nation whose economic system differed from our own. Stalin and the other members of the Politburo were dedicated to the spread of Communist ideology. They operated from a belief that America would resort to aggressive wars in order to maintain its power. It was the economic failure of capitalism that led to the rise of Germany's Adolf Hitler, Italy's Benito Mussolini and Japan's Hideki Tojo and to the disastrous war that followed. It was the failure of capitalism to grow that led to the First World War.

Since history tends to repeat itself, there was more than a distinct possibility that a failing capitalist system in America would resort to the same practice. This was the rationale for Stalin's speech to the Central Committee of the Communist party in January 1946. The Soviet system represented more than the practice of state socialism; people were prepared to die in order to usher in a new and just world. Communism alone, they felt, held the keys to this new kingdom of heaven on earth. America viewed the Cold War as a result of Soviet aggression; the Soviet Union viewed America as a capitalist aggressor whose intent was the destruction of the Soviet system of state socialism.

It is only in retrospect that the so-called Cold War can be understood. Each side believed that sooner or later their competition would lead to direct conflict and that overwhelming military superiority was the best protection. Once both sides fell into this belief, nature took its course. On both sides weapon systems were added to already existing weapon systems, until both countries had climbed to the apex of asininity, mutual overkill. From that long drawn out process, in succeeding decades, would emerge the Almighty Dollar. Nobody foresaw its arrival on the world scene, least of all the United States government. Nor did its elevation happen overnight. Nor did anyone fully grasp its implications. What was clear when President Richard Nixon announced to the world in 1971 that the United States no longer would redeem dollars for gold was that the cupboard at Fort Knox, Kentucky, had been denuded of most of its stock of gold. A piece of paper, the dollar, had been exalted to a position unique in history.

King Midas finally was dead as far as international commerce was concerned. Nations intending to build up their gold reserves would have to buy the precious metal on the open market. Gold might be dead as far as its former role was concerned, but it was not buried. Once released from its artificial price of $35 for an ounce of gold, it would soar into the stratosphere, rising at one point to a high of $850 an ounce before settling down to an average price of $350. Because of its inflated price, gold mines formerly considered too expensive to operate were reopened. Gold Bugs and Silverites prayed for its return. Some economists believed that international commerce would collapse unless gold assumed its former role. There were too many dollars afloat in the world for gold ever to return. Gold's doom was firmly sealed with the escalation of oil prices during the 1970s. The inflation that followed, as the OPEC nations steadily increased the cost of a barrel of oil from $3 in 1973 to a high approaching $40, finally signaled gold's burial. Crude oil now was referred to as liquid gold. (See Appendix, Figure 1.)

Those nations largely responsible for the demise of the gold standard were America's former enemies, Germany and Japan. Neither of them had been present at the Bretton Woods conference, so their currencies were not pegged to the dollar until the late 1940s when the policy of the Truman administration was to reconstruct their economies to prevent Communists from taking hold, and to alter their political systems towards a democratic form of government. These dual purposes went hand-in-hand. On the surface, the more difficult political system to reform was Japan, which had never experienced any form of democracy in its history. Giving that job to General Douglas MacArthur, who had accepted the official unconditional surrender of the Japanese, was a brilliant choice. Making no effort to charge the Japanese Emperor as a war criminal, MacArthur was able to establish a rapport with the Japanese people. In essence, MacArthur became the Cardinal Richelieu of the newly formed government. Bringing in experts from the United States, a new Constitution was established. But before that came to fruition, an entirely new currency was established. MacArthur's reason was to prevent those Japanese still in Shanghai, where they had amassed huge fortunes over the war years, from making use of their ill-gotten gains by converting them into dollars. But the newly issued yen still had to be ascribed a value in relation to the dollar if trade between the nations was to be resumed. With the fall of Nationalist China to the Communists in 1949, the growth and strength of the Japanese economy took on a new urgency. Strategically, Japan now was America's first line of defense in the Pacific region.

As the Japanese economy slowly began to recover, thanks to an infusion of US dollars from the occupation army, along with modern machinery from the United States, the newly elected, democratic Japanese government saw no reason to adjust the value of the yen as the peacetime economy took root. Furthermore, the same drive and energies of the Japanese people that had been harnessed to create a modern war machine now were directed to producing civilian products for export. In contrast to the pre-war era, when Japanese exports had been focused on inexpensive merchandise, Japan now made a 180-degree turn and concentrated on higher priced goods. American manufacturers producing television sets saw a golden opportunity in having them assembled in Japan where the cost of labor was far less than in the United States. The Japanese were quick to grasp onto the technology, and while initially producing sets for local consumption, they soon turned to exports. The same held true for cameras, copying German models and improving upon them. Despite its growing favorable balance of trade with the United States, the Central Bank of Japan made no effort to adjust the value of its currency with the dollar. Instead, it used its surplus dollars to acquire gold. By the late 1960s, Japanese labels on television sets and cameras had become household names in America. Part of the Japanese success in developing this technology was the result of Sears Roebuck, the largest retailer in America at that time, using Japan's cheap labor to produce private label televisions for its stores.

The same held true for Germany. Although the occupation authorities were late in converting the old German mark to one that was pegged to the dollar, once they did, the German economy became revitalized. Ironically, it was this conversion from the old German mark to the new one that brought about the Berlin Blockade. Of course, the Marshall Plan played a major role in the revitalization of German industry. The successful export of the Volkswagen, as an inexpensive second car, along with the restoration of Germany's famous chemical and dye industries, created a similar imbalance of trade with the United States. Like the Japanese, the Germans made no effort to readjust the mark to its actual value. Instead, the German Central Bank was determined to amass as much gold as possible. The rapid recovery of the German and Japanese economies, starting in the late 1950s and reaching its peak in the 1960s, with its resultant drain on America's gold supplies, did not go unnoticed. President Dwight Eisenhower would warn President-elect John Kennedy of this problem. Unfortunately, there was nothing any President could do to stem the outflow of gold. US foreign policy was geared to sustaining democracy in Germany and Japan, and a strong economy would ensure that neither of them would stray from that path.

The Cold War dominated the thinking of every administration. Once the United States had embarked on a policy of containing the spread of communism, this had come to take precedence over every other aspect of America's future. The conservative Republicans who surrounded Eisenhower might have believed that fiscal prudence should be high on the agenda of any President, but the potential threat from the Soviet Union was considered to be a matter of life and death. Thanks to the Marshall Plan, the United States had prevented Western Europe from falling into the hands of Communist parties in Italy and France. But the success of the homegrown Cuban revolution, 90 miles off of the coast of Florida, had served to exacerbate America's paranoia about a worldwide Communist threat to its security. Eisenhower had also warned Kennedy about potential Communist takeovers in Laos, the Congo, and perhaps Algeria. The so-called Domino Theory did not originate in the Kennedy administration but had been present in Eisenhower's. The world was in a state of flux; colonialism was on its last legs, leaving the door open to Communist takeovers. The leadership in both political parties had convinced themselves that the current and future policy for America was to prevent the spread of communism any place in the world.

It was this belief that sparked its policy towards the Soviet Union. American policy makers were convinced that the Russians were involved behind the scenes every time Communists came to power. The Soviet Union did not foster Castro's overthrow of the Batista regime, nor did it influence his decision to socialize the Cuban economy. Neither was Russia responsible for the Communists' success in China. It did arm the North Vietnamese in their war against the French, but Vietnam had been a united country under Ho Chi Minh immediately after the war, until President Harry Truman allowed the French to retake their former colony. Neither Kennedy nor Lyndon Johnson was willing to recognize past history, which is how the United States became involved in the Vietnamese quagmire. It was by following this policy of containment and rearmament that the budget deficit grew throughout the Kennedy-Johnson presidencies, and along with it, the growing debt that served to weaken the value of the dollar, and to accelerate the outflow of America's gold.

By the time Nixon took office in 1969, the national debt left by Kennedy and Johnson, which reflected fighting a major land war in Vietnam, had increased by $76 billion, or almost four times the $20 billion debt accumulated under Truman and Eisenhower. And, unlike under Truman and Eisenhower, when the GDP increased almost two and one half times, under Kennedy and Johnson the GDP only advanced from $529.9 billion to $868.5 billion, a 63% increase. Defense expenditures over that period rose from $49.6 billion to $81.9 billion. The war cry of the Republicans — that the nation couldn't afford both guns and butter — was only accurate if you placed the guns in the hands of soldiers. The major cost of fighting the war in Vietnam was sustaining troop levels of more than 500,000 men, 10,000 miles away. The soldiers stationed in Vietnam may have enriched a certain class of Vietnamese, but they did nothing to increase the GDP on the domestic front. Even though Nixon began the withdrawal of troops in 1969, completing their withdrawal in 1973 when the peace treaty with North Vietnam finally was signed, the deficits increased substantially — adding $101 billion to the national debt. It was the combined debts incurred by the three Presidents that kept driving the value of the dollar down, in relation to other currencies, and resulted in the drain of gold from the Treasury.

It was not only defense that was contributing to the budget deficits. The increased costs of Johnson's Great Society were beginning to take a toll, which is revealed when we track "Human Resource" allocations, which included health, education, Social Security and other social services. In 1967, when Johnson's Great Society programs were still in their infancy, defense expenditures were $71.4 billion, and human resource expenditures were $51.3 billion; by 1971, human resource expenditures exceeded defense expenditures and would continue along that track. Specifically, in 1971, defense expenditures were $78.9 billion, and human resource expenditures were $91.9 billion. (See Appendix, Table 4.) Ten years later, human resource spending was more than double that of defense. Once the United States had removed itself from the gold standard, it was able to have both guns and tons of butter. It was the Almighty Dollar that paid for the escalating prices of crude oil, while still funding America's defense needs and the programs of the Great Society. It was a new form of capitalism. The government no longer paid for the goods and services it provided for its citizens; the interest on the national debt performed that function.

Looking back to the period immediately following the end of the Second World War, it would be difficult to discern the events that were to come over the next 45 years. Certainly no one could imagine the role that the Almighty Dollar would play in helping to bring about the collapse of the Soviet Union. The United States dollar occupied a unique position now that gold was a commodity. The US, as the custodian of the dominant currency in the world, was free to run up huge deficits with impunity. As the number of dollars in circulation increased, America's financial position became stronger. On the surface, this outcome would appear to be a contradiction. Without gold, the value of the dollar with respect to other currencies was declining. Starting in 1971, America's overall balance of trade turned into the negative, and remained that way with rare exceptions until the present. (See Appendix, Table 3.) Even with the readjusted values of the German mark and the Japanese yen, both countries continued to export more than they imported from the United States.

When the OPEC oil crisis emerged in 1973 and the price of crude oil soared into the stratosphere, while large double-digit deficits had a major impact on the US economy, the long-term effect of the oil price increase on the Western European and the Japanese economies was far worse. In addition to the inflationary effect it would have on their economies as well as our own, it flooded the world with billions of unexpected dollars. A certain percentage of this newly acquired wealth would be invested by the OPEC nations in real estate, both in the US and in Europe; another percentage would be devoted to the modernization of their countries; but the majority of these funds would be invested in enterprises either domestically or throughout the world. The US dollar was now omnipresent. Therein lay its aforementioned strength. Its intrinsic value might depreciate vis-à-vis other currencies, but there were too many dollars in circulation to dispense with it, and nothing available to replace this monetary standard.

At that moment in world history, perhaps nobody realized the significance of the dollar. The escalating rise in the price of crude oil not only released unprecedented inflationary pressures but also dramatically increased the growth of the US national debt. From 1974, when the initial impact of increased crude oil prices first served to escalate the budget deficits, until 1981, when mandated mileage standards for cars broke the OPEC monopoly, the national debt grew from $483.9 billion to $994.8 billion, more than doubling. At the same time, the GDP increased from $1.4 trillion to $3.1 trillion, matching the percentage increase in the deficit. (See Appendix, Table 5.) Critics, of course, would counter that this increase in the GDP was largely the result of inflation. But then again, inflation also contributed to the increase in the deficit. Nevertheless, the escalation in the price of crude oil, and the concomitant inflation it brought on, did have a profound effect on three areas of the US economy: Social Security, the savings and loan institutions, and the Big Three automobile manufacturers. While recipients of Social Security were covered for any increase in inflation, their monthly checks being tied to the rise in the Consumer Price Index, the Social Security Trust Fund, which dispensed these monies, had never factored in this excessive inflation. Unless the payroll taxes were increased, the monies wouldn't be there for future retirees. Although payroll taxes are regressive, affecting the poor disproportionately compared to the rich, and they increase employers' expenses, in 1977 and again in 1983 Congress passed the necessary legislation — reluctantly.

The second sector of the national economy that faced a calamity as a result of the steep rise in inflation was that of the savings and loan institutions. In 1979, in an effort to slow down the rate of runaway inflation, Paul Volcker, Chairman of the Federal Reserve Board (which controls the nation's money supply) began raising the Fed's discount rate to 12%, then 13%, forcing the banks to raise their rate of interest to their most creditworthy customers to between 15.2% and 16%. Those bank clients that did not enjoy a triple-A credit rating found themselves in the position of having to pay 20% or more to borrow money. Volcker, who ultimately pushed the discount rate up to 14%, achieved his objective. The nation's economy fell into a deep recession from which it didn't recover until 1983, when the 1981 Reagan tax cuts kicked in and the price of a barrel of oil descended to below $30. The S & Ls were caught in the middle. With most of their funds tied up in long-term, low-interest loans, and restricted by Congressional law from raising their interest rates to attract depositors, they sought and received Congressional relief. The S & L debacle is described in detail in another chapter. When the dust finally settled eight years later, thousands of S & Ls had either been absorbed by stronger institutions or had gone out of business. To pay for their losses, the federal government added about $253 billion to its deficit; and the original concept of savings and loan institutions disappeared into the history books.

The third sector of the economy that would be impacted by the steep rise in oil prices was Detroit. In 1970, Nixon signed into law the creation of the Environmental Protection Agency. Designed to salvage the American environment from the 100 years of abuse that it had suffered from unrestricted industrial expansion, the legislation covered every aspect of American life. Among its major provisions was the Clean Air Act. Industry was forced to reduce significantly the amount of pollutants that emanated from the smoke stacks of its factories. But the real villains were the 100-million-plus cars and trucks that spewed carbon monoxide into the atmosphere 24 hours a day, seven days a week. Major cities such as Los Angeles and Denver were covered with heavy smog that never lifted. Since there was no possible way to eliminate these vehicles, the legislation called for a different approach. Leaded gas, which was cheaper to refine and cost less, would be gradually phased out. The sudden increase in the price of crude oil in 1974, however, forced Congress to focus on a more immediate and necessary concern — that of conservation. After much debate and despite pressure from the Big Three in Detroit, in 1975 Congress enacted the Energy Policy & Conservation Act, which established Corporate Average Fuel Economy (CAFE) standards for passenger cars and light trucks. The standards were set for vehicles weighing 8,500 pounds or less and were to be averaged out over each new line of cars. Beginning in 1978, any line of cars sold for use in the United States would have to average 18.5 miles per gallon, gradually increasing the average mileage until it reached 27.5 miles per gallon by 1985. To satisfy the United Auto Workers union, the CAFE standards defined two vehicle fleets — a "domestic" one for autos with 75% or more of US/Canadian content, and an "imports" one for all others. These two categories had to meet the standards separately, thereby preventing Detroit from meeting the standards by simply importing more fuel-efficient cars.

To the executives at General Motors, Ford and Chrysler, this new government mandate was a petty annoyance. In order to meet these standards they would have to develop a line of smaller and more fuel efficient cars to compensate for the gas guzzlers from which they drew the bulk of their profits. Having established this attitude, these executives were ill-prepared for the steady increases in the price of imported crude oil, which translated into higher gas costs for consumers when they filled their cars. Moreover, as the cost of gasoline continued to escalate during the 1970s, Detroit manufacturers made no effort to improve the quality of the small cars they first produced to meet the initial standards. Their eyes remained focused on the bottom line, and big cars were far more profitable than the smaller ones they had to manufacture in order to meet the CAFE standards.

In comparison with other industrialized nations, gasoline had been relatively cheap in this country. Until the post-war expansion of the economy, US oil production was able to satisfy consumer demand without resorting to imports. The Seven Sisters, those major domestic and international oil producers and refiners that controlled more than

90% of the world's oil production, had managed to keep costs down. In the United States, there was fierce competition between the domestic producers for a share of the domestic market. In Japan and Europe, where no domestic production existed, and where there were far fewer cars on the road, gasoline not only was far more expensive but was heavily taxed by the respective governments. As a result, Japanese and European auto manufacturers had concentrated on building automobiles that would deliver high mileage for each gallon of gas. Furthermore, the Japanese and European cars were engineered to last for years. Unlike Detroit, which prided itself on offering an array of different colors for car interiors, Japan provided less choice. Whatever harmonized with the exterior color is what the consumer got. The old leadership at the Big Three was blind to this threat. Had Detroit executives taken into account what had happened to the television and camera industries, they might have reacted. Instead they reassured themselves that the American public would never be tempted by such Japanese brand names as Toyota, Honda and Nissan. They forgot that a new generation had come of age, which did not view Japan as a wartime enemy.

The executives of the US automobile industry were so isolated from reality that they did not understand or admit that a sexual revolution had taken place during the 1960s and 1970s. Despite the success of Playboy magazine, with newsstand sales of five million, and a pass-along readership of four, Detroit's car makers refused to advertise in what they deemed to be a salacious publication. In the consumer magazine business, if you don't advertise, you don't get editorial credits. For a decade, the only cars advertised or featured in Playboy were foreign cars. Because of this attitude, coupled with Detroit's unwillingness to invest in small fuel-efficient cars, the Japanese auto manufacturers captured 20% of the American car market right under US car producers' noses. Coerced by the Reagan administration to limit their exports to 20%, the Japanese responded by opening plants in the United States. Instead of 20%, they now own one-third of the US auto market, and the Toyota Camry has been the number one selling car in America for a number of years. Furthermore, the Japanese joined the Germans in entering the luxury car market, dealing a serious blow to Cadillac, Lincoln and Buick.

The complacency of executives to the threat of foreign competition was not restricted to the automotive industry. At the end of the Second World War, with the rest of the industrialized world in ruins, America's basic industries faced no competition except from domestic competitors. Moreover, as a result of the Depression, no effort had been made to update or modernize existing machinery in the years prior to the war. As a result, those firms that had been engaged in supplying basic industries with new developments in manufacturing methods had, with the exception of one or two, disappeared from the business landscape. The few corporations that sought to invest and modernize their existing equipment were limited in their selection. Even more troubling was the fact that those still in existence, because of their virtual monopoly, saw no reason to innovate and to develop updated versions of their previous offerings. On the other hand, in Western Europe (where basic industries started from ground zero, but a renewed infrastructure was established, thanks to the Marshall Plan), and in Japan (once China had fallen to the Communists, and Japan represented America's first line of defense in the Pacific), the latest innovations in machinery were developed. Thus, the basic machinery used for steel and textile mills was far superior to what was currently available or in use in the United States. Moreover, this superiority in equipment was not limited to steel and textiles but encompassed other industries as well. By the 1960s, the Japanese dominated the ceramic tile business; the British, the four-color printing presses; the Germans, the textile and knitting machine equipment. Where at one time American industry had been in the forefront of innovation, exporting its equipment for secondary use, now those US companies who sought to update their facilities turned to imported equipment.

When Ronald Reagan assumed the presidency in 1981, the economic crisis caused by the escalating price of crude oil was already on the wane. Thanks to mandated CAFE standards, and the growing penetration of fuel-efficient Japanese cars, the United States consumption of crude oil began to decline. Since America consumed 25% of the world's oil supply, and one-third of that amount was used by cars and trucks, OPEC no longer was in the driver's seat. With the oil crisis resolved, Reagan turned his attention to the US economy, which was in a deep recession as a result of the inflation and the decision by the Fed to reduce the nation's money supply by raising interest rates. Most remarkable is that economists in all camps — Supply Siders, Keynesians, monetarists and Gold Bugs — seemed to ignore that the overriding reason for the inflation that was choking the economy was the escalation in the price of oil. Oil not only was used for transportation and home and business heating, but was also a mainstay of such basic industries as plastics and man-made fibers. Wherever plastics were used, and they were omnipresent throughout the economy, the increase in oil prices was reflected in the finished product. The same held true for man-made fibers, whether in textiles, apparel, home furnishings or carpeting. It was also used for the development of pesticides used in agriculture.

Once the price of crude oil declined to the mid-to low-$20s, and for a brief time as low as $10 a barrel, the specter of inflation disappeared. The Fed responded by lowering interest rates, and with the across-the-board Reagan tax cuts, the US economy rebounded. Much ado has been made about the theory of Supply Side economics, or as its detractors labeled it, Voodoo economics. As is the case with all economic systems, it is formulated in an academic vacuum. There is no room for contingencies or drastic changes such as occurred with OPEC. It is as simplistic as the Keynesian theory or the monetarist one of Nobel-winning economist Milton Friedman. The strengths of capitalism are continued growth and an increase in productivity. How the growth is to be attained, the Supply Siders had the answer. The model upon which Supply Side economics rested was the writings of the French economist, Jean-Baptiste Say. Originally an entrepreneur in a cotton mill, and later a professor of economics at the College de France, Say was both a pragmatist and a theorist. However, Say's theories were written for early nineteenth century France, when French capitalism had yet to emerge from its swaddling clothes. What intrigued the Supply Siders about Say's writings was his opposition to any government interference in the economy, and his belief that capital investment in production was the driving force for a successful economy. To Say, if there was overproduction in a consumer product, the invested capital should be transferred to another segment of the economy, where demand could be created. To try to apply Say's nineteenth century concept to capital-intensive industries in the twentieth century was an absurd exercise. The only industry France possessed at the time Say espoused his theory was textiles. The Frenchman, whose actual experience was limited to the production of cotton fabrics, visualized using the same equipment to produce woolens or silk in the event there was a glut in the production of cottons. In the modern textile industry, with high speed power looms, it made no sense.

Say's economic theories had been discarded during the Depression and replaced by the Keynesian theory of the necessity for the federal government to pump-prime the national economy through deficit spending. Keynes also believed that once the economy was back on its feet, the government should leave, and the private sector once again should take over. Now, with Reagan elected, it was time for the modern interpreters of Say's theories to have their place in the sun. In their interpretation of Say's theories, the key to economic growth was to release the private capital for use in the marketplace rather than having it confiscated by the government through high personal and corporate tax rates and a repressive capital gains tax. Once these monies were released through an across-the-board tax cut, they would be invested in either old or new businesses, which in turn would create jobs and expand the tax base through increased employment. The Democratic Congress, over the objection of its liberal wing, passed the Reagan tax cuts; as the Supply Siders predicted, the economy not only recovered but entered a period of extraordinary prosperity. In the 1984 presidential election Reagan carried every state except Minnesota, the Democratic candidate's home state. At the same time, Reagan was determined to increase defense expenditures, and launched an expensive plan to devise a shield system to secure the nation against intercontinental ballistic missiles. Labeled the Strategic Defensive Initiative, it was satirized as Star Wars by those who opposed the increased spending or doubted the viability of such a plan. At the same time, the programs of the Great Society were also increasing the cost of the federal government. Despite increased revenues from taxes, the national debt continued to soar. During Reagan's eight years in the White House the gross national debt grew from $909.0 billion to $2.6 trillion. At the same time, the gross domestic product rose from $2.7 trillion to $5.0 trillion. In other words, it duplicated exactly what had taken place during the Ford-Carter years, when inflation was out of control. Eureka! This was almost a carbon copy of Keynesian pump-priming used by the New Deal during the Depression, when the increase in the deficit corresponded with the growth of the GDP. Comparing 1933 and 1941, both the debt and the GDP approximately doubled. (See Appendix, Table 6.)

It was not Supply Side economics that produced the prosperity but deficit spending by the government. The Great Society programs of Johnson were having their impact on the economy. In addition to the growing costs of Medicare and Medicaid, overall health costs escalated as the average lifespan of Americans was increased. Although the federal tax on gasoline had paid for the construction of the six-lane interstate highways, the Department of Transportation was now paying for their maintenance. The Department of Health, Education and Welfare grew like Topsy. It was the federal government that was pump-priming the economy through increased deficit spending, not only on defense but on civilian projects as well, including the pork-barrel spending used by congressional representatives and senators to ensure their reelection.

The notion of Supply Side economics was applied in the form of across-the-board tax cuts in 1981. Putting more money in the hands of the consumer enabled the economy to grow. This was reflected in the GDP, where consumer spending now accounts for 72% of total volume. Unfortunately, the predicted growth in domestic manufacturing did not take place. Instead, more and more US businesses began the slow but steady practice of outsourcing their production to other countries in order to remain competitive and grow their dollar volume and profitability. When Say postulated his theory in the early nineteenth century, he had not taken this into account.

The first bull market on the New York Stock Exchange of the post-war era began in the late 1950s and extended throughout the 1960s and early 1970s, until the US Treasury abandoned the gold standard and the value of the dollar was allowed to float freely on international currency markets. The bear market that followed was further exacerbated by the ongoing oil crisis. This bull market began with the revolution in the field of electronics. The invention of the transistor, followed by the invention of the micro-circuit, dramatically altered the production of radios and television sets as well as other electronic equipment. It also spearheaded the movement of US industry to overseas locations since the primary cost for implementing the new technology was in labor. The transistor and the micro-circuit, as revolutionary as they appeared to investors on Wall Street, paled in comparison with the introduction of the personal computer and the use of the Internet, ushering in the Age of Information, which changed the way that the world communicated. This bull market would last for almost two decades, until the bubble burst and Wall Street took a breath before resuming its upward climb. At the time that the first bull market surfaced, a less noticed innovation occurred in the financial community, which in it own way was more revolutionary than either the micro-circuit or the Age of Information in altering the US economy.

The introduction of the stock option, at first for top executives in a corporation and gradually extended to other executives, was to change the conduct of American business. Until its introduction sometime in the late 1950s, executives in the upper income levels were subject to a tax of 91% on their salaries and bonuses. When Johnson was able to pass the Kennedy tax cut in 1964, this figure was reduced to 70%. On the other hand, when stock options were cashed in they were taxed at the capital gains rate of 20% on 50% of the income, allowing an executive to retire with a handsome nest egg. Under the Reagan tax cut, the 50% was increased to 60%. As the bull market of the 1960s advanced towards the 1,000 mark, with concomitant increases in the value of a corporation's stock price, the importance of the stock option took precedence over any other consideration of executives. It was during this period of time that the conglomerate and the agglomerate emerged. Through the acquisition of other companies, the value of the stock would increase, and with it, the value of the stock options held by the key executives. On the negative side, the leaders of major corporations were loath to use their profits for plant modernization since this investment would not be reflected in the price of their stock holdings. Executives from both the acquiring corporation and the acquired one profited from these mergers and acquisitions. The monies accrued by the acquired corporation, whether purchased for cash or stock or a combination of the two, would be taxed as capital gains, and the key executives would emerge as wealthy men and women. The acquiring corporation would see the price of its stock rise, reflecting the increased value of the merged entity. During the bear market of the 1970s, this trend towards mergers and acquisitions would slow down. But, with the emergence of the personal computer, which led to the Age of Information and the new bull market, this trend accelerated even more than previously. Actually, the Age of Information is a misnomer. Ever since IBM had patented the mainframe computer and attained almost a worldwide monopoly on its use, it had transformed the exchange of information. Retailers and manufacturers could keep track of their inventories; it obsolesced how publications set their type since it could now be done electronically rather than manually; it allowed for computation at lightening speeds, opening the door for advances in mathematical theory, which led to advances in science and technology, including the use of robots to replace manual labor; the personal computer merely advanced it to a new stage of use.

In this instance, venture capital played the major role in bringing these innovations to market. But it was expenditure by the federal government that developed the Internet and satellite communications, and provided the single largest market for the personal computer and its software. It was the federal government that was providing funds for the states and the cities. It was the federal government that funded the relief for disasters — whether hurricanes, earthquakes or flooding. None of these seemingly limitless expenditures, which added to the growing debt, would have been possible without the Almighty Dollar. Private money could not support the growing interest on the national debt. Only the central banks of creditor nations could afford that luxury. Given the number of excess dollars they possessed, they had no alternative. If the United States government should default on its interest payments, its economy would collapse, and it would take the rest of the world with it. The only element missing from this equation was how these central banks were amassing these excess dollars. The oil producing states certainly were flooded with dollars, but what about the other nations such as Western Europe, Japan and beginning in 1986, China?

The transformation of the US economy from one geared to manufacturing to one dependent upon services occurred over a period of 40 years. Its origin could be traced to the Cold War and the policy of containing Communist expansion, first into Western Europe and then throughout Asia. By the 1960s, the economies of all these nations had recovered from the ravages of war; their infrastructures were in place; and the next stage in their growth and development was to build up their currency reserves. Since the dollar was the official currency for international commerce, it was necessary to acquire dollars now that gold had disappeared as a means of exchange. From the inception of the post-war era, the single largest consumer market for exports was, and still is, the United States. With the largest and most affluent population in the world, it was a natural magnet for every nation seeking to export its products. It is also the most competitive nation when it comes to retailing. Unlike Europe and Japan, where strictures were placed on competition, in the United States with its philosophy of free enterprise the retail sector had no restraints imposed upon its growth. The emergence of the discounter was to revolutionize the distribution of merchandise in this country. By emulating the supermarket and eliminating the cost of labor through self-service, it radically altered the retail scene. The discounters' focus was centered solely on price, and when it came to merchandise that did not require customer service but was guaranteed by the manufacturer, they possessed an advantage over the traditional store with its high labor overhead. Although excluded from the conventional shopping malls where traditional retailers were housed, the lure of price overcame that disadvantage. By the late 1960s, the traditional department and specialty stores had abandoned attempting to compete with discounters in the field of electronics, major appliances and small electrics. By the late 1970s, discounters had become a major factor in the sale of apparel, home furnishings, footwear, toys and luggage. Like the two major retail/catalog chains, Sears and J.C. Penney, they were sourcing their merchandise overseas, especially in the Orient. At the same time that the discounter emerged on the retail scene, so did the concept of specialty store chains in the apparel, home furnishings, footwear and toys. Like the discounter, they too began sourcing their merchandise in the Far East. Unlike the traditional department and specialty stores, which purchased their merchandise from domestic manufacturers, by buying directly the specialty chains were able to eliminate the middle man. With the advances in transportation and communication it was possible to ship merchandise overnight by air; at the same time, via the computer and the FAX machine instant contact could be maintained with their overseas factories. US manufacturers, especially those that were unionized, soon found themselves unable to compete.

By the 1980s, the retail scene for apparel had undergone a drastic transformation. The traditional department store and the independent specialty store were either forced out of business or turned to consolidation. Manufacturers that had depended upon these outlets for their customer base were driven out of business. The domestic production of apparel was being transferred almost in its entirety to the Orient. As a result, domestic mills and converters, who had serviced these manufacturers, also went out of business. With their departure, the producers of man-made fibers followed. Not only did the flight of labor-intensive industries lead to the dismembering of the American manufacturing sector, but the very concept of free trade, which was espoused by both political parties, contributed as well. Although organized labor was vehemently opposed to free trade, seeing it as a threat to labor's political power, there was nothing it could do to prevent its occurrence. The United Steelworkers union had tried; the result of their efforts to prevent the loss of jobs by opposing any innovation that would make domestic steel more competitive was to see the domestic steel industry disappear in the face of less expensive imports. The United Automobile Workers union was more pragmatic. Faced with competition from non-unionized domestic Japanese and later, German automakers, it reluctantly acceded to the Big Three sourcing some automotive components from less expensive overseas suppliers in order to remain competitive with foreign auto producers. As a result, small and medium-sized cities in Ohio and Michigan, which at one time had supplied parts to the Big Three, found their factories abandoned and the good-paying union jobs now part of ancient history. Little by little, the UAW was obliged to give ground in order to sustain the majority of its unionized labor force. The opening up of China to capitalist enterprises, with that nation's vast population of inexpensive labor, further accelerated the demise of labor-intensive industries. It was not only the obvious labor-intensive industries that sought the advantage of less expensive labor but other manufacturing industries as well. Except for Dell, the largest manufacturer of personal computers in the world, which assembled its computers domestically, the other manufacturers of computers, printers and other peripherals had theirs assembled in the Far East. Accelerating the demise of the domestic labor market was the increased rate of mergers and acquisitions, leading to further layoffs as the operations were consolidated to improve profitability. This transformation and consolidation of the retailing and manufacturing sectors of the US economy would lead to greater efficiency and productivity. At the same time, the service sector of the economy was growing thanks to the programs initiated by Johnson's Great Society. This is the genius of American capitalism. Once the greatest manufacturing center of the world, it has abdicated that role without creating an economic crisis. This transition was inevitable once the dollar had become supreme in world commerce. It was our negative trade balance with other nations that was providing their central banks with the surplus dollars to support the interest on our growing debt. With the passage of the North American Free Trade Agreement (NAFTA) in the mid-1990s, the United States developed a negative balance of payments with Mexico as US manufacturers moved their assembly plants south of the border. This continuous acceleration by industry to move its manufacturing operations to countries where the cost of labor was far less expensive was to produce an unforeseen dividend for the American consumer. Where at one time inflation was viewed as a serious problem, by the late 1990s it had all but disappeared. (See Appendix, Table 7.).

To use debt to foster growth runs counter to the original principles of capitalistic theory. But capitalism has no principles beyond making a profit. Its very strength is its ability to adapt to new circumstances. When Keynes and White settled on the dollar as the official currency for international commerce in 1944, they hadn't the remotest idea that a Cold War between the United States and the Soviet Union would dramatically alter the economy of the United States. Capitalism is less constrained by ideology than Communism. In its flexibility lies its genius. If debt is the answer to growth, so be it. The simple fact is that you can't go home again. The national debt will continue to increase, as does the debt of most major corporations listed on the New York Stock Exchange. Thanks to the Almighty Dollar, this new form of capitalism will continue to progress and evolve.

There are purists, especially among economists, along with politicians, who view the nation's growing deficit as a calamity. Members of Congress in particular see the growing deficit as a burden that is being placed on America's children and grandchildren, while at the same time our elected representatives are adding amendments to spending bills to reinsure their reelection. State and city governments complain because federal mandates require them to supply health care, education and other social services, while at the same time they are still sanctioned by their constitutions to achieve a balanced budget. Ignored is the fact that all of them are up to their necks in debt through the issuance of long-term tax-free bonds. It is not only the federal government that is living off the Almighty Dollar but state and local governments as well. The European Union, now that it has its own currency — the euro, created in 1999 — suddenly has to cope with a declining dollar, which makes American exports cheaper and European exports more expensive. While the facts are accurate, it has not affected the balance of trade with the countries of the European Union appreciably. The United States still imports more than it exports to the three leading economies of the European Union — Germany, France and Great Britain.

Those who remain pessimistic about the future of the US economy tend to overlook one simple fact. Whether the world likes it or not, we are all sleeping in one economic bed. There is no currency capable of replacing the dollar. There are trillions of dollars currently in circulation and trillions more to follow in the succeeding years. Moreover, the economies of other nations are so integrated into our own, thanks to the dollar, that this integration compels them to support the interest on the growing US debt. The alternative would produce a collapse of every economy in the world. In essence, that is what makes the dollar almighty.

CHAPTER 2. THE AMAZING US ECONOMY

The US economy appears to be a paradox. Here is a nation that over the past three decades has consistently run ever-increasing trade deficits; the value of its currency continues to depreciate; at one time the largest industrial power in the world, today its economy is increasingly dependent upon the service sector; its national debt now exceeds $8 trillion and continues to mount every year; its population, both male and female, is more interested in sports than any other subject (with the possible exception of sex); its education system, in comparison with that of other evolved nations, ranks near the bottom. Yet the US remains the world's only superpower, militarily and economically, and its economy continues to be the economic machine that drives the other economies of the world. Its population has the highest standard of living in the world, and its popular culture dominates that of every other nation.

Is it any wonder, then, that these contradictions have produced a number of Cassandras who continue to predict the decline and fall of this US empire? In the 1980s they put their money on Japan, Inc. as our likely successor. By the year 2000, there was the European Union (EU), with its expansion into Eastern Europe and it own currency, the euro. With its larger population and its greater gross domestic product, it seemed only a matter of time before Europe would reduce the United States to a second-rate economic power. Overlooked in the assessment of the flourishing economies of the European Union is the fact that its growing GDP is largely a result of adding the economies of new members to the overall total. There also is a high rate of unemployment in Germany and France, the founding members, which hovers around 10%. Not only does this unemployment impede economic growth but it also represents a drain on the financial resources of both countries as they struggle to maintain the standard of living of the unemployed. As for the expansion of the European Union into Eastern Europe, it is largely an effort by Germany and France to exploit the less developed economies of these nations. The EU is not about to supplant the United States as the driving force for the world's economic growth. It is more concerned with economic security than leadership.

Today, the Cassandras have seized upon the thunder coming out of China and India, with their potential growth from huge, highly educated populations. Now that their political leaders have come to understand the importance of a free market economy, the doomsayers prognosticate that these economies are certain to grow to dwarf that of the United States. The administration and Congress have been quick to respond with the infusion of money and government regulation into the US educational system. Place more computers in every classroom; improve the quality of the teaching staff; raise the standards for promotion from one grade to the next; reduce the size of classes. This accent on quantity rather than quality defies historical facts. Over the course of the nineteenth and twentieth centuries, Americans developed more major inventions, which served to improve economic growth and living standards, than all the other nations in the world combined. It is this creativity that characterizes the amazing American economy. (Go to Encarta.msn.com; search: notable inventions.) There is no better example than the leadership exhibited by young and old Americans in bringing the Age of Information to the world, not only via the Internet but through the micro-chip and the software systems to operate personal computers and their offshoots. The world listens to music on Apple's iPods; tracks its business activities on Microsoft's Excel spreadsheet software; and uses Google as the number one source for information. Absent the leadership and contributions of the US, there would be no Age of Information.

The influence of the United States on the culture and economy of every nation in the world is enormous. English, or actually American vernacular, is a mandatory second language. There has been no reciprocal cultural movement or economic development that has influenced American society, or for that matter any other nation in the world. It may be one world on the currency exchanges and in the domain of commodities, but aside from those two areas of international business, the economic and cultural machine that influences the rest of the world is located in the United States. America is the single largest market for consumer goods, setting aside necessities. Europe may have succeeded in creating a union of European nations but its popular culture is American. And should the US economy catch a cold, as it did in 2001, people from Brussels to New Delhi will come down with a fever.

What makes the US economy unique and the envy of the world are the circumstances that determined its evolution. What distinguished early Americans from their counterparts in England and Europe was their exposure to a new and strange world that was not constricted by the boundaries of a civilization that had evolved over numerous centuries. At the same time, the colonists brought with them a working knowledge of all the advances their former homelands had made. This was the first time in history that a new social organism would be created with all the advantages and few of the negatives that burdened the society they had left behind. Where in England all the lands were already possessed by those who had preceded their generation, in the colonies there was land available to all. Where the mother country had long been divided into a society dominated by classes, none of these trappings pre-existed in their adopted land. In addition in these colonies there was an independence from authorities. This and the availability of resources were two factors that would shape the economic development of this nation, and in turn, the political system that would evolve.

Class distinctions (other than wealth) meant less in the new society and the goal of wealth was open to all those capable of attaining it. In America as in England, land constituted wealth. While indigenous peoples did occupy some of these lands, as far as the early colonists were concerned, "might makes right." Like the ancient Israelites when they entered Canaan and Jehovah enjoined them to slay the local inhabitants to make room for his chosen people, the colonists took it upon themselves to eliminate those tribes that would not cede their lands.

Continuing the tradition of pulling up roots and moving ever farther westward, Americans to this day are more open than many others to trying what is new and novel; many Americans relish change. As a corollary, they remain opposed to outside authority dictating to them. These unique characteristics of Americans — individualism, intolerance for constraints, mobility, and the quest for wealth — defines the difference between the evolution of the US economy and that of the European countries. There never was a rigid class structure among the whites in America. This astounded Alexis de Tocqueville. There were always rich and poor in this country, but at the same time, the society always was open to upward mobility. In the early stage of American history, wealth was sought after through the acquisition of land or through commerce by sea. The cause for the American Revolution could be traced to the insatiable lust of Americans for new lands to settle and conquer, and in turn, amass wealth.

British Lieutenant Governor Robert Dinwiddie, in conjunction with wealthy Virginia planters, financed George Washington's first effort to claim the lands beyond the Appalachian Mountains, then possessed by the French; this foray precipitated the French and Indian War and led to the removal of France from North America. Following the surrender of this immense territory, extending from the Appalachian Mountains to the Mississippi River, the British attempted to restrain the colonists from expanding into these new lands, which might lead to the creation of a nation more powerful than the mother country. As far as the Americans were concerned, the vacant land was theirs to expropriate for their own wealth. The British sought to contain these adventurers by posting an armed force of 10,000 soldiers; then they demanded that the Americans pay for the soldiers' upkeep. For the first time, 13 disparate colonies possessed a common interest — the acquisition and exploitation of this vast, untouched territory. It was George Rogers Clark, with a force of 175 frontiersmen and with the aid of French settlers, who drove the British out of these territories and allowed these lands to be secured for the United States in the peace treaty that followed the end of the war. The Duke of Wellington, Britain's greatest hero, who had defeated Napoleon at Waterloo, made the astute judgment that the expanding America was too vast a land ever to be conquered and he used his influence to bring the War of 1812 to an end.

Those engaged in commerce by sea were as aggressive as those acquiring land in their pursuit of wealth. Prior to the outbreak of the Revolutionary War, they violated all the regulations imposed by the British Admiralty that forbade them to trade with foreign possessions in the Caribbean. Smuggling became a way of life that led to personal fortunes. To the British, this attitude of flouting the law for personal gain seemed inexplicable. Now that Britain was master of the seas, and no longer had the need to prey on Spanish galleons, it assumed its colonies would honor its supremacy. In British society, every one knew his or her place and acted accordingly. In the American colonies, the acquisition of wealth took precedence over British tradition or customs. Without consciously realizing it, psychologically these British possessions had cut the umbilical cord that bound them to the mother country. Although these colonies were separated from each other by geography, economies, climatic conditions and religions, they all possessed one thing in common, freedom. The British allowed them the freedom to develop their own societies. Because of that, they never were colonial possessions in the strict sense of that term. Nor could they be considered Protectorates since they managed their own finances and were free to develop their own economies, other than certain restrictions on trade. This was the reason why they resented the direct taxation that eventually led to the American Revolution. To Parliament and the members of the British establishment, the colonists were spoiled children who ought to have been spanked. To the Americans in these disparate colonies, after 150 years, they were sufficiently mature to make their own decisions without Papa disciplining them. This analogy is not farfetched. American merchants imposed a boycott on the importation of British merchandise in a protest against the Stamp Act. When it was finally withdrawn, a letter expressing this exact attitude was sent to the American merchants in New York by their British counterparts.

These early examples of Americans seeking wealth and independence from authority would characterize the growth of the nation's economy. In a classless society, wealth was the only distinction. While the Revolution was made possible by men from all walks of life, the American establishment — those in the forefront of the Revolution — had no intention of establishing a democracy. Only men of means were selected to go to Philadelphia to draw up a constitution for the nation. Their intent was to create a system that would prevent the establishment of a democracy. The United States was founded as a republic, and the specific role of the Senate, whose members were appointed by the state legislatures, was to block any excesses committed by the executive branch of government or the House of Representatives. This apparent contradiction between a free society, where every man was the equal of his neighbor, and the creation of a form of government that protected the assets of those who had acquired wealth, was deliberately omitted in the

Declaration of Independence. Jefferson's famous phrase "life, liberty and the pursuit of happiness," adopted from the writings of the English philosopher John Locke, did not include the word "property," which was consciously removed from his original text. There was a good reason. Most of the colonies were the property of the King of England. The American Constitution would rectify that strategic omission on the part of Jefferson. Private property was to be as sacred in this country as it was in Great Britain, with one major difference. Britain was a closed society; whatever land existed already was possessed. To insure that these lands remained intact and were not splintered into smaller parcels, primogeniture was the law in Britain. In the new world, with its vast open spaces yet to be populated, there was no need for primogeniture, given the potential for new settlements on unoccupied virgin lands.

How a fortune was accumulated in this new nation was immaterial. Once a man acquired wealth, he joined that club of successful Americans who came to view themselves as the bastion of a republican form of government.

Millionaires became America's royalty, especially if their fortunes had been made starting from scratch. The attitude of the average American was that even with a minimum education, those blessed only with an overwhelming desire to succeed could indeed make a fortune. Lady Luck favored the self-confident risk taker. The newly rich were attracted to Wall Street, and further fortunes were made and lost as entrepreneurs lured investors to fledgling industries. Money equaled power, and corruption pervaded state legislatures and the judicial system. The myth that the streets of America were paved with gold was fostered by Horatio Alger's rags-to-riches novels, which were published one after another during the late nineteenth century. To sophisticated people, it may seem corny, but hundreds of thousands, or perhaps millions, of immigrants read and believed in these stories. Each one recounted the same tale of a poor boy who made good by dint of virtue, discipline and hard work. To immigrant boys first learning the new language, these books were a source of inspiration and the requisite perspiration. They inspired many to succeed; others spent their lives serving to make their employers rich. However, it can be said that the robber barons made most of their money not so much by stealing from the poor as by bilking other men who were just as greedy and unscrupulous as they were.

With a constant flow of new immigrants following the end of the Civil War, no powerful labor movement developed in this country. The American Federation of Labor, launched by Samuel Gompers, consisted of craft unions and did not attempt to pit labor against capital. In essence, it was more a fraternity of men in the same profession than an activist labor movement. Until Congress in the early 1920s enacted legislation severely limiting immigration, in particular from eastern and southern Europe, labor leaders suffered from a terrible disadvantage — an endless supply of labor prepared to work for less money and longer hours. It was only when that supply was cut off that labor was able to organize.

The industrial revolution that took place in the United States, beginning with the railroads, would catapult this country into the position of leading industrial power in the world. The sheer size of the nation dwarfed that of any European power. Opportunities existed from the eastern seaboard to the Pacific coast. Even in the former Confederate states, which remained mired in an economic depression during the period of phenomenal economic growth in the North and West, individuals emerged to create a monopoly on the burgeoning cigarette market that would replace chewing tobacco and cigars. It was the period of inventive genius that distinguished this country from all others. Every section of this vast, empty space had special needs. It would be a housewife who would help to invent barbed wire to keep the livestock from straying. America was a country continually reinventing itself. By the beginning of the twentieth century, a rural society had become a nation of large, overcrowded cities. The farm boys who became the robber barons of the post-Civil War period would be succeeded by other boys off farms, such as Henry Ford, who would develop the concepts of the assembly line and of paying his workers what was then considered a munificent wage, so they could afford to buy the cars they produced.

The new breed of millionaires that emerged devoted their energies to the development of industry rather than concentrating on railroads and stock manipulation. American industry was expanding and contracting at the same time. Competition was fierce, and in the end, the larger companies swallowed up those less successful. The merger of United States Steel into the largest corporation in the world was preceded by dozens of consolidations between small steel producers. It would be duplicated several decades later, with the consolidation of the automotive industry.

All of these consolidations would take place on a much smaller scale in industrialized Britain and Western Europe. There were two major differences that distinguished the pattern of economic expansion on the two sides of the Atlantic. Because of Europe's caste system and the absence of mass immigration, workers would organize into unions in the Old World. From these unions would emerge Socialist parties in an effort to raise the standard of living of the working class. In the United States, no comparable political movement took place. Thanks to its open-door policy on immigration, there was always a supply of cheap labor. Even the effort to organize the independent farmers succeeded only for a brief period of time. The other major difference between these two worlds was in the standard of living. With all the examples of exploitation, the take-home pay of the average American worker far exceeded that of his European counterpart. It was this differential that allowed the US economy to grow at a faster pace than that of Europe. This relative economic wellbeing also played a major role in curbing any movement towards unionization or the development of Socialist organizations. To the European immigrants, especially the last to arrive, those from southern and eastern Europe, the standard of living in their new country was a miracle compared to conditions in their native countries. Except for a few intellectuals, the idea that labor was being exploited never entered their minds. Any man or woman willing to work could find employment. Most of them were uneducated and naïve. Some were foolish enough to invest their life savings in the stock market or in some scam, with the hope of getting rich. But as long as jobs were available, almost every American believed this country was the best of all possible nations.

The crash of the stock market in 1929 and the Depression and massive unemployment that followed was to shatter that American dream. To many, it now appeared that the days of swashbuckling individualism and eternal optimism were gone forever. For the first time since the founding of this nation, a large percentage of the population was frightened and bewildered. The laissez-faire capitalism that had developed the greatest economy in the world no longer seemed to have an answer.

It was not yet time to change the system, but rather to reform it. The New Deal, espoused by the academic experts that newly elected President Franklin Roosevelt brought to Washington, would set in motion what many of the old establishment believed to be a revolution. Armed with a newly elected Democratic Congress, as uncertain about the future of the economy as their constituents who elected them, they rubber-stamped whatever legislation the administration requested. Despite the contention of its critics that the New Deal was leading the country towards a Socialist economy, it never had such aspirations. The legislation proposed by Roosevelt's Brain Trusters and enacted by Congress was designed to ameliorate the plight of America's farmer and unorganized labor by providing a basic safety net for them. The New Deal programs — of price supports for farmers; a minimum wage for labor; the ability for unions to bargain with management; Social Security for the aged and the infirm; and the use of government monies to provide employment on worthwhile projects — were efforts to stimulate the economy through deficit spending while at the same time providing economic justice for the less fortunate. To the old establishment, it was nothing less than socialism; to those in the vanguard of the reform movement, these reforms were a necessary antidote to the excesses of laissez-faire capitalism that had dominated the US economy since it inception.

The legislation enacted during the first two terms of the Roosevelt administration was revolutionary in permitting labor to organize and bargain with management; in subsidizing the farm population; and in supporting the aged and the disabled; as well as in imposing regulations on the financial markets by establishing the Securities and Exchange Commission. However, Roosevelt's New Deal was not as revolutionary as most old guard Republicans perceived it to be. Rather its was plain vanilla Keynesian economics instituted to resolve an economic downturn, such as had existed prior to the collapse of the gold standard, by pump priming a sluggish economy through government spending. In the 1930s, free trade was almost non-existent because every country tried to protect from competition what remained of its industries. Thus in 1938 massive unemployment returned when the Roosevelt administration decided that the US economy had rebounded sufficiently to reduce government expenditures and reduce the budget deficit, to allow the free market economy to take over. It was only the outbreak of the Second World War in Europe, followed by the build-up of the nation's military, that brought an end to the Depression. By the time victory came in 1945, after four years of prosperity for the majority of the American public, the

Depression was viewed as an economic aberration. Americans had more money in their pockets than ever before.

At the close of the Second World War, Congress rewarded the 16 million men and women who had served in the armed forces with a generous G.I. Bill of Rights, providing every honorably discharged veteran a sum of several hundred dollars and an opportunity to further his or her education. In addition, Congress guaranteed home loans for up to 90% of the property's value. This largesse on the part of the federal government would pay off. Once armed with college degrees, returning veterans would become tomorrow's engineers, scientists, doctors, dentists, lawyers and businessmen. In the late 1940s and early 1950s, a college degree had far more significance than it possesses today. Making a degree more widely available was significant in redistributing wealth and adding further flexibility to the economic class structure. The upper middle class expanded from a few to more than 20% of the population. More important, professions that had closed their doors to all but Anglo-Saxons gradually were infiltrated by ethnic groups. This diversity would serve to bolster creativity through the cross pollenization of ideas and a broader base of participation.

The widespread shortage of affordable housing, a consequence of the Depression, left a tremendous void to be filled. In the New York area, this was partially resolved by two returning veterans, the Levitt brothers. In their approach to housing, they ignored historical paradigms. Instead of constructing a series of individual homes to be sold off one at a time, they would bring to home construction Henry Ford's concept of mass production, through the use of an assembly line. Purchasing thousands of acres of unused potato fields on Long Island, NY, for a dollar an acre, they proceeded to construct one model home, with a picture window in front, on a quarter of an acre, completely outfitted with kitchen cabinets and major appliances. This two-bedroom one-bath home with a living room would serve as the prototype for the additional 7,000 homes that would be constructed at the same time. Every home that was built would be a replica of the model home. There would be no deviations. All the framing, windows, walls and the roof would be pre-fabricated, mirroring an assembly line used for automobiles. The amount of time necessary to complete a house was calibrated. With every element of the finished product the same, the cost savings through bulk purchasing were enormous. There were no middlemen. Using non-union labor not only lowered the cost, but equally important, avoided union regulations dictating the amount of time required to complete each project. Full-page ads in the newspapers announced the sale of a two-bedroom house, complete with appliances and ready for occupancy at the unbelievable price of $7,500.

The migration to the suburbs that Levittown signaled would transform the US economy. Where there was population, retailers soon followed — first in strip centers; then in shopping centers; finally in huge malls anchored by four or five major department stores and mail order chains. Eventually, realizing the advantages of inexpensive land and a growing workforce nearby, corporations would follow. Truck farmers who had barely eked out a living soon found that the lands they tilled were worth far more to developers than the money they could make in a lifetime from farming. Where before the war the suburbs had been viewed as a place only the wealthy could afford, now they became a necessity for the average family. For the growing middle class, the suburbs became the only place to raise a family. Little by little, small cities became metropolises as the city limits were pushed out farther and farther. Dallas and Houston, Texas, once small non-descript cities, soon would boast of a population of more than a million. The same would hold true for Phoenix and even Las Vegas. Los Angeles, the daddy of them all, with its ideal climate conditions, would continue its sprawl, with people now commuting to work from adjacent Orange County. The automotive industry would prosper since almost all families now required two cars. Roads and highways would have to be built to accommodate the increased traffic. The mobility of the early Americans as they set out to conquer a continent was being duplicated a century later.

The move from the city to the suburbs also changed the face of the apparel industry. Daily life in the suburbs was informal. There were no streets with retail stores; women got in and out of their cars either to go shopping at a supermarket or a mall or to deliver their children to an activity. Slacks and jeans served as their dress code. Unless they were members of a country club, where dress was more formal, casual wear fit their lifestyle. Around the house men wore a pair of jeans or shorts. Within a few decades, the acceptable dress for restaurants and even many churches in the suburbs largely meant casual wear. Even in the workplace, acceptable attire became more casual. The sexual revolution of the 1960s and 1970s further eroded formality in dress. With the invention of pantyhose, the mini-skirt was born, and the girdle died. This undergarment had become an anachronism. The modesty it once represented was passé, and its practical application — to anchor stockings — was obsolete. Eventually the change in US dress codes migrated to Europe and other developed countries

The rise of suburbia also forced a change in retailing, in the form of the supermarket. By consolidating every food product under one roof, this innovation not only tended to even the flow of traffic, but more importantly, led to the concept of self-service. The need for sales help was greatly reduced because all the merchandise was checked out at a cash register. The supermarket set the stage for the emergence of the discounter, which would lead to the demise of most traditional retailers. The basic concept of discounting was to maintain a low overhead, which would enable it to undersell the competition and make up for the difference in profit margins through the volume of merchandise it sold. As was the case with the supermarket, it depended upon self-service to minimize its cost. It first made its appearance in New York City, undercutting the traditional department store on such big-ticket items as television sets, major appliances and small electrics. A 1962 *Time* magazine cover story on Korvette's, a pioneer discounter, inspired both the chairman of S.S. Kresge and Sam Walton of Bentonville, AK, to enter the field, eventually populating the US with Kmarts and the world with Wal-Marts.

Continually losing share of market to these new types of retailers and off-price specialty chains, the department stores initiated a policy of leasing out space to individual vendors, which at least guaranteed the retailers a profit; at the same time, they embarked upon mergers and acquisitions in order to show growth for Wall Street. Therein lay the problem. The executives at every type of retail organization had their eyes fixed on the price of their stock and the stock options they held. So, they opened more retail outlets in markets already oversaturated, or bought independent department stores. Entire chains of stores were acquired, sold, or closed down. After a series of bankruptcies and near bankruptcies, the industry is much consolidated; Federated-Macy's now owns almost every major department store in the country.

A given in US retailing is that it is always in the process of reinventing itself. Many current retail giants were start-ups in the mid 1970s and 1980s. The Price Club, the first warehouse club, which was designed to offer unbeatable discounts for volume purchases by small businesses and restaurants, inspired the development of such chains as Sam's Club and BJ's, which greatly expanded the audience and offerings. The 1970s also gave rise to "category killers" — chains that focused on a single category of merchandise, housed in "big box" buildings, with their own large parking facilities, enabling the store to offer breadth and depth of inventory. Foremost among these was the Home Depot. Designed to attract the do-it-your-selfer and the small contractor, this huge warehouse stocks every imaginable piece of merchandise for the home owner, including plants, shrubs and flowers, at discounted or highly competitive prices. In addition, if the homeowner wants a professional to do the job, Home Depot will recommend contractors and guarantee the quality of the workmanship. This has revolutionized the do-it-your-self business. During the same time period, another innovator — Circuit City — would apply the same concept to the electronics business. The Sports Authority would use the same formula for sporting goods; Staples would for office supplies. Efficiency and price have been the hallmarks of recent success in retailing. In the process, these colossi are leading to the demise of the independent merchant.

The growth of the US economy, whether on the manufacturing or retail level, is predicated on debt. Most of the corporations listed on the New York Stock Exchange grew because of the debt they accumulated by issuing stock. If forced to come up with cash to pay off all the stock that had been issued over the years, at the current selling price, they would be unable to meet the amount of debt outstanding without resorting to loans, which would place them in further debt. Furthermore, without the indebtedness of the American consumer, whose purchases account for more than 70% of the gross domestic product, the economy would collapse. Until the early 1970s, the debts incurred by the consumer were generally the mortgage on his home, payments on his car, and in certain instances, payments on such big ticket items as major appliances and carpeting. All debt limitations were to be removed with the emergence of the ubiquitous credit card. Over the next 30 years, the amount of credit available to consumers would expand enormously and, with it, the growth of the GDP.

The early history of the credit card revolved around convenience for the well-to-do. Upscale specialty stores issued credit cards to their most favored customers, with the bill due at the end of the month. Macy's was to come up with a better gimmick; their customers could deposit money in Macy's bank and draw upon their account for their purchases. In the early 1950s, the concept of a credit card was extended to upscale restaurants, both domestically and in Europe, with the creation of Diners Club International. To meet the competition from Diners, American Express, which already had a dominant position in Europe with its Travelers Checks, issued its own credit card, which soon outstripped Diners in importance. American Express included hotels as well as restaurants and promoted its card as a written record for expenses. In 1958, a vice-president at the Bank of America decided to experiment with its own credit card for favored customers. It was so successful that other banks joined in. All of these credit cards, like Diners and American Express, were for convenience only. Credit was only extended until payment was due on the monthly bill.

In 1970, a major breakthrough took place with the invention of the magnetic tape. Thanks to this tape, credit information could be stored and transferred electronically. It would take another group of inventors to show how the data collected could be instantaneously transferred to a central terminal, where it could be read and acted upon. To do this would require setting up machines in each retail location, capable of transmitting this information. This led to the development of bank credit cards, which put credit in the wallets of a wider base of consumers. The basic attraction for a bank to join the fray was the potential interest it could charge by extending credit to the consumer. Holding credit cards from different banks expanded the amount of credit the consumer could use when making purchases. If his credit limit was $500 on each of three cards from different banks, the cardholder now possessed $1,500 of credit. Moreover, since cardholders were required to pay only 10% of the unpaid balance each month on each of the cards, they tended to buy more than they ordinarily would.

This ability to indulge soon was reflected in the increase in consumer spending. Where prior to the credit card explosion, consumer expenditures accounted for 67% of the gross domestic product, over the ensuing years it would increase gradually until today it accounts for 72% of the GDP. When American Airlines introduced the concept of frequent flier miles for those using its airline, Citicorp bank saw this innovation as an opportunity to expand its customer base. In an arrangement with the airline, any dollar expenditures made on its credit cards could be applied toward frequent flyer points.

The US economy is astonishingly flexible in adjusting to changing circumstances. From its very inception, the US economy had all the advantages of being able to create its own formula for success. It consisted of one part independence for the individual; one part mobility or freedom of movement; and a third part that could be termed unbridled determination. For the early colonists, there was always a tomorrow if today failed to meet expectations. As a result, little by little, the frontier was pushed back to make room for development and from this expansion, a complex and diverse economy would emerge.

When Jefferson described the goals of this new nation as being life, liberty and the pursuit of happiness, his words reflected the way that those in the forefront of the American Revolution viewed the future direction of the nation's economy. The political system that emerged was designed to protect the economy that had been built since the original settlements. Our political system was a reflection of the economic situation already in place. It was only with the advent of the Depression, with the resulting massive unemployment, that our original economic system seemed to have run out of steam. From Roosevelt's New Deal and thereafter, the federal government assigned to itself a major role in the development of the economy. Despite the checks and balances placed on the economy, first by the legislation enacted during the Depression and later by the legislation that created Lyndon Johnson's Great Society, the original ethos from which had emerged the American economy still remains in place. There are no restrictions on upward mobility and the accumulation of wealth. Indeed, the rich are quite free to get richer, and the disparity between the wealthiest and the least wealthy only continues to grow. In the late nineteenth century, the exemplar of a man who knew how to seize opportunity was John D. Rockefeller, who achieved domination of the crude oil market by acquiring all the refineries in the country; in the late twentieth century, the exemplar was Bill Gates of Microsoft, who achieved domination of the operating system market for personal computers.

The possibility of such successes has lured Americans into the forefront of innovation. If today's economy is directed towards the service sector rather than manufacturing, Americans now will seek their fortunes in these new industries. The American economy has undergone drastic changes since the first European settlers arrived on these shores 400-plus years ago. The one constant throughout those four centuries has been the ability of the American economy to adjust to changing circumstances. It is this fact which marks the difference between the American economy and that of other nations. From its very inception the American economy has been a work in progress. Its only tradition is the accumulation of personal wealth.

Chapter 3. Beyond Good and Evil: A Different Portrait of Joe Stalin

When Ronald Reagan proclaimed the Soviet Union to be an "evil empire," he was the first US president to promote this attitude in such primitive terms, although by then many Americans had been brought up in much the same thinking. Liberals, who had already classified Reagan as a dangerous war monger, feared that he could convert the Cold War into a hot war and trigger the unthinkable — mutual destruction. But if Joseph Stalin, soundly asleep in his coffin for 30 years, had heard these words, in all likelihood he would have smiled and retorted: those are the ravings of a two-bit Hollywood actor, now the leader of a bourgeois society on the verge of collapse. To Stalin, the words good and evil were tools used by the ruling capitalist elite in order to maintain their control over society.

Only by setting aside such terms as good and evil can a true picture of Stalin emerge. Every action he took was calculated to erase the last remaining vestiges of a bourgeois society, where the wealthy exploit the workers, in order to open the door to the future of a more equitable Communist society. He viewed the elimination of any dissenters in the same fashion. To re-make an entire society along new lines required total and unswerving discipline and obedience. Had he opened up the leadership to debate, the result would have been at best confusion and gridlock. The Western democracies were a prime example. When Hitler marched German troops into the Rhineland, in violation of the Treaty of Versailles, the French Assembly debated whether to send in troops to drive them out. In the end, France did nothing and Hitler consequently felt himself free to rearm Germany. More important, he had proved to the general staff of the German Army that he understood the attitude of the French and that Germany could proceed to scuttle the other terms of the treaty.

Had Stalin allowed for debate among the members of the Politburo, there would have been no Five Year Plan and the Soviet Union never could have developed the industrial base that put the country on its feet and enabled it to defeat the Wehrmacht. To this day, even after most of the archives of the former Soviet Union have been opened, the West still doesn't understand Stalin. There is good reason for this. Westerners measure him in terms of their own projective system. The words good and evil, which are part of Western man's baggage, meant nothing to Stalin. He viewed them as an anachronism of Judeo-Christian theology, which teaches that man is not master of his own destiny but is merely the creature of an imaginary God. The words good and evil have been ascribed by man's imagination to represent the divine thoughts of this imagined figure. Over centuries, organized religion has made good use of these words to cement its hold on people's minds. When Karl Marx described religion as the opiate of the masses, he was describing the way many Christians, Jews, Muslims and others put belief above knowledge, and accept what they are told rather than making the effort to think for themselves. Stalin made every effort to exorcise religion in the Soviet Union. It was divisive. It challenged the authority of the state. Stalin saw organized religion as another remnant of bourgeois thinking that was counter-revolutionary.

Students of Soviet history are well informed on the general outline of Stalin's early years. He had eight years of schooling in the town of Gori and then was enrolled as a student in the seminary at Tiflis, now Tbilisi, the capital of the Georgia. While a student at the seminary, he was exposed to Marxism and began his career as a social revolutionary. After being expelled from the seminary for his efforts to organize labor, and after a brief position as a clerk, he devoted himself to a revolutionary career, joining the budding Social Democratic Party. Imprisoned by the tsarist police seven times and dispatched to Siberia, he managed to escape each time; his longest sentence lasting from 1913 to 1917. In between, he had met Vladimir Lenin, the leader of the Bolshevik faction of the Social Democratic Party at congresses held in Finland, Stockholm and London. But he remained a minor functionary in the party apparatus until he planned and helped execute a spectacular robbery in Tiflis, which provided the party with much needed funds. In 1912, Lenin elevated him to the Central Committee of the Bolshevik Party and prior to his four-year exile in Siberia he edited the party newspaper, *Pravda*. Upon his escape in 1917, he resumed editorship of the paper and took an active role as a Political Commissar during the revolutionary war.

The Russian Revolution was the explosion of a pressure cooker that had been hissing for a long time. In February 1917, the monarchy was overthrown and a provisional government was formed. The country was in a crisis, already exhausted by three years of war. Yet, due perhaps to an excess of democratic debate, decisive action was impossible. Lenin stepped into the vacuum and seized power in November, with the backing of the Petrograd Soviet. One of Lenin's most appealing populist promises was to give the *muzhiks* the land owned by their absentee landlords for their own personal use. This may seem a strange start for a government dedicated to state socialism, but above all Lenin was a pragmatist. What he termed his New Economic Policy in 1921, which he described as taking one step backward in order to move two steps forward, was a necessity. Unlike the American Civil War, which had been waged largely in the South, the Russian Civil War encompassed the entire range of the tsarist empire — from Petrograd in the north to the Caucasus in the south, from Poland in the west to Siberia in the east. It had been a long and bloody struggle; even the victors were exhausted and needed a breathing spell. Unlike the French revolutionaries, however, Lenin knew from the outset what direction the revolution would follow. The new government he and his colleagues formed, the Union of Soviet Socialist Republics, was to become a Communist state once the scars of the Civil War had faded away. In this dictatorship of the proletariat there would be one party, the Communist, and the leadership and direction of the party would be in the hands of an appointed Politburo, with Lenin as its chief executive.

The basic problem facing the members of the Politburo, after Lenin suffered a disabling stroke in 1923, was who would succeed him when he died. Until then, the succession had been left in limbo. By January 1924, when he died, the newly created Soviet Union had largely recovered from the ravages brought about by the Civil War. It was time to implement the Marxist-Leninist doctrine and socialize the economy. The two leading candidates, neither one of whom Lenin had endorsed as his successor, were Leon Trotsky, who had led the victorious Red Army during the Civil War and who also served as Foreign Minister; and Stalin, Secretary General of the Communist Party, who was responsible for the functioning of the far-flung party apparatus. There were many reasons why Lenin had refused to anoint a successor. He had made the revolution possible single-handedly. It was he who had insisted that the Soviet Union should emerge as a federation of socialist republics; he had rebuffed the efforts of some of his collaborators to admit the Mensheviks and other offshoots of the Russian Social Democratic party, unless they agreed to be subservient to the will of the Bolshevik party. He defeated the efforts of the Russophiles to control and direct the party apparatus. Before his last stroke left him totally paralyzed, he had produced a paper indicating which direction the Communist Party should follow. Lenin, like so many men of extraordinary brilliance, was jealous of his creation and he wasn't sure how anyone else could fill his shoes.

On the surface, the choice should have been Trotsky. Brilliant, mercurial, a master orator who could hold an audience spellbound, a superb administrator, he had been Lenin's leading lieutenant during the war years, in total charge of the Red army. Working against him was his enormous ego. From his earliest published writings, he doubted that a Socialist state could be created in such a backward country as Russia, which had yet to develop a flourishing bourgeois society. Even after the German Communist Party failed to seize power in 1923 when the German economy had totally collapsed under extreme inflation, he still believed that, while the Soviet Union could set an example for the future of socialism, its success was contingent upon it being spread to more advanced economies. There was another factor that mitigated against his being chosen and that was his supercilious attitude toward other members of the hierarchy, and toward Lenin himself. While Lenin admired Trotsky, he also felt that once he was in power Trotsky would shape the revolution as he saw it, not as Lenin did.

Stalin, on the other hand, represented a different problem. For one thing, he was not a good administrator. Lenin had appointed him General Secretary of the Party with the task of reorganizing and rationalizing the cumbersome bureaucracy that had emerged in the immediate years after the war. He had failed miserably, and Lenin had chastised him for his failure. On the other hand, Stalin had written the program for the absorption of the nationalities within the framework of the Soviet Union. It was his lucid understanding of the problems that had to be overcome that had made possible Lenin's concept of a federalized nation. During the Civil War, Stalin had played a major role as a commissar overseeing the former tsarist officers that Trotsky had enlisted to fight on the side of Communist Party. In addition, Stalin was more likely than Trotsky to hew to the general direction of the party that Lenin envisioned.

The struggle for power between these two determined individuals would be played out within the confines of the Politburo. In 1924, there were two viewpoints on how to implement the industrialization of the nation. One was to take a gradual approach, using the wealth from collectivizing the farms to pay for building the necessary infrastructure; the other, advanced by Trotsky, was to act immediately. He wanted to establish a Five Year Plan, set goals, and hold those responsible for administering the various projects accountable. To the members of the Politburo, accountability sounded risky. Stalin quickly sensed this unease and decided to exploit it. With Lev Kamenev and Grigory Zinovyev on his side, Stalin challenged Trotsky's proposal as being counter-revolutionary. In place of moderation, Trotsky was prepared to jeopardize the very survival of the Soviet experiment in a highly risky venture, which if it failed, would destroy the very system Lenin had been in the process of creating. Stalin had thrown down the gauntlet, and Trotsky now found himself in the position of defending himself. With the heads of the two leading Soviets, Moscow and Leningrad, on Stalin's side, Trotsky sought support from the other members of the Politburo. It was his supercilious attitude toward other members of the Politburo that did him in. In gradual stages, he was first dismissed from the Politburo; then from the Communist Party; and finally sent into exile in Siberia.

Having successfully removed the main obstacle in his plan to take absolute control of the Politburo, Stalin now maneuvered to rid himself of his only possible challengers, Kamenev and Zinovyev. Individually, each of them believed that he would succeed to be head of the Politburo, once Trotsky was out of the way. Both of them would soon discover that their heads were next on the chopping block. With the backing of Nikolai Bukharin and Alexei Rykov, Stalin reintroduced Trotsky's original Five Year Plan for the industrialization of the Soviet Union. As he expected, Kamenev and Zinovyev immediately opposed the concept, citing all the reasons that Stalin had proffered at the time. Stalin's retort was that the situation had changed; that instead of the economy growing, it was drifting; that Lenin's New Economic Policy had run its course. He proclaimed that unless a crash program was immediately instituted, the very concept of a successful Socialist economy would be doomed. Even though the two men controlled the leading Soviets, Stalin had enough votes in the Politburo to remove them from that body. Unlike Trotsky, however, they were not removed from the Communist Party but were given minor posts in obscure ministries. With the departure of his two potential rivals, Stalin now had a free hand in directing the future of the country's economy.

The continuous American effort to pillory Stalin for his record of ruthlessness fails to take into account the rationale behind the deportations and killings that were carried out. Among the many heinous crimes attributed to Stalin, the most egregious was the slaughter and deportation of millions of kulaks in order to collectivize agriculture. Viewed through the perspective of a socialist state, where all the means of production are controlled by the Communist Party, in order to ensure equitable distribution, the decision to collectivize agriculture was mandatory. While Marx had never touched on this subject in his writings, from Lenin forward it was assumed that this process was inevitable if a true socialist state was to be created. Supporting the feasibility of this thesis was the success of the kibbutzim in Palestine. Not only were there Socialist kibbutzim in Palestine but there were Communist ones as well. While the Communist Mapam was a minority party, and most of the kibbutzim and industry were controlled by the Mapai, the Socialist labor party, the Mapam was still a political factor among the early settlers, the majority of whom had fled Russia to avoid anti-Semitism. In making the decision to collectivize Soviet agriculture, agronomists pointed to the success of the kibbutzim in making the desert bloom. Thus it was naturally assumed, given the rich soil in the Ukraine, once the breadbasket for Western Europe, the results would be phenomenal.

One small drawback was overlooked. The pioneers who moved to Palestine, whether Communist, Socialist or capitalist, were Zionists, dedicated to creating a homeland for Jews. Their political and economic interpretations of the future state were secondary to that fact. The independent farmers who had sided with the Soviets during the Civil War had done so on the premise that the land of the absentee landlords that had been turned over to the farmers was theirs to keep. Moreover, when Stalin announced his plan to collectivize Soviet agriculture, they had experienced almost a decade of relative prosperity. As in any market economy, the more successful among them had expanded their original land holdings. Among all layers of Soviet society, during the 1920s, they had fared the best.

To believers of Marxist-Leninism, the collectivization of agriculture would increase productivity because the system now could be scientifically rationalized. The profits taken by the kulaks, in selling their product to the state, now would disappear and be replaced by lower prices for the Soviet consumer. Among the leadership at the Politburo, there was no dissent. None of them had ever farmed; and none of them understood the symbiotic relationship between the farmer, his land and his livestock. Whereas in industry the workers could be provided with an eight-hour day, farmers worked from before dawn until after sunset. Industrial production was not contingent upon the weather or an invasion of pests that could lay waste to a season's labor. Stalin and the other members of the Politburo actually believed that the independent farmer would accept collectivization and subsume his personal interests for the good of the socialist dream, in which the fruits of everyone's labor would be enjoyed by all of society.

To this day, Stalin has been attacked for the ruthless measures he took in his effort to collectivize Soviet agriculture. Discounted, and rarely mentioned, is the reaction of the kulaks to collectivization. Determined to maintain their independence, in retaliation the kulaks began to slaughter their livestock, to set their fields on fire or to pour salt into the ground. If they couldn't maintain their status, then let the Soviet experiment wither on the vine. It was their effort to sabotage Soviet agriculture that produced Stalin's fury and led to the executions and mass deportations to Siberia. Stalin took these depredations on Soviet soil personally. To him, the kulaks' attempts to destroy the goals of the revolution were treasonous. Critics lament the fate of the kulaks without taking into consideration the situation the new nation faced. Without a sufficient supply of food, the government would collapse. In fact, the real criticism of Stalin was his failure to act more quickly and put down this insurrection. The actions taken by the kulaks were not only counter-revolutionary but potentially lethal. Throughout the 1930s, the people of the Soviet Union were forced to live on short rations. The German invasion in

1941 provided a second deathblow to Soviet agriculture, which would not recover until the early 1960s.

The setback in collectivizing agriculture did not deter Stalin from pursuing his overall strategy of creating a modern industrial state. While there were mishaps and the quotas set were often unrealistic, there was continual progress. Soviet engineers were as capable as those in any other nation. Coal and oil production increased rapidly. Steel mills were constructed. Dams to generate hydroelectric power were soon in place. The decision to electrify the entire country, including the nationalities, was implemented. In essence, what the Soviet Union accomplished — although, on a much larger scale — was no different than what the Roosevelt administration fostered with the creation of the Tennessee Valley Authority. The United States government provided the capital and the plans that would curb flooding by constructing dams, and in turn, provided inexpensive electricity to millions of homes. This was also the case with the Rural Electrification Act. Since the population was too sparse to provide a return on invested capital for private companies, the government stepped in, and with its own funds, solved the problem.

Of course, the scope of the Five Year Plans dwarfed those efforts by the Roosevelt administration. An entire Socialist economy was to be built which would cover every facet of a Soviet citizen's life. The job undertaken was monumental. While there were remnants of the old economy under the tsars upon which to build, the plans for a new, Socialist economy far exceeded what was in place. One of the most pressing tasks was to address the dire shortage of housing, a result of the migration to cities that everywhere accompanied industrialization, exacerbated by three years of warfare during the revolutionary period. Another was the expansion of the textile and apparel industries. Hospitals and clinics as well as schools had to be constructed over a landmass that covered seven time zones. To unify all the "nationalities" or ethnic groups encompassed in these vast territories, Russian was declared the primary language.

For the young people growing up in this socialist environment, where advancement in education was predicated on merit, it was a time of excitement. They were part of a great experiment designed to bring economic justice to everyone. While the shortage of food was the most prevalent complaint, and the housing projects were shoddy, there were compensations in the cultural life that abounded. This included theater, cinema, symphony orchestras, opera, ballet and regional dance troupes.

The Moscow circus was as world famous as the Russian and Ukrainian dance groups. Celebration of national folklore was allowed but religious practices were not. And with successive Five Year Plans, the economy grew stronger. The only problem that Stalin was unable to resolve was that of agriculture. Not only had the kulaks done major damage to the soil and the livestock, but the most intelligent and knowledgeable among them had been either massacred or deported.

Except for the agricultural sector of the state Socialist economy, major progress was being made throughout the economy. At the same time, there was a darker side which threatened the success of this socialist state. In describing the hierarchy of the system he had envisioned, Marx co-opted a phrase from the 18th century French advocate of a socialist state, Gabriel Bonnet de Mably: "from each according to his abilities, to each according to his needs." That was not the way the system operated in the early days of this socialist experiment. Members of the Communist Party had priority in awarding and being awarded assignments. Nepotism was rampant throughout the Soviet empire. Especially in the nationalities, positions were awarded on the basis of family connections. Skillful members of the bourgeoisie who had accepted the new regime were shunted aside for loyal Communists. Mistakes in judgment were covered up by Commissars in order to protect their own positions in the new society.

The concept that adopting quotas would provide accountability boomeranged. Quantity replaced quality. This was most apparent in the field of construction. If materials didn't arrive on time, or the quality wasn't up to the standards set, this did not delay construction. All that mattered was production of the right number of units, if a person was to hold onto his position and the benefits that came with it. Inefficiency and sloppiness permeated the entire Soviet economy. Early on, state socialism would develop the characteristics that would distinguish it throughout its lifespan — indifference to quality.

The one aspect of Soviet life that was threatening was the omnipresence of the secret police, the Cheka, which Lenin had established at the beginning of the revolution. He modeled it after the secret agents of the tsarist regime, whose role was to infiltrate revolutionary organizations. The Cheka's original function was to prevent sabotage of the new regime. The rationale for the secret police stemmed from the Communist leaders' own personal experiences. All those who had been caught up in the revolutionary movement, and had been caught, had spent time in exile in Siberia. New to power, and with the nation still in a fragile state, the threat of a counter-revolution was foremost in their minds. The European powers had yet to recognize the country's very existence. British and US troops, which had fought on the side of the White Russian Army, were withdrawn only in 1921. What some might classify as paranoia was actually prudence. In its early years, the Cheka focused its attention on any remaining royalists, bourgeoisie and dissident Social Democrats. But any organization given such enormous power has a tendency to become self-perpetuating, by continually uncovering plots against the state. It was only with the demotion of Trotsky from the Politburo and his eventual exile that the Cheka took on a secondary role.

Stalin feared sabotage from within the ranks of the Communist Party by those who had been Trotsky's supporters. The specter of Trotsky and his supporters, both within and outside the Soviet Union, was a source of serious concern to Stalin, until Trotsky's assassination in Mexico in 1940. Moreover, Stalin had good reason for concern. In a sense, he had stolen Trotsky's birthright by using his proposed Five Year Plan to eject him from the party and then turning around and adopting it as his own.

Stalin's bloody reputation grew with the purges of the 1930s. Opponents of Stalin have convinced most people that the charges against Kamenev and Zinovyev during those purges were patently false — that Stalin had used trumped up conspiracy charges as a red herring to deflect criticism from the failings of his Five Year Plans. That Kamenev and Zinovyev had been ousted from the Politburo for their opposition to the Five Year Plans is factual. On the other hand, their self-confessions may have been an effort to save the lives of their families and friends. In no way, however, does all of the foregoing axiomatically exclude the possible eventuality of a plot to overthrow Stalin. The economic situation in the Soviet Union in 1936 was not all that bleak. Despite its cumbersome bureaucracy, its false starts and the errors committed, and the enormity of creating an industrial state almost overnight, major progress had been made. There was the grand opening of the Moscow subway, the most modern in the world; and, thanks to the construction of dams and hydroelectric facilities, electricity was being brought to the entire nation. If everything wasn't *comme il faut*, the broad outlines already were in place for the future completion of a modern industrial state. If there was any conspiracy to overthrow the one-man regime established by Stalin, the time for action was now, before the Five Year Plans had come to fruition. Viewed from that perspective, the possibility of a coup appears reasonable. Whether it was directed by Trotsky may be subject to question, but on the other hand, neither Kamenev nor Zinovyev possessed either the reputation or the following to replace Stalin as head of state.

For Stalin, their self-confessions provided a golden opportunity to shake up the bureaucracy and eliminate real or potential enemies. In all likelihood, before making their own confessions, the two of them implicated others who were in on the cabal. Was there really a plot underway to overthrow Stalin? Of course there was. The evidence displayed by the prosecutor, Andrei Vyshinsky, was not fabricated, as some are wont to believe. Were the confessions of their subordinates in the cabal extracted under torture? Of course. Stalin knew that unless Vyshinsky had overwhelming evidence of their perfidy, never would they have confessed publicly. Foreigners who viewed them on the witness stand could see no physical evidence of torture because there was none. What Stalin wanted and got from their confessions was to prove to the Soviet people that the conspiracy against the government went as far as those two men who had been instrumental in creating the revolution. In other words, it gave him the license to undertake a wholesale cleansing of the existing bureaucracy. Nikita Khrushchev was appalled that it swept up innocents as well as the guilty; he failed to understand Stalin's purpose. The success of the Five Year Plans was contingent upon those in the lower echelons of the bureaucracy being fearful for their lives and those of their families. Stalin believed that only that level of fear could provide adequate motivation to implement the nation's ambitious plans.

No European Socialist leader took the potential threat to communism from the rise to power of Adolf Hitler more seriously than Stalin. Outside of the Soviet Union, Germany possessed the largest Communist Party. Its failure to seize power in 1923-24, when the German economy had collapsed totally, was viewed as a lost opportunity. It was the fear of a Communist takeover that led the US government and private interests, including some from Britain and France, to bolster the German economy with the introduction of the Dawes Plan. Thanks to the wartime reparations imposed by the victorious Allies, the value of the German mark had experienced a collapse. The Dawes transfusion that pumped hard currency into the German economy was not an altruistic gift. It was specifically designed to prevent a takeover of the government by the German

Communist Party. In addition to returning the mark to convertibility in the international marketplace, the plan also tailored back the amount of reparations to be paid to the Allies.

It was also in 1924 that the aborted coup launched in Bavaria by Hitler, in conjunction with the private armed forces of Ernst Rohm, the founder of the Nazi party, took place. Rohm fled to Bolivia in order to escape arrest; Hitler went to prison for four years, for his part in the conspiracy, where he would write *Mein Kampf*. In 1928, when it became obvious that the German economy still couldn't meet its reparation payments, a second effort was made to stabilize the German economy. This was the Young Plan, which further reduced the amount of reparations and extended their due date. In the fall of 1929, the US stock market felt its first seismic shock and it reverberated throughout the world, striking hardest at the already weak German economy. Massive unemployment followed, touching every facet of the German population.

Meanwhile Hitler, now out of prison, set about reorganizing the Nazi party on a national scale. Hitler's basic appeal was to the lower middle class, white-collar worker. The SA, the name attached to Rohm's Brown Shirts, his new national paramilitary, soon were engaged in street brawls with the Communists. As the Depression deepened, the size of Rohm's private army grew into the millions. Furthermore, at the polls, the number of Nazis elected to the Reichstag advanced. With the 1933 elections, the Nazi party, under Hitler, held the largest number of seats of the various minority parties. He now demanded of ailing President Paul von Hindenberg that the Nazi Party be allowed to organize a government. The German Communist Party would shortly be decimated. It was already infiltrated by members of the SA; they made short shrift of its leadership before taking on its rank and file. The longstanding strife between the German Socialists and Communists made the job easier. By 1934, when Hitler attained total power, neither the Socialists nor the Communists represented any threat to the Nazi party.

Stalin was well aware that the first item on Hitler's agenda, once he came to power, would be the destruction of the German Communist and Socialist Parties, the only political organizations capable of opposing a fascist regime. However, Stalin was powerless to influence events. The Soviet government was still considered a pariah by England, France and the United States for refusing to honor the debts owed by the tsarist regime. In addition, the Communist parties within these European countries were openly dedicated to the overthrow of their existing forms of government. Except for Germany, they had failed to gain much of a foothold.

By 1933 the Soviet regime had been recognized by many countries in Europe and Asia, but not by the US. Given the threat posed by Hitler, Stalin decided it would be helpful to restore official relations with the United States. Anyway, it would be far easier to operate a spy apparatus if Soviet agents were officially on the premises. With the Democratic Party coming to power in 1933, he dispatched to Washington his affable Jewish Foreign Minister, Maxim Litvinoff. When Litvinoff succeeded in his mission, ambassadors were exchanged and Soviet consulates opened in New York, Chicago and San Francisco. While the US Communist Party never was a factor in American political life, certain members did insinuate themselves into the federal government and into industrial unions. There were also large contingents that were either actual Party members or sympathizers throughout academia, the arts, music, journalism and book publishing, as well as in Hollywood and in the New York theater. During the Spanish Civil War, the US Communist party was instrumental in the organization of the Abraham Lincoln brigade, which fought on the side of the Loyalists. And during the Nazi-Soviet non-aggression pact, the US Communist Party and its sympathizers were active in opposing the Selective Service Act, as well as America's Lend Lease of 50 old destroyers to Great Britain. When Hitler invaded Russia, the US Communist party became jingoist and promoted America's early entry into the conflict. When the US did enter the war after Pearl Harbor, the party members were strident in their demand for a second front. While some Party members and sympathizers served Soviet interests well during the war, both in terms of espionage and propaganda, in the post-war era they proved to be a detriment to Soviet-US relations. The idea of any foreign nation attempting to influence America's foreign policy helped to foster the anti-Communist sentiment already in existence.

While Stalin was successful in establishing diplomatic relations with the United States, he was less successful in his efforts to reestablish a loose military alliance with France. Pierre Laval did make an effort when he became Prime Minister in the mid-1930s to establish better relations with the Soviet Union by visiting Moscow, but this rapprochement remained in the state of conversation. Laval was far more interested in courting Benito Mussolini. Until 1935, France had avoided the worst aspects of the Depression that had debilitated the economies of Great Britain and the United States. But, by 1935, it too was forced to abandon the gold standard and face the same economic plight as other capitalist nations. The Depression was to strike France with a vengeance. The French franc went into a freefall. Strikes broke out in every major industry as consumer demand declined sharply. Workers were laid off by the tens of thousands, and those still employed had their wages reduced. Even before French industry had begun to make serious cutbacks in its labor force to meet reduced consumer demand, fascistic parties began to emerge in France, Belgium, Holland and England. Like Hitler's original storm troopers, they wore uniforms and were armed. The most notorious were the French Cagoulards and Sir Oswald Mosley's British Union of Fascists. Most of them were virulently anti-Semitic as well as anti-Communist. In France, there were constant street brawls between the Cagoulards and the Communists. Part of the rationale for the emergence of these neo-fascist parties was the seeming success of Mussolini's fascistic government in eliminating the Italian Communist Party. Most of the support for these Fascist parties was drawn from an insecure lower middle class who were latently or overtly anti-Semitic and prone to believe the Nazi propaganda that all Jews were either capitalists, out to exploit middle-class citizens, or Communists, who wished to reduce them to mere ciphers in the amorphous working class.

In 1935, unexpectedly, Mussolini invaded Ethiopia. Whatever pretext he used for this display of Italian military power, the attack on an innocent nation was viewed by a few as the first spark that would light the fuse of military power for aggression against weaker nations. The failure of Mussolini's vaunted army and air force to achieve a quick victory; the use of poison gas in violation of the Geneva Conventions (to which Italy was a signatory); and the inept failure of economic sanctions imposed by the League of Nations, from which the Soviet Union had been excluded, convinced Stalin that the Soviet Union would have to prepare itself militarily. While an arms buildup would impede the growth of the civilian economy, there was no other alternative. The failure of Great Britain and France to intervene indicated that the Soviet Union would have to look to itself if it was going to survive.

In 1936, with France in the depths of the Depression, for the first time the French Socialist Party won a majority in the National Assembly and formed a ruling government. At the same time, in light of the economic disaster facing the nation, the French Communist Party, which had yet to become a political factor, increased its representation in the Assembly from 10 to 72 members. As a result of this strong showing in the election and in an effort to expand his majority in the National Assembly, Leon Blum, the titular head of the Socialist Party and now the first Jewish Prime Minister in French history, invited the French Communists in the Assembly to join the Socialists and form a coalition government, labeled the Popular Front. Since the French Communist Party was under the control of Moscow, no decision could be made without Stalin's approval. To the shock of most Party members, Stalin would initiate a fundamental change in the philosophy of the Soviet Communist Party. In a major break with his mentor Lenin, he would allow the French Communist Party to join communism's bitterest enemy, the Socialists, as part of the ruling government. This step violated Lenin's basic premise against any joint political action with the Socialists. The reasons for this deviation from Lenin's dogma were, first, Hitler's decision to expand the German army to 16 divisions, in violation of the Treaty of Versailles; and more important, the German reoccupation of the Rhineland in March 1936, another abrogation of the treaty. While the French government called for immediate mobilization of the French army, and Hitler had warned his generals to vacate the region without a fight should the French army advance, the Conservative government of Neville Chamberlain in Great Britain stayed the French from taking any action. In all his speeches, and in *Mein Kampf*, Hitler had reiterated that the greatest threat to European civilization was Soviet Communism. Part of his rhetoric and writings were sincere; but in 1936, his aim was to seduce Great Britain and France into believing that his real goal was to eradicate the Communist regime in Moscow. The capitalist leadership in both countries was quite willing to swallow this propaganda. The simple and obvious fact — that in order to attack the Soviet Union, Hitler first would have to conquer Poland — was conveniently overlooked. Stalin had hopes that with Communists represented in the Popular Front government, they might exert some influence in the conduct of foreign affairs. But when the Communists were offered only token representation in the government, with no input into the direction of foreign policy, they refused to participate in the Cabinet.

If Stalin had any doubts about the nefarious influence that British foreign policy had on France, they were soon dissipated with the outbreak of the Spanish Civil War in 1936. With a legitimate Socialist government elected in Spain, General Francisco Franco, commanding Spanish troops in Spanish Morocco, crossed to the mainland in an attempt to overthrow the Socialist government. Despite the presence of a Socialist government in France, once again Great Britain persuaded France's Blum to join Britain in an embargo on all arms shipments to both of the adversaries. It was Ethiopia all over again. While Germany and Italy provided Franco with armaments to wage the war, and Mussolini went one step further by sending in troops and air power, only the Soviet Union sent arms and military advisors to the legitimate Republican government.

Hitler, now firmly in power, would establish first with Japan, later with Italy, the Anti-Comintern Pact. Its sole purpose was propaganda, aimed largely at the British Conservative government, and to a lesser extent, France. Since the Communist Party had been eliminated in both Germany and Italy, and never had made any inroads in Japan, it may have appeared as a cynical gesture on the part of Hitler. In fact, the Fuhrer was still taking care to confuse Britain and France about Germany's future intentions. Shortly thereafter, the Soviet Union and Germany signed a non-aggression pact that opened the door to a trade agreement between the two nations. Since German gold reserves were non-existent, trade between the two nations was carried out under the primitive basis of barter. Germany required crude oil and the Soviet Union was in need of specialized industrial equipment. As the Civil War in Spain continued to rage, the Russian military advisors that were sent along with the war equipment being provided to the Spanish government soon became aware of the superiority of the German military equipment being provided to Franco's army. Alerted to this, Stalin now insisted that if the barter arrangement were to continue, German military equipment would replace industrial products. Since Germany was desperate for crude oil, Hitler acceded to Stalin's demands. In place of industrial engineers visiting the Reich, now it was the turn of the Russian General Staff.

Stalin was playing a dangerous game, but he had no alternative. The Soviet military had to be updated. Since Soviet generals did the negotiations with their Germans counterparts, Stalin's natural suspicions were aroused. The purges in 1937-38 were not conducted in public. Except for

Bukharin, Rykov and Mikhail Tomsky, there were no major civilians who fell under the axe. However, military officers were a different story. Marshall Mikhail Tukhachevsky, one of the heroes of the Red Army during the Civil War, and some of his associates in the Red Army and Air Force were executed. A few other major officers were shot, but most were dispatched to labor camps in Siberia. Stalin's major prey was the second level of Soviet bureaucrats. Almost two-thirds of the members elected to the Central Committee of the Communist Party were removed from office. But his hardest blows, once again, were directed against the officials in the nationalities, where nepotism still was a major factor. Stalin, a Georgian, was familiar with the problem of integrating the nationalities into the Union of Soviet Socialist Republics. For the Soviet Union to survive, however, he had to eliminate the family and tribal loyalties that impeded their integration. For Stalin the quickest and most efficacious solution was terror and fear. At the same time, Stalin appointed his fellow Georgian, Lavrenty Beria, to head the secret police, whose name had been changed to the NKVD. Beria, who at one time had commanded the secret police in Georgia, was a master administrator. An indefatigable worker, within a short time he purged the organization of its inefficient members; established total discipline; and created new labor camps in Siberia to handle the flood of so-called political prisoners who had been caught up in the purges.

The Spanish Civil War dragged on and it became convenient to blame the Soviet Union for the military wrangling that took place among the Socialists, the Communists and the Anarchists. As Franco's troops moved forward to capture Madrid, Hitler now felt certain that France was umbilically tied to Great Britain and its policy of appeasement, and that the German army could move forward with impunity. In 1938, having established a strong Nazi base in Austria, Hitler marched German troops into Austria, overthrew the legitimate government, and incorporated Austria into what Hitler termed the Third Reich. With the seizure of Austria, without a shot being fired, the Popular Front government of France, headed by Blum, was turned out of office, and a centrist, right wing government under Prime Minister Edouard Daladier was formed. Stalin now recognized that the situation in Europe was at the boiling point. In 1938, when Hitler made known his demands for incorporating the largely German population in the Czech Sudetenland into Germany, Stalin dispatched Russian generals to confer with their French counterparts in an effort to stop Hitler once and for all. France, after all, in an effort to surround Germany, had entered into alliances with Czechoslovakia and Poland, to which the British had adhered. Although remaining suspicious of British intentions, he assumed that with Britain having signed a formal alliance with both countries it was finally serious about bringing a halt to Hitler's expansion plans.

Although the Soviet Union was not militarily ready for a major war, Stalin felt that the threat of an alliance between France, England and the Soviet Union would deter Hitler from taking any precipitous action. As the talks in Paris seemed to progress, Hitler realized that his only hope for preventing such an alliance was to bring Britain into his camp. There were other factors as well. In order for Soviet troops to link up with the Czech army, they would have to pass through the southern part of Poland. Given the Soviet attempt to subjugate Poland following the end of the First World War, the Polish government refused. The Poles would pay a bitter price a little more than a year later. A more grievous error was committed by the French government. Because its foreign policy was dictated by Britain, it did not insist that the Soviet Union be included in the *pourparler* with Hitler at Munich. Shortly after Britain and France gave in to Hitler over the Sudetenland, he gobbled up the rest of Czechoslovakia, including the famous Skoda arms factories.

For Stalin, the British and French sell-out of the Czechs was the moment of truth. The great hope of the leaders of both these countries was that Hitler would turn his attention to the Soviet Union before attacking them — once again ignoring the fact that Poland stood in the way. The problem facing Britain and France was that they had a binding treaty to come to the aid of Poland in the event that Germany attacked. Hitler, of course, understood that there was no physical way that the French army could come to the aid of the Poles. His problem was that in conquering Poland, his army would now sit on the border of the Soviet Union. Faced with the threat of a two-front war, which Hitler believed resulted in the eventual defeat of Germany during the First World War, he decided to undertake what British and French military intelligence believed to be impossible. He would attempt to replace the original non-aggression pact with the Soviet Union with a formal treaty between the two nations, which would allow him to concentrate first on the war with France and Britain.

In a certain sense, Stalin was following in the footsteps of Lenin with his New Economic Policy. He was prepared to take one step backward so he could later take two steps forward. Stalin accepted the German proposal for several reasons, two of which turned out to be based on erroneous reasoning. He assumed, like most of the world, that the French and Germans would get bogged down in a long war which would allow the Soviet Union the necessary time to rearm. Second, he no longer trusted the French since Great Britain was the senior partner and the French would follow wherever the British led them. Stalin also was convinced that the British Conservative government preferred even Hitler to communism. It was this animosity towards the Conservative regime that would have Stalin dismiss Prime Minister Winston Churchill's warning that the Nazis were about to invade the Soviet Union. Finally, he guessed correctly that Hitler was the suitor and that he could gain territorial advantages if he adhered to the non-aggression treaty. Reluctantly, Hitler did give in to the Soviet demands for possession of the three Baltic States as well as a slice of the Polish pie. The announcement of the pact between Germany and the Soviet Union caught the British and French totally by surprise.

Unlike the Finnish people, who were prepared for the Soviet invasion of 1939 and inflicted one setback after another before finally succumbing, the unsuspecting Poles were surprised by the Russian invasion from the east coordinated with the German from the west. In six weeks, the war was over except for some cleanup activities. For the German High Command, Poland was a practice run. The basic lesson that the German generals learned from their attack on Poland was the effectiveness of low flying aircraft strafing the fleeing civilian population. In panic, the civilians would clog the roads and prevent the Polish army from reforming its battle lines. The second important lesson gleaned was the effectiveness of paratroopers as a surprise weapon. This was only a prelude to what would happen later in France and in the Soviet Union.

The effectiveness of the German military, with its coordination between air and motorized ground forces, awoke Stalin to the inadequacies of the Soviet military machine. With his Five Year Plans, Stalin had concentrated on building up Soviet heavy industry and electrifying the country at the expense of every other project. Now, while the Soviet army had greater reserves of manpower, it lacked the speed, agility and concentrated power necessary to fight a modern war. His new General

Staff advised him that it would take four years before the Soviet forces would be on a par with the Germans. Political prisoners who had been shipped off to Siberia at the time of the military purges were rehabilitated and put to work on Soviet defense needs. Among them was the architect of the Tupelev fighter plane, which would be instrumental in driving the Germans from the air and establishing Soviet air superiority. Time was of the essence, and Stalin was placing all his hopes on the French Maginot Line effectuating a long, drawn out war. Even though Germany had invaded France through Belgium during the First World War, and had come close to an immediate victory, the French government made the decision not to extend the line to the Atlantic coast, which would have prevented the German army from outflanking the French and British armies. The firebomb raids on Dutch and Belgian cities, coordinated with the dropping of paratroops to seize key locations, took the French and British high commands by surprise. Even more of a shock was the ability of the German army to punch a hole through the so-called impregnable Maginot Line. As in Poland, German fighter craft proved effective by strafing the fleeing civilians who were crowding the roads. Despite having witnessed the techniques employed by the Germans in their invasion of Poland, the French and British Generals acted as if they had never seen the Blitzkrieg before. With the surrender of the French army in six weeks, Stalin should have known that the Soviet Union was Hitler's next land target. The failure of Hermann Goering's vaunted air force to bring Britain to the bargaining table could only serve to reinforce that opinion.

Which brings up the question: why did Stalin not heed the word from his own spy in Japan, Richard Sorge, who told him the Germans were about to attack the Soviet Union. The answer generally accepted is that Stalin couldn't believe that Hitler was going to attack. Stalin haters are willing to accept this fairy tale, but Stalin was anything but naive. The most logical explanation is treachery among the Russian army and air force generals. The 1938 purge of the upper echelons of the Russian generals must have embittered the officer class. Whether they were paid or merely wished to see the demise of the Stalinist regime is immaterial. Given the size of Hitler's invasion force, before it launched its combined air and ground attack, it would have been impossible for the Russian generals on the ground to be unaware of the massive German buildup.

Stalin's reaction to the speed with which the German army overran the Soviet forces remains inexplicable. It was as though he had been blind to the success of the German army and air force in Poland and France. With the German air force in complete control of the skies, it was *déjà vu*. Civilians clogged the roads, impeding Russian troop movements, so that the Russian defenders were unable to reform and do battle; one city after another was overrun by the German soldiers, until they approached the outskirts of Leningrad and Moscow. It was only the intervention of an early Russian winter that prevented both cities from falling into the hands of the Germans. When all appeared to be lost, Stalin lived up to his revolutionary pseudonym, which in Russian means "steel." He took over the overall command of the Russian forces. By this action, Marshal Stalin made himself personally responsible for the success or failure of the Soviet war effort. His insistence on remaining in Moscow and defending the capital provided a shot of adrenalin to the Soviet people. Despite mass starvation, neither Moscow nor Leningrad surrendered. Meanwhile, the Russian winters were taking a terrible toll on the German war machine, its officers and its soldiers. Frostbite was common; tanks were disabled by sub-freezing temperatures. By the winter of 1943, with neither Moscow nor Leningrad captured; with large segments of the German army now replaced by soldiers from Hungary, Bulgaria, Romania and Italy; with the German army stretched thin, since it had to maintain troops in Greece and Yugoslavia; with the Germans defeated in North Africa and forced to replace Italian troops in defending Italy, Hitler and the German High Command launched a major drive towards the south and the rich Baku oil fields. The failure to capture Stalingrad marked the beginning of the end. Soviet factories had been dismantled and moved to the safety of the Urals; US military aid was now pouring in new supplies. Hitler's orders not to retreat resulted in the surrender of the 6th German Corps and the capture of 600,000 officers and men. Russian fighter planes now dominated the skies. The cost, in lives and property damage, was horrific. But the Soviet Union, the first great experiment in state socialism, had been saved.

By late November 1943, at the first meeting of the Big Three at Tehran, the Germans were forced to lift their sieges of Moscow and Leningrad. Throughout the eastern front, the German army and its satellite forces were in retreat. Actually, the presence of Churchill was unnecessary. President Franklin Roosevelt had vetoed Churchill's plan to invade Europe through what he called "its soft underbelly," the Balkans. Stalin was no fool. He knew what Churchill had in mind. A successful invasion through the Balkans would act as a brake against Soviet expansion into the center of Europe. As it was, the Allied forces were bogged down by the mountainous regions of Italy. Unlike almost all Americans, who then and today view Churchill as a heroic figure, standing up to Hitler when Britain alone was fighting the war against Germany, Stalin saw him as another British imperialist whose basic concern was maintaining Britain's far-flung colonial possessions and containing the Soviet Union within its borders. Stalin's estimate of Britain's heroic leader was on the mark. Privately at Yalta, Churchill asked Stalin if Greece was to be included in Stalin's post war Eastern Europe. Stalin informed him that the Soviet Union had no interest in the Balkans since they hadn't been liberated by Russian troops, and he kept his word.

When Roosevelt, Stalin and Churchill first met at Tehran, General George Marshall outlined the plans for the Allied invasion of Western Europe. The bulk of the Allied forces would land in Normandy, followed by a second invasion a few months later through southern France. Stalin also refused to take up the post-war question of Poland. Stalin was well aware that Roosevelt, in particular, knew it was the Soviet armies that had broken the back of the Wehrmacht. He also recognized that neither the British nor the Americans realized the terrible price the Soviet Union had paid, or knew the overall weakness of its economic situation.

At the same time that the Big Three were meeting in Tehran, Hitler had issued orders to withdraw some of the crack German troops from the eastern front and shift them to defend against the expected invasion of Normandy. Hitler was determined to prevent an American landing and the possibility of facing a two-front war. Stalin was pleased with the results of his first meeting with Roosevelt. He was doubly pleased that a US general would head up the invasion and that another US general would draw up the plans for the actual assault. Stalin must have been more than amused by Roosevelt's efforts to charm him. On the domestic front, Stalin did not face the many challenges the President had to contend with at home. Congress, while still under the control of the Democratic Party, was deeply divided between conservative Southerners and liberal Northerners. Stalin had never been so secure on the domestic front. His personal command of the Soviet armed forces had led to the retreat of the Germans and guaranteed his popularity with the overwhelming majority of the Soviet population, and the armed forces as well. In late 1943, while it was obvious that the tide was turning against the Germans in the west and against the Japanese in the east, the American public still did not comprehend the enormous number of lives that would be sacrificed before the Germans and Japanese would surrender. Stalin faced no such problems on the home front. Unlike the civilian population of the United States, which remained unscathed by the war, the number of casualties among the Soviet civilians, either through starvation or German brutality, almost equaled the losses suffered by the Soviet armed forces.

In 1947, when the Republicans took over Congress after a hiatus of 14 years, it became fashionable in some circles to believe either that Roosevelt had given away the store at Yalta, or, more likely, that Stalin had pulled the wool over the eyes of an ailing president. In fact, when the Big Three met at Yalta from February 4-11, 1945, nothing new was added to the agenda agreed upon more than a year earlier at Tehran, other than the addition of France as a fourth occupying power in Germany. Stalin had never agreed to free Polish elections at Tehran, and he only confirmed his position at Yalta, and again when he met with President Harry Truman at Potsdam. As for Stalin allowing free elections in Bulgaria, Romania and Hungary, after they had fought on the side of the Germans throughout the war, that would be comparable to calling for free elections in Germany and Austria. Since the Baltic States had been incorporated into the Soviet Union in 1939, prior to the German invasion of Russia, Stalin saw no reason why their future should be put on the table. Nor did the Americans or British protest very much, since the basic concern of Roosevelt and Churchill was Poland. As far as Stalin was concerned, the Soviet Union had borne the brunt of the war in Europe; had suffered the greatest number of casualties; had had more than one-half of its industrial infrastructure and agriculture destroyed during the conflict; and was entitled to reparations over and beyond what the other Allied countries would receive. To Stalin, it was as simple as that, and he would not surrender an inch of any territory now under Soviet control.

Today, historians point to Stalin as the architect of the Cold War — starting with his refusal to allow for free elections in Poland when he met with Truman at Potsdam, and followed by his reluctance to vacate northern Iran, as promised at Yalta. No mention was made of the atomic bomb, until Truman informed him at Yalta that the United States had developed a powerful weapon that it intended to use against Japan in the hope of ending that war. History records that Stalin appeared blasé when informed by Truman. Knowing as we do that Stalin was aware of America's and Britain's joint efforts to create the super weapon of mass destruction, thanks to information passed to the Kremlin by Klaus Fuchs and Ethel and Julius Rosenberg, Stalin's nonchalance seems perfectly in keeping with his attitude towards his so-called allies. Little wonder that Stalin had been amused by Roosevelt's efforts to assure him that this wartime alliance would be binding.

Stalin's decision to join the United Nations was defensive — defensive in the sense that being a member would give the Soviet Union enough time to attain military parity with the United States by creating its own atom bomb. As long as any one member of the Security Council was able to exercise a veto over the majority, the Soviet Union was safe from any hostile actions taken against it. The decision by the US government not to share its secrets with the Soviet Union, as it had done with Great Britain, convinced Stalin that the so-called wartime alliance was nothing more than a *mariage de convenance*. Despite all the toasts that had been drunk at Tehran, Yalta and Potsdam, America still looked on the Soviet Union, with its Communist ideology, as an enemy. Stalin had come close to losing the Second World War when he failed to heed the warnings from his spy in Tokyo. He would not repeat that mistake again.

In fact, the United States did debate whether to share the secrets of the atom bomb with the Soviet Union. Having witnessed the damage done by the first two bombs, a serious discussion ensued not only within the government but within the scientific community as well. The obvious question then posed is: would there have been a Cold War had this information been shared with the Soviet Union? Two things are certain. It would have assuaged some of Stalin's fears about a preemptive attack coming from the United States. It would not have changed his mind that the Communist system of state socialism was the best future course for all humanity. It would not have changed his mind on free elections in Poland, nor would he have relinquished his hold on Eastern Europe. If he believed that state socialism was the wave of the future, then the more countries it encompassed, the greater the possibility of it advancing westward until all Europeans came to realize their own destiny. Stalin, the revolutionary, never had any doubts about the efficacy of the Communist system. While he was prepared to live in peace with the United

States, in his mind capitalism had to fail because of its internal contradictions. In that sense, he was a Marxist; in protecting the Soviet Union, he was a Leninist. The crucial issue for Stalin was the future of Germany. As a result of the war on the battlefields, the United States and its allies had been awarded with the rich industrial sector of that country. The Soviet Union, which had borne the bulk of the casualties, was allocated the poorer Eastern section of the country and the city of Berlin that lay within it, which Soviet troops had liberated at a terrible cost in lives. In Stalin's first meeting with Truman and Churchill following the unconditional surrender of Germany, held in Potsdam, East Germany, Stalin was to commit his first blunder. Anxious to appease his allies after refusing to hold free elections in Poland, he offered to share the occupation of Berlin and Vienna with the Americans, British and French, as a symbol of allied unity. Those areas conquered by the allied armies would remain under their occupation; those conquered by the Soviet armies would be theirs. The same held true for Austria, which because of its size and industrial capacity, was less important.

Stalin, who prior to the war had kept the Soviet Union isolated from the Western, capitalist world in order, in part, to avoid invidious comparison with Western lifestyles, now was exposing the Soviet officers and soldiers stationed in Berlin to just that. For the moment, it meant nothing. Soviet troops, which hadn't been paid in three years, received their back wages in German marks. Since Berlin had been devastated by the Soviet assault on the city and the determination of Hitler's SS troops to fight to the bitter end, there wasn't much that could be bought with their new-found wealth.

The question left unanswered was: what was to become of the future of the Germany, and the four-power occupation? Would it remain divided or would the two sectors be united? The resolution of Germany was foremost on the mind of the Truman administration. Stalin was in no hurry. Post-war Europe had been decimated by the war. The Germans had stripped France, Belgium and Holland of most of their industry. What was left had been destroyed by the Allied armies in fighting the war. All of Europe, including Germany, was destitute. Members of the Communist parties had led the resistance movements in France and Italy. Since the Soviet armies had taken no part in the liberation of these countries, they would have no input into their future, any more than the United States would have in the final disposition of those countries under Soviet occupation. The Cold War in Europe began the day that Germany surrendered.

It would be impossible for any president, or for that matter, for George Kennan, the Soviet expert at the State Department and the author of the US policy of containment, to understand Stalin unless he set aside the concept of good and evil. Marxism-Leninism viewed itself as a product of historical determinism, tied to the principle of societal economic development. The United States possessed a history of 175 years, during which time its economy and mores changed dramatically. It had been a work in progress, moving from a republic to a democracy. Over the centuries, the US economy would evolve from one largely based on agriculture to one driven by industrial development. In the process, its population would shift from the largely rural areas of the country to the urban cities.

The Soviet Union also was a work in progress, and its economy too was shifting toward more industry and urbanization. The project had been set back by the German invasion. The fundamental difference between the two works in progress was that the Soviet Union defined its end game at its very inception. Stalin and those who succeeded him firmly believed that an economic system of state socialism was the final stage in societal development. In other words, there was no compromise, no give and take. As Lenin informed those within the Party who wanted to include the Russian Social Democrats in the revolution, they were only welcome provided that they followed the orders and directions laid down by the leadership of the Communist Party.

The title for this chapter, *Beyond Good and Evil*, was borrowed from the great nineteenth-century German philosopher Friedrich Nietzsche who, like Marx, had nothing but contempt for the Judeo-Christian concept of good and evil. In a sense, the judgment of both men was as accurate as those who continue to define the words as they evolved in the Western civilizations over several thousand years. To view Stalin's deeds as evil when he committed them in order to create and develop a viable socialist state, which he viewed as the best thing for his nation, is absurd. Instead, viewed objectively, the Western world owes a great debt to the man. Had he not initiated the Cold War in an effort to expedite the spread of communism, the only viable capitalist nation, the United States, would not have responded to the threat as it did. Stalin's challenge to capitalism resulted in enormous and unpredictable changes to its system. Communism posed a threat not only to the Judeo-Christian concept of morality but more importantly to Western civilization's interest in protecting the "sanctity" of private property, and that is what led to a life-and-death struggle as to which system would triumph. By labeling this drama as a struggle between the forces of good and evil, the United States and its allies justified all of their actions. Many people may consider Stalin to have been an evil man, but at one time, in the minds of millions of other people, he was considered to be the prophet who would lead his followers into the Promised Land.

It is commonplace today to denounce Stalin as a tyrant almost on a par with Hitler. With the passing of each year more books detailing his cruelty and insane savagery emerge from survivors of the former Soviet Union. If that is not the portrait painted here, there is a very logical reason. In the space of 15 years, single-handedly, he totally revamped the former tsarist empire of 250 million people, composed of different races, speaking different languages, practicing different religions and with multiple customs, and unified them into a single state speaking a single tongue. He provided these diverse races of largely illiterate peasants with such basic necessities as education and health care. He forced them to create a modern industrial society that is light years from what the overwhelmingly majority of these disparate peoples had ever experienced — albeit, it is in no way comparable to our own or those in Western Europe. When viewed from that perspective what he accomplished was nothing short of a miracle. Those who condemn him for his methods lose sight of one important thing. Had Stalin not succeeded in his quest to remake tsarist Russia into a modern state, there is more than a good likelihood that Hitler and his minions might still control all of Europe, the Middle East and perhaps even Asia today.

The Cold War, which set in motion the armament race, altered forever the concept of capitalism while at the same time forcing the Soviet Union to expend more than one-fourth of its gross domestic product on armaments. What set it off? At the end of the Second World War, Stalin was physically and mentally exhausted. In addition he was frustrated, especially when Palmiro Togliatti and the Italian Communists were not elected to power in Italy in 1948; they would have given the Communists a base in the West. Moreover, in acquiring all the countries of Eastern Europe he had overextended his ability to control events. The Berlin Blockade is a prime example. The success of the Marshall Plan and the establishment of a West German government, followed by the creation of the North Atlantic Treaty Organization, made him realize that Western Europe was now lost to communism. The final blow was his failure to actuate his promise to Mao Tse-tung that the People's Republic of China would replace Nationalist China on the UN Security Council. Furious and frustrated, he allowed Kim Il-sung of North Korea to invade South Korea, hoping thereby to embarrass the United States. He died before a truce finally was arranged.

Chapter 4. The Contradictions of State Socialism

By definition state socialism, or communism, is a system whereby the government owns everything — from the nation's land and the capital to its means of production, transportation and distribution. It is the nation's sole employer. The technocrats in the hierarchy make all the decisions. Governmental leaders, and the officials reporting to them, allocate raw materials; decide on how much land should be devoted to each particular crop; fix production schedules and quotas; and decide on the level of salaries that are to be paid to managers and workers. They determine which consumer products are to be produced — the quantity, the quality and the price — and how they are to be distributed. When viewed in that perspective, the job is enormously complicated for those at the top and for those who are responsible for implementing the decisions further down the hierarchy.

The goal of the Soviet leaders was to create and to develop an entirely new social organism while at the same time jettisoning all the remnants of the old regime. This was assumed to require tight control by the administration in order to avoid confusion and waste. The Herculean task of altering the lives and lifestyles of 250 million people with diverse customs and religions was to be achieved without the discipline that financial accountability brings to a capitalist system. Because a Communist state dispenses with the profit motive, success in each segment of the economy can only be measured in terms of whether targets and projections are met. In essence, Marxist thinkers sought to rationalize the means of production; then the cyclical nature of capitalism could be eliminated, the financial security of the workers assured, and the benefits of an industrial society equally distributed. As corollaries to this economic system, the number of hours required for labor would be standardized to an eight-hour day; free education and health care would be available to all; child labor would be eliminated; and a decent retirement plan would be assured for the aged and disabled.

Marx had arrived at the conclusion that capitalism could not be reformed and that for a true Communist society to be attained, it would be necessary to uproot capitalism's basic motive — profit. That surely sounded like an "evil" concept to the business owners in the leading capitalist nation. Yet the goals sounded good to Americans, too. Thus, to fend off any appeal the foreign-backed Communists might have in the US, similar goals would lead to Roosevelt's New Deal legislation.

The concept of a Socialist community had been bruited about long before Marx arrived on the scene. Attempts at establishing agricultural communes had been tried, not only in France but in the United States as well. Efforts in both these nations failed after several years because human nature was not yet prepared to subsume the ego of the individual to the greater interest of the community. Marx dismissed these initial failed experiments in agricultural socialism as doomed because of their timing. The days of a society where agriculture had been the predominant economic force had passed with the advent of the industrial revolution. It was the economic power of the bourgeoisie that had triggered the revolutions of 1848. Thanks to the growing wealth of this class, it sought not only representation in the government but also a voice in determining public policy. Society had advanced to a superior economic stage in which industrial capitalism would shape and determine the economics of a nation, and by virtue of that, its politics as well. To Marx, this was the next to last stage in humanity's exploitation of its surrounding environment.

Once the bourgeoisie had seized power, following Hegelian dialectics, the seeds for capitalism's self-destruction would sprout. By virtue of its necessity to grow and expand, capitalism would suck into its system more and more of the landless lower classes. This premise was the fundamental flaw in Marx's analysis of capitalism. Focusing his studies on the means of production, he lost sight of the necessity for the concomitant growth of distribution. For a capitalist system to grow in its internal market, it has to facilitate the distribution of its products.

Marx's contemptuous referral to Britain as a nation of small shopkeepers could be applied to France as well. The growth of the petite bourgeoisie took place at the same time as the evolution of industrial production. Distribution was an important adjunct to the capitalist system. When Marx wrote of capitalism, it was in its early stages of development. As it grew, not only did it suck more of the landless labor into the industrial workforce but it also opened up opportunities for those engaged in the wholesale and retail business. As a capitalist society evolved, it became more complicated. To collect taxes, federal and local governments expanded the number of tax collectors. Given its need for skilled employees, educational opportunities were opened up to a larger portion of the population. The growth of capitalism was not limited solely to employment in its mines and factories but extended to every facet of a growing economy. It was not the industrial working class that supported the rise to power of Benito Mussolini and Adolf Hitler but the growing class of petite bourgeoisie whose jobs as clerks and functionaries were threatened by the collapse of the industrial system.

A major error Marx committed in his prognostication of capitalism's future was his view of profit motive as a negative force and not a positive one. He also viewed competition as a negative force only, and not at the same time as a positive and beneficial element of capitalism. The fundamental fallacy in his reasoning was demonstrated by the failure of the Soviet economy to grow once its means of production had been rationalized. Once the USSR had met the quotas originally established for each segment of the economy, there was no incentive to advance the system any further. Without the presence of competition, the economy remained static. It was only in the areas of defense and space, where the USSR was competing with the United States, that the Soviet administration found it necessary to continually introduce change. When President Vladimir Putin came to office, he was the first former member of the Soviet hierarchy to admit that the economy of the Soviet Union was analogous to that of a Third World nation. The reasons for this situation were clear. Capitalism ordinarily aims to increase productivity, which in turn should reduce the cost of merchandise; but under state socialism, every man and woman was guaranteed full employment. Even in the US, when job creation is taken as a greater priority than productivity, mechanization and technological advances are set aside and production costs may remain higher than necessary.

But state socialism suffered from other weaknesses as well. Because the theory of Marxism had centered on production, Stalin gave short shrift to distribution. As a result, there was little planning when it came to the best methods to bring perishable produce to the consumer before it rotted. Soviet agricultural production was focused on the production of grains, which could be converted into the basic necessity of bread, and fodder for livestock. The entire effort was geared to providing a secure supply of the basics, like root vegetables that could last throughout the winter months, and little consideration was devoted to anything else. Even meat was considered a luxury. By the time Soviet agriculture was recovering from the massive destruction of its livestock during the government's effort to collectivize the farms, the German invasion occurred. The only protein-rich foods available, and they were hardly within reach of most of the population, were chicken and eggs. While it is easy to criticize the incompetence of Soviet officials, it is also necessary to bear in mind that the Soviet economy was a work in progress. It took time for Soviet agricultural institutions to graduate agronomists who would apply scientific methods to increase agricultural production.

Probably the biggest drawback the USSR faced was that the direction of every phase of the Soviet economy was in the hands of party members. Fluency in Marxist ideology was often given more respect than practical experience. The elimination of the old elite — composed of bourgeois, potential counter-revolutionaries — created a void of competent and experienced managers. In the new and perfect society to be developed, Marxist doctrine took priority over pragmatism. None of the original members of the Politburo was selected because of his expertise in any particular field of endeavor. Moreover, managerial positions were reserved for members of the Communist party, who were not necessarily the most competent. Aside from those problems, difficult enough to overcome, there was the basic philosophy of socialism, which focused on efficiency and full employment at the same time. To devotees of Marxism, there was no contradiction. They were convinced that having eliminated the profit motive, they had resolved the basic contradiction of capitalism and this would result in a cornucopia of wealth. Their belief that their economy was on the right track enabled them to discount all the errors and inefficiencies that plagued it throughout its history. The one element that the Soviet people had in superabundance was enthusiasm. They were going to lead the world into a system where economic justice prevailed. Unlike under capitalism, where the worker was just a cog who could be dismissed from his employment without just cause because profits were more important than the dignity of the worker and the needs of society under socialism, every man and woman who labored for the system's realization was contributing to the creation of a new society where resources would be distributed fairly and one class would no longer take advantage of another. The "bottom line" was not the measure of success in a Socialist society, as it is under capitalism; rather success is linked to the greater good of all its citizens.

This enthusiasm was contagious and was continually reinforced by the public information campaign issued from the state. Throughout the 1930s, documentary films showed the long soup lines in the United States; pictures of men standing on corners selling apples; hoboes sitting on wooden boxes around makeshift campfires; and every so often a picture of a Negro being lynched. There was plenty of evidence to suggest that capitalism was a failed system in the last throes of survival. Equally important, incentives were offered to Soviet workers who exceeded the quota allotted to them in the coal mines. Not only were they given increased rations during the 1930s, but they were given awards — which were prized in an illiterate society made up largely of unsophisticated peasants.

According to Marxist doctrine, the advent of a Communist state was only possible in an advanced bourgeois society. However, in an advanced bourgeois society, the industrial working class never has constituted the majority of the population, even in such a highly industrialized society as Germany or the United States. Because capitalism's basic concern is profits, its direction is geared to expanding its market by reducing cost through increased productivity. The industrial sector was never in a position to replace the existing system. Both the Labor party in Great Britain and the Popular Front in France were able to reform the capitalist system in place, but they were unable to replace it with a Socialist economy. The combination of the agricultural sector, the *petite bourgeoisie* and the *bonne bourgeoisie* in a democratic form of government constituted too strong an element in the society to be overturned. Furthermore, as was witnessed in the Soviet economy, Socialist doctrines impeded growth.

This was not the case in the early stages of economic development in the Soviet Union. Because there was little infrastructure in place when

Stalin initiated his first Five Year Plan, every stage of economic development was an addition to the existing facilities. No dams were in place that could be used to generate electric power. Hospitals were found only in the major cities; clinics had to be established for the rural areas. Primary and secondary schools, and colleges and universities, had to be erected if the illiterate population was to be educated. Russian was to replace local languages as the principal means of communication. Steel and aluminum mills had to be erected; the mining of coal had to be improved; oil refineries had to be modernized, and a system of roads and highways had to be developed. On the level of personnel, there was a desperate need for doctors, nurses, engineers and agronomists. A diverse society, much of it still living in a primitive state, had to be uplifted and brought into the twentieth century. It was a massive and daunting undertaking and only could have been accomplished by imposing a harsh discipline on the population. Nobody understood this better than Stalin. Brought up in Georgia, he realized how backward the various nationalities were and how much effort it would take to integrate them into a modern industrial society. Those who criticize him for his purges among the nationalities did not understand the difficulties of breaking down the cultural barriers that impeded progress. Viewed objectively (which is difficult for most Westerners to do because of the brutal methods he used to accomplish his goals), his accomplishments have never been acknowledged. Prior to the German invasion he had transformed a largely primitive people into a modern industrial society, with an educational system that had all but abolished illiteracy; with modern medical facilities; and with the introduction of electricity to a land mass that extended over seven time zones. On the negative side, he had not solved the problem of adequately feeding the vast Soviet population, nor had he been able to provide decent housing facilities

Despite its limitations, state socialism has proved its system capable of developing the structure for an industrial society. This was the great appeal of the system to less developed countries. In addition, the fact that it had been accomplished in 15 years made it even more attractive. When Khrushchev criticized Stalin for his excesses at the Twentieth International Congress of Communist Parties in February 1956, China's Mao Tse-tung lashed out at him. The leader of the largest undeveloped Socialist state, as China was in 1956, viewed Stalin's accomplishments as the standard to be followed. And if Stalin used tough measures to achieve his goals, those used by Mao were even tougher. This was the blind spot of state socialism. Although less efficient than capitalism, it was fully capable of setting in place all the elements required. It may have taken longer to duplicate the principal socialistic product developed in the United States, the Tennessee Valley Authority, but the dams and hydroelectric plants developed by US engineers provided the same services as those developed in the Soviet Union during the 1930s. The dilemma that state socialism proved incapable of resolving was: how could its economy grow once the infrastructure was in place? The leadership of the Soviet Union, once Stalin had died, was stumped, as was that of China — until Deng Xiaoping set China on a new course, which led to a form of capitalism.

When building an economy from scratch, basic goods can be produced cheaply, in great quantity, to meet the basic needs. After that it gets more complicated, and less efficient, as the requirement for more and more specialization arises. In the Soviet Union, the civilian industrial sector was never fully developed. Since prices were fixed and there was no financial incentive to offer more and more enticing products, consumer goods remained at a basic level. And then, enduring two terrible wars, building the entire national infrastructure, and providing social security for the entire population does expend resources; there was little left over to pay for individual indulgences. The people in the upper echelons of Soviet society had access to company stores stocked with merchandise produced in capitalist economies, and they could enjoy all the amenities available to people in the West. In short, in terms of consumer goods, there was neither the supply nor the demand that we take for granted.

Because tsarist Russia had been the least evolved of any European nation, the majority of the population accepted these conditions. The West fails to comprehend this. Compared to life in the US, the former Soviet Union looks like a Third World country; compared to with living conditions two generations ago, it is a working man's paradise. Although amenities the West takes for granted are absent, everything is relative. Under the old regime, the majority of people had lived under far worse conditions. Most of the population lived in hovels, without running water, without sanitation, with no electricity or the possibility of health care or obtaining an education. If it was necessary to wait on long lines to acquire the necessities of life under communism, waiting in line was better than starving.

The Soviet Union collapsed not because the majority of its people were dissatisfied with their condition but because its excellent educational system had developed a growing middle class that demanded change. This is illustrated in the voting patterns during an election for representatives to Russia's national assembly. The older generation continues to vote the Communist ticket. It also explains why Putin remains popular with the majority of the Russian people. After 60 years of security under a strong centralized government and five years of financial anarchy under Boris Yeltsin, a large percentage of the Russian people feel more comfortable with the former. Everyone knew what to expect in the old society; now, with a fledgling free-market economy and attempts to move toward democracy, the majority of the population remains confused and disoriented.

As Marx had prophesized, the individual was subordinated to the general welfare of the society. While that did produce the most good for the most people, for a while, it seems that after some time the dearth of individual incentives and lack of competition, and the adherence to a strict hierarchical structure of command, retard the further development of the economy. Where the economy of the Soviet Union did compete — in the areas of the military and space exploration, because it was engaged in a Cold War with the United States — it managed to maintain parity.

CHAPTER 5. THE COLD WAR BEGINS: THE TRUMAN PRESIDENCY

When Harry Truman assumed the Presidency upon the unexpected death of Franklin Delano Roosevelt, he carried with him three basic principles: he was a born and bred Democrat; he was a devout New Dealer, and he held a firm belief in the principles of American democracy. A man who had never enjoyed the privilege of a college education, he nevertheless found time to immerse himself in the history of this country. When he suddenly found himself the new leader of the non-Communist world, these values — combined with a heavy dose of common sense — were all he could depend on when he took office. He had no experience in foreign affairs, and the man he had appointed as his Secretary of State, James S. Byrnes, although far more experienced than the President, had none either. Of course, Truman could count on the professionals within the State Department for the necessary background and for briefings. Nevertheless, the new role he was undertaking was fraught with unresolved problems. He would soon learn their number and how difficult they would be to resolve.

In August 1945, when Truman met Stalin and Churchill for the first time, at Potsdam, the only war cloud in the sky floated over Japan. True to the agreement Stalin had made with Roosevelt at Yalta, Russian troops had invaded Japanese-held Manchuria as part of the Allied war effort to bring about an unconditional surrender on the part of the Japanese Emperor. Truman informed the Russian leader of a special weapon the

Americans now possessed that might induce Japan to surrender. Stalin had already heard about this weapon from his own sources. The Soviet Union officially might be an equal member of the Big Three alliance, but its equality was provisional and did not extend to a true partnership. Stalin knew the Soviet Union would not be trusted beyond a certain point by the US and British establishments.

Following the dropping of the bombs on Hiroshima and Nagasaki, a serious debate took place among members of the administration and the scientific community as to whether the United States should share its technology with the Russians. Its proponents stressed the importance of the alliance in defeating the Nazis, and the scientific community was certain that eventually Russian scientists would be able to duplicate what the joint US-British teams had accomplished. But the American establishment decided that it was best for the foreseeable future to keep the secrets of the bomb locked up in the United States.

Did the Cold War begin then? Or did the Cold War begin earlier, pursuant to Bretton Woods in July 1944, when Stalin reneged on the Russian delegate's agreement to join the World Bank and the International Monetary Fund? Or was the Cold War inevitable, given the basic conflict between two ideologies — state socialism and capitalism? But, the Cold War was far more than an economic, ideological conflict. It was an overpowering series of events, over a period of 45 years, which dominated the lives of two generations. The threat of a devastating atomic war that could destroy both civilizations never left the public consciousness. Many historians have come to the conclusion that the actions of one man, Joseph Stalin, set the wheels in motion. They point to his refusal to conduct free elections in post-war Poland; his unwillingness to negotiate a final peace treaty with divided Germany; his use of local Communist parties in Western democracies to destabilize existing governments; and finally, the air of secrecy about what was taking place in Eastern Europe.

All these factors contributed to the tension, including Stalin's reluctance to vacate the oil fields of northern Iran, but by themselves they do not constitute a Cold War. Ugliness as well as beauty is determined by the eyes of the beholder. There existed in the United States a powerful and influential group who were unalterably opposed to the very concepts of socialism and communism. Such systems were inherently incompatible with their own interests, and they viewed the wartime alliance as a *mariage de convenance*. This political group, which had been isolationist before the war, was prepared to retreat behind the security of our exclusive possession of the atom bomb. Supported by Midwestern Republicans and Anglo-phobic Irish Catholics, among others, they saw the Cold War as a blessing in disguise — in their shortsighted view of the post-war world. They were prepared to leave Western Europe to its deserved fate, and as for Britain, now that it had turned to the Labor party for its economic salvation, it was best for the United States to dissociate itself from that nation. In their own way, they contributed to the fever of the Cold War. As a counterpart to this anti-Roosevelt coalition, there were American Communists, Communist sympathizers, and well-meaning liberals, all of whom rallied around such respected figures as Eleanor Roosevelt and Henry Wallace, former Vice President under FDR. They were pro-Soviet Union and tended to lay the blame for the increasingly frayed relations between the two countries on the policies of the Truman administration. Finally, there were the internationalists, led by Truman and the ex-New Dealers, who positioned themselves somewhere between these two extremes. They sought to maintain cooperative relations with the Soviet Union, but were skeptical of where Stalin was leading the Soviet Union.

Truman was naïve. He believed that Stalin would live up to the other agreements made at Yalta, namely free elections in Poland. But that provision was in deliberately obscure language, composed in such a fashion as to induce Stalin to agree to enter the war against Japan. Stalin had no intention of allowing the Brits and Americans to consolidate their influence in a territory that was now under the Soviet army, least of all Poland, which bordered the Soviet Union and which stood between it and East Germany. Churchill might remonstrate that the pre-war government in Poland, housed in England, had contributed soldiers, sailors and airmen to the Allied war effort, but Stalin was adamant. Stalin knew that neither the United States nor Great Britain was prepared to go to war over Poland. Truman then embarrassed himself and Churchill when he called for free elections in Romania and Bulgaria, two countries that had fought on the side of the Nazis. Stalin did uphold the provisions of the Yalta agreement that called for a joint four-power occupation of Berlin and Vienna, both within territory occupied by the Russian army. He also agreed to have France as the fourth occupying power.

From a political point of view, the Potsdam meeting proved to be a disaster for the Democratic Party. In the 1946 mid-term Congressional elections, the Republicans recaptured both houses of Congress. The large ethnic voting blocs of immigrants from Eastern Europe, which had previously been a mainstay of the Democratic Party, believed that Roosevelt, and in turn the Democratic party, had sold out their native lands to Stalin at Yalta. Most of the voters in these ethnic groups had families still living there. Instead of being able to practice their religion, their relatives were about to wake up under an atheistic regime.

Six months after Potsdam, Stalin addressed the Central Committee of the Soviet Communist Party. The theme of his speech was dark and foreboding. In the immediate post-war era, the population of the Soviet Union could expect no amelioration in its living conditions. The government was forced to use its capital and energies in preparation for a potential attack by the United States. Analyzing the events that had led to the outbreak of World War I and II, Stalin had determined that Russia must be able to defend itself. Stalin's interpretation of past and recent history was accurate. However, it didn't necessarily apply to the current post-war period and that was a fatal error. Many economists in this country assumed, as Stalin did, that once the empty pipelines for civilian goods had been filled, US manufacturers would be faced with a static economy and would resort to reducing wages and/or laying off workers in order to survive. As was the case in the early 1930s, when supply exceeded demand, an economic depression would follow. In a great irony, Stalin's actions based on this theory resulted in the phenomenal growth of the US economy. His hard-line attitude toward the United States propelled it towards rearming to prevent a war with the USSR, and thus the US escaped the predicted Depression. By contributing to the synergy that fueled the Cold War, Stalin saved the US economy.

In March 1946, at a small college in Fulton, Missouri, Churchill (now out of office) would enunciate the first ringing rhetoric of the Cold War: "From Stettin in the Baltic to Trieste in the Adriatic an 'iron curtain' has descended across the Continent." A guest of Truman, Churchill had cleared the thesis of the speech first with the President; it called for the Western democracies to bond together to counter the threat now posed by Soviet expansionism. Churchill's speech reflected a strategy that was evolving within the State Department at that time. The previous month the Secretary of State had received a long telegram from George F. Kennan, deputy head of the US mission in Moscow, detailing what American foreign policy should be with regard to the Soviet Union. Short of engaging the Soviet Union in war, he suggested, there was nothing the United States could do to liberate the nations in Eastern Europe currently under Soviet hegemony. Instead, the policy of the US government should be to contain communism within the areas the USSR already controlled by strengthening Western institutions at risk of Communist takeover.

A year later, events caused Truman to signal his support of Churchill's thesis and Kennan's recommendations publicly. The venue, however, was not Western Europe, but Greece and Turkey. At Yalta, Stalin had told Churchill that Greece lay outside of Soviet post-war interests; the Soviet Union's army had not liberated it. Moreover, Russia had no objection to its return to a constitutional monarchy. As was the case with so many other occupied countries, a Greek government in exile had been set up in London. When the king returned to Athens, the population was divided. There were those who had fought against the Germans and before that, against the Italians, and those who had collaborated with the occupiers. This had been true throughout the war in every occupied country. Those who had been in the avant-garde of the resistance, generally speaking, were the local Communists. When the British troops arrived with the Greek king and his entourage to restore order and assemble a ruling government, they discovered they had an insurrection on their hands. The local Communists were determined to establish a Socialist government. It was not the Soviet Union that was supplying the rebels with arms but neighboring Yugoslavia, which had established a Socialist regime of its own under Joseph Broz Tito. The post-war Labor government of Great Britain was almost bankrupt. It could not afford to support the governments of Greece and Turkey. In desperation, it turned to the United States. Truman reacted immediately. On March 12, 1947, he addressed Congress and announced a policy of containment, which was later termed the Truman Doctrine. In essence, the doctrine stated that the United States was prepared to lend its financial support to any regime defending itself against communism. Although he was faced with a hostile Republican-dominated Congress, when the issue at stake was the prevention of Communist expansion, Congress willingly voted for the $400 million required to support the current anti-Communist regime. That summer, *Foreign Affairs* magazine published an anonymous article by Kennan elaborating on the US policy of containment. The author's identity soon was leaked. Because Kennan was now head of the

State Department's Policy Planning Staff, the article was deemed to state official policy. The message to the leadership in the Soviet Union was clear. The United States policy would be to prevent the spread of communism.

The Democratic Party that Truman inherited from Roosevelt was a mélange of conflicting interests bound together by the power inherent in controlling the government's purse strings. There was the solid Democratic South that had voted the straight Democratic line since the end of Reconstruction; there were the Big City bosses, who still retained their power thanks to the large immigrant population they had coddled; there were the industrial labor unions, who owed their success in organizing labor to legislation passed by the Democratic Congress under the New Deal; finally, there were the liberals, concentrated largely along the Boston-Washington seaboard, with the majority residing in New York City. In their approach to liberalism they ranged from Communists to Trotskyites, from Socialists to followers of John Maynard Keynes, who believed that the government had a responsibility to pump-prime the economy at the first sign of an economic slowdown. Both the liberals and the industrial unions believed that the government had a major role to play in directing the economy.

As a result, some of the labor unions, whose leadership was in the hands of Communists, and a large percentage of the liberal community looked favorably on the Soviet Union and the post-war policies it was pursuing. Except for the Communists, who adhered to whatever line the Cominform demanded, a certain percentage believed that socialism was the best way forward for society. They pointed to the fact that during the Depression, only the Soviet Union had experienced full employment. Many of them shared the belief that in a few years, the United States once again would sink into a post-war Depression.

The Republican majority in both houses of Congress and the Democratic South saw things differently. Over Truman's veto they passed the Taft-Hartley Act, which not only allowed for an "open shop" but also forbade unions to make contributions to political parties, and obliged them to open up their financial records for inspection. In addition, they passed the Loyalty Act, which Truman signed. When America entered the war in 1942, Roosevelt and Congress had enacted a similar piece of legislation. At that time, its focus was on nationals from Germany and Italy, who might be serving the interests of the enemy. Only a minor effort was made to seek out Communists in government. The new legislation, signed into law in peacetime, was directing its efforts towards the greatest potential enemy on the horizon, Communists. Over four years, the FBI would check the records of three million government employees. While none was indicted, thousands left rather than be investigated, and 122 were terminated. This, too, was part of the Cold War that was still on the horizon. While labor and the liberals viewed this Act as an intrusion on civil rights, the majority of Americans were in favor of it.

In retrospect, it could be said that the Truman Doctrine was the first blatantly overt statement by the President and Congress that the United States was opposed to communism, per se. Despite the fact that Stalin had no interest in Greece, his obduracy on Poland and his reluctance to remove Russian troops from northern Iran made him suspect in the eyes of the Truman administration and most Americans. A major cause for this attitude was a sense of frustration at the possibility of an uncertain future. Despite petty annoyances like rationing and the terrible losses sustained by so many families during the conflict, Americans were anxious to put the war behind them. They thought any differences between nations in this post-war world should be handled by the United Nations. It would take the imposition of the Berlin Blockade to awake Americans to the fact that while the Second World War was over, the threat of a new conflict was on the horizon.

In the poker game that would be played out prior to the Korean War, Stalin was at a serious disadvantage. The only high cards he held in his hand were the Communist parties in France and Italy, which he would subsidize through the newly reorganized Cominform. He did have control of East Germany, but the big prize, industrial West Germany, with its Saar Basin and its Ruhr Valley, was in the hands of America and its allies. His only trump card was the condition of the economies of Western Europe. Between the German occupation, which had stripped their economies bare, and the Allied invasion from the West, all of Western Europe, including Germany, was in a shambles. While the United States had been rebuffed in its demand for free elections in Poland, of far greater importance to the policy makers in Washington was the reunification of Germany. In order to arrive at that goal, a peace treaty would have to be put in place by the occupying powers. Stalin was no fool. Without a formal peace treaty, Germany would remain an occupied, divided nation. Conditions throughout Western Europe would continue to deteriorate, which in turn would accelerate the growth and influence of the Communist parties in all Western European countries.

When all four nations occupied Germany following the unconditional surrender, they retained the existing German currency, the Deutsche mark. Soviet troops, which hadn't been paid in three years, received their back pay in Deutsche marks. Unfortunately in war-torn Berlin or any other part of Germany, there wasn't much for sale. Berlin was unique in that the former capital of Hitler's Reich was occupied by the Four Powers, each nation controlling a section of the city. There was no wall, and freedom of movement between the occupied zones was relatively normal.

Nothing transcends languages and cultures like visual depictions. In the twentieth century, the two most widely spread visuals were the silent motion pictures of Charlie Chaplin and the animated cartoon figures created by Walt Disney. In every corner of the world, the adventures of Mickey and Minnie Mouse and the other characters created by Disney entertained millions. A good capitalist is someone who not only senses opportunities but also knows how to exploit them. Among the troops stationed in Berlin, there were a few neophyte capitalists who saw the opportunity to make a killing of a nonmilitary sort. Whoever was the first genius to recognize the potential market for Mickey Mouse wristwatches is unknown. Not only must he have made a fortune, but also in a strange way he might have accelerated the onset of the Cold War. A G.I. on leave might head for Paris or he might go to Switzerland. If he was smart, he'd go to Switzerland where he could buy Mickey Mouse watches for a dollar. When he returned to Berlin, he could visit the Russian soldiers laden with three years of back pay and with nothing to spend it on. Novelty always has its appeal, and within a short period of time, the going price was $300 in Deutsche marks.

Before they were repatriated, the Deutsche marks could be converted into US dollars. Some G.I.s made a fortune selling these watches. Other scams to exploit the Soviet soldiers were soon conceived. Until the new German mark was issued in the American zone of occupation, in 1948, it was estimated that it cost the United States Treasury Department close to $2 billion in exchanging Deutsche marks for dollars. That would represent a large number of Mickey Mouse watches and fountain pens. Commanding General Dwight Eisenhower and his subordinates were caught sleeping on the job. In Japan, General Douglas MacArthur had the old Japanese Yen replaced by new currency within six months of the start of the American occupation.

Meanwhile, the negotiations over a German peace treaty taking place in Paris between Secretary of State Byrnes and the Russian Foreign Minister Vyacheslav Molotov were going nowhere. Molotov's role was to procrastinate. Byrnes was an experienced man; his credentials as a politician and an administrator were superior to that of any other American. A former governor, senator, and Supreme Court justice, he had been Roosevelt's right hand man during the war, taking charge of the domestic economy while the President concentrated on the war and foreign affairs. But while Byrnes had been Truman's choice for Secretary of State, and the President had total confidence in his abilities, Truman was frustrated by the lack of progress in the negotiations. A misunderstanding over a speech that Byrnes was to deliver on his return to Washington caused a tiff between the two men. The result was Byrnes' resignation.

There was only one man to whom Truman could turn, whom he trusted implicitly and who would be certain of confirmation by a hostile Republican Senate — General George C. Marshall. Marshall had directed the nation's overall war effort in both the European and Asian theaters. In 1946, he had been called out of retirement by Truman in a hopeless effort to arrange a joint government between the Chinese Communists headed by Mao Tse-tung and the Chinese Nationalists led by Chiang Kai-shek. It was a thankless job; nothing could be resolved. Each of them assumed that they would emerge victorious from the civil war then raging in China. In addition to being a brilliant military strategist, Marshall was an astute observer of men. As Chief of Staff of the Army, he had made the decision to promote Eisenhower over other men with higher rank to lead the invasion of North Africa and then France. He had made this decision based on the need for a US general who could be an astute politician as well as a strategist. As commander of the allied forces invading Normandy, not only would Eisenhower have to contend with the inflated ego of British General Bernard Montgomery, who believed he should have had the commander position, but with the continued second guessing of Churchill, who also fancied himself a military expert. Eisenhower also would have to deal, later on, with the likes of General Charles De Gaulle. That Eisenhower had been able to adroitly acquit himself faced with these prima donnas, as well as such a brilliant but non-political general as George Patton, was confirmation of Marshall's judgment.

Upon taking up his new job as Secretary of State, Marshall conferred with his predecessor and with the President. Instead of waiting for a meeting with Molotov in Paris, he decided to go directly to Moscow. His translator, Chip Bohlen, also considered to be extremely knowledgeable about the inner workings of the Soviet Union, had counseled him that only one man made the decisions in the Soviet Union — Stalin. As the former commanding general of the US Army and Air Force, Marshall was wined and dined by the Soviet Generals. Both sides knew this was all part of a giant charade. He had come to Moscow as the new Secretary of State, and he had come to talk about Germany and a final peace treaty with the former enemy of both countries. As Bohlen had warned, Marshall would get nowhere with Molotov. Molotov attempted to forestall a meeting between Marshall and Stalin, but Marshall was adamant. Finally, Stalin agreed to meet with him. At the conclusion of the meeting, Marshall was convinced that Stalin had no intention of addressing the German problem, either now or in the future. A divided Germany fit in with Stalin's plans for the future of Western Europe.

On his return trip to the United States, Marshall made stops in Berlin and Paris. In both cities, he was briefed on the extent of damage to the economies of both countries. A great military strategist has to measure the strength of his own forces on hand, compared to those available to the enemy. That is the way that Marshall viewed Western Europe after visiting with Stalin and receiving an assessment from the US military commanders on the ground. The economies of Western Europe, given their present state, would continue to deteriorate. There were shortages of everything from coal in the winter to food and electricity. The infrastructure of these countries was a total disaster. Unless this condition was addressed immediately, the general public would turn to radical elements to change the status quo. This explained Stalin's attitude. If nothing were done to alleviate the current economic situation, Western Europe would turn to communism as a last desperate measure. Nor was the remedy to be attained with loans. The job was too big to be financed by banks. In order to save Western European capitalism, the United States Treasury, namely the Congress and the President, would have to deliver huge grants of money with no strings attached. All the European countries were in desperate need of a transfusion if their economies were to become viable once again.

The sum of money needed to implement the Marshall Plan is a mere bagatelle by today's standards. But in 1948 it was the most audacious scheme ever conceived. Truman greeted the plan enthusiastically; the Republican Senate would present the problem. There was the matter of the unpaid debts dating back to the First World War, which the United States government had absorbed. Now, instead of loans, the United States would be playing Santa Claus to nations who might become our future competitors. In addition to the cost, there was the equally problematic decision as to which nations should be offered the proposed plan. Should the Soviet Union and its satellite nations be included? In early 1948, the ensuing Cold War was barely visible. If aid were offered only to Western European nations, this decision would signify that the United States formally recognized Soviet hegemony over all of Eastern Europe. Secondly, this decision could have been construed by Moscow as an American act of hostility. On the other hand, it was highly doubtful that the Republican Congress would allocate funds to promote the stability of communism. Even without the component of extending aid to Communist regimes, the Marshall Plan was a difficult sale to Congress. The key to its passage by the Senate was Arthur Vandenberg, Chairman of the Senate's Foreign Relation's Committee. Nevertheless, had Byrnes, a Democrat, remained as Secretary of State, the bill appropriating the requisite funds never would have left the committee and reached the floor of the Senate. The strength of Marshall's arguments was buttressed by the fact he was apolitical.

Marshall's State Department was walking on a tightrope. Kennan and other Soviet specialists drew up a plan that they believed Stalin never would accept. In March 1948, all the nations from Europe were invited to Paris where Marshall laid out the details of his plan. The United States would help finance the rebuilding of the infrastructure of all of Europe. There were only two conditions. All projects undertaken had to be approved by US specialists; second, Americans would be on hand to supervise, in order to insure that the US materials were utilized only for that project and not transferred to other end uses. There was another condition that applied to the Eastern European satellites: the Soviet Union would help subsidize their projects. As Kennan had predicted, the deal was dead on arrival. The last thing Stalin wanted was American capitalism to insinuate itself into a Socialist economy. While some of the satellite nations were anxious to participate, especially Czechoslovakia, which was under almost total Soviet domination, the answer was always a resounding *nyet*.

With no Communist nations participating, the Marshall Plan passed both Houses of Congress. Of course, the original projection of approximately $6 billion soon mushroomed to $17 billion, or close to 10% of the total cost of fighting the Second World War. The Communist-led longshoremen unions in France and Belgium tried to prevent the unloading of materials coming from the United States. While there were delays, there were enough members of Socialist and Catholic longshoremen unions to insure the landing and delivery.

The intent of the Marshall Plan was to enable Western Europe to get back on its feet. At the same time, it gave a much-needed boost to America's economy. Thanks to the largesse of the Marshall Plan, a huge export market was opened that wouldn't have existed otherwise. The Marshall Plan not only was stimulating Western Europe's recovery but also was adding to the gross domestic product at home. Instead of the expected layoffs that had been predicted by Stalin and left-wing economists in the United States, the post-war boom continued. Steel mills were operating at full capacity. European rail tracks, locomotives, and freight and passenger cars had to be replaced. Lumber was required, as well as electrical equipment. An entire infrastructure that had been destroyed by five years of war had to be rebuilt. The Western European coal industry had to be put back on its feet. It would take four years before the impact of the Marshall Plan produced a positive effect on Western European economies. At the same time, under MacArthur, the Japanese economy was being revived through US aid. This program was given even greater emphasis once China had fallen to the Communists. Under these unforeseen circumstances, Japan now would become America's first line of defense in the Pacific region.

Before the rebuilding of Western Europe could come to fruition, a major crisis arose in the relations between the United States and the Soviet Union — the Berlin Blockade. It began when the US High Commissioner for Germany arrived at the conclusion that the reconstruction of the German economy in the American zone of occupation required a viable currency that could be exchanged in the international market. Since the Bretton Woods agreement of 1944, it had been decided that all the major currencies in the world would be pegged to the US dollar. Using the current Deutsche mark was a joke since the Soviet Union had access to the plates, inks and paper used for printing the currency. Once the Truman administration, in conjunction with Britain and France, had made the decision to rehabilitate the West German economy, a new dollar-based currency would have to be issued.

In the fifteenth century, Sir Thomas Gresham, keeper of the English Royal Exchange, informed the English monarch that good money drives out cheap money. In the nineteenth century, this was rediscovered and proclaimed as Gresham's Law. Since the dollar now was accepted as the world's official currency, with a newly backed Deutsche mark pegged to the dollar, the old Deutsche marks depreciated in value. While the sale of Mickey Mouse watches no longer was possible, of far greater consequence in the Soviet zone of occupation in Berlin was the threat to the value of the old Deutsche mark. There had been a free flow of trade between the four occupied zones, as well as with East Germany, but once the dollar-backed mark was circulated, the value of the old Deutsche mark declined precipitously. Gresham's Law had swung into action. Not only would this affect the economy of East Berlin, but it would affect that of East Germany as well. The trade between the Russian zone in Berlin and East Germany with those zones of the Allied sectors was immediately affected. The result was a runaway inflation in both East Berlin and East Germany. Even more disastrous was its effect on the overall East German economy. It was caught in a giant trap. If it cut off trade with West Berlin, its economy would suffer. If it continued, inflation truly would get out of hand. The entire East German economy was on the verge of collapsing since only the new Deutsche mark was prized.

The head of the Russian zone in Berlin called for a meeting with his Allied counterparts. He insisted that the new Deutsche mark be withdrawn and replaced with the old. This was impossible. The Allied zones in West Germany traded with their counterparts in West Berlin. It was impossible to conduct business with two different currencies. Stalin and his advisors in the Kremlin were stumped. From its very inception, the economy of Soviet Union had been isolated from that of the West. Its trade with Hitler's Germany had been conducted on the basis of barter. This had enabled Stalin to hide the actual value of the ruble. It also explained why Stalin had rejected the Bretton Woods agreement. The only possible solution to this economic conundrum was to remove the Allied forces from Berlin.

The method chosen was to have the East German government impose a blockade that would shut off all commerce between West Germany and Berlin. Since Berlin was located inside East Germany, all truck and rail traffic had to pass through sovereign East German territory. East Germany would force the three Allied powers either to vacate the city or to reinstall the old Deutsche mark. In effect, Russia's demand was tantamount to a declaration of war. The Allies were faced with two alternatives. Either they could attempt to force their way through with an armored train and test if the Soviet Union was bluffing; or they could attempt to supply a city of 2.5 million people, in the three Allied sectors, with food and fuel through an airlift. By a strange coincidence, the year was 1948, and a Presidential election was in the offing. The blockade imposed certain risks for the Soviet Union as well as the United States and its allies. If the Allies attempted to push an armored train through the blockade, and the East Germans resisted, the Allied troops stationed in Berlin could be overwhelmed by the superior military force of Russian troops still stationed in East Germany. Furthermore, given the minimal number of Allied troops still under arms in Europe, the Soviet army could sweep through Western Europe and reach the Atlantic Coast. For the Soviet Union, the risk was far greater. By now the United States had a large supply of atomic bombs. Moscow and Leningrad could be wiped off the face of the map.

The decision for war or peace lay in the hands of two men, Truman and Stalin. Neither man could be certain how the other would react. That would seem to be the normal conclusion to be drawn from the position of the two parties. Yet Stalin was too shrewd to challenge the United States with its arsenal of atomic weapons. It was not the Soviet Union that was acting confrontational. The blockade was being imposed by the sovereign state of East Germany. As later in Korea, Stalin would use surrogates to challenge the United States. And the United States would blink. But if an armored train had been sent through, the East Germans would not have contested it. Stalin merely had borrowed a page from Hitler when he reoccupied the Rhineland. The German generals were told that if the French army moved against them, they were to retreat. During the 14 months that the airlift went on, United States and British aircraft were violating the sovereign airspace of East Germany. If Stalin had been prepared to go to war, the airlift would have been impossible.

The blockade finally was lifted by the East German government. Cut off from all commerce with the West, unemployment soared and the East German economy went into a tailspin. This gradually would spread to the other Soviet satellite nations. Until the Berlin Wall was erected in 1961, the East German economy struggled along, even with the disparity in the value of the two Deutsche marks. The 14 months had proved to be an exercise in insanity. The Soviet Union might be self-sufficient but its satellite countries weren't. Stalin had lost on every front. The Marshall Plan was accelerated; a 14-nation North Atlantic Treaty Organization was developed in 1949 with the express purpose of coming to the defense of any nation that would come under attack by the Soviet Union; and in that same year, the three occupied zones of West Germany were incorporated into the German Federal Republic, with Konrad Adenauer as its first chancellor. All the hope that once was placed in the United Nations, with the Soviet Union and the United States acting together as the peacemakers, had vanished. Thanks to the Berlin Blockade, the concept of a Cold War had been established. At that time, the American public was unprepared to accept the possibility of another war. Truman was praised for his forbearance. After all, all's well that ends well.

Churchill's assertion that an Iron Curtain had descended over Eastern Europe now was taken for granted. Then, to the surprise of everyone, a crack in the Iron Curtain emerged. Marshal Tito of Yugoslavia made the decision to make his country independent of Soviet foreign policy. Yugoslavia would continue to develop its economy along the lines of a Socialist state, but in foreign affairs it no longer would take its instructions from the Kremlin. Tito viewed Stalin's policy towards the United States as uncalled-for adventurism. Tito was the first man to stand up to Stalin. There was the threat of a Soviet military invasion, but nothing came of it. The last thing Stalin wanted was internal warfare between two Socialist states. This did not deter Stalin from attempting to overthrow the regime internally. But Tito employed his own secret police, and whatever conspiracy was afoot was soon put down.

In that same year, 1948, the Truman administration was faced with another seemingly insoluble headache — the recognition of the new state of Israel. While none of the members of the Security Council had voiced any opposition to the United Nation's plan to partition the British mandate over Palestine into two nations, one Arab and the other Jewish, there was strong opposition within the Truman administration to the recognition of the Jewish state. Both Marshall, Secretary of State, and James Forrestal, Secretary of Defense, were highly vocal in their opposition. Their view of the geo-political world was measured in terms of America's best interests rather than the emotionally charged atmosphere that surrounded the creation of a homeland for the Jewish people. Their concern was the reaction of the neighboring Arab states, especially those producing oil, all of which were vehemently opposed to a Zionist state in the Middle East. In addition, an influential segment of the American-Jewish population was opposed to recognition of the new state. These opponents were led by Henry Morgenthau, the Secretary of the Treasury under Roosevelt, the Ochs family, the publisher of the *New York Times*, the most influential newspaper in the United States, and Lessing Rosenwald, the single largest stockholder in Sears, Roebuck and Company, the largest retailer in the country and founder of the American-Jewish Committee (organized as a competitor to the American-Jewish Congress, which supported the creation of a Zionist state in Palestine). Their motives were different than those of Marshall and Forrestal. Their fear was a backlash of anti-Semitism against American Jewry. Most of their supporters, like themselves, were American Jews of German extraction who had preceded the more recent waves of Eastern European Jewish immigrants. It was this latter, much larger, group of American Jews who were responding to the plight of Jews in Eastern Europe, especially given the slaughter of millions of Jews (as well as Slavs, Gypsies and others) under the Nazis, and they had supported the Zionist cause with generous contributions of money.

Truman had to take into account another factor. This was a presidential election year, and to carry the all-important vote in New York required the support of the large Jewish population in New York City. He also had to contend with pressure from his friend and former business partner Eddie Jacobson, an ardent Zionist. Finally, there was the moral issue. During the war, Roosevelt had turned away a shipload of German Jews seeking asylum in this country and sent the ship back to Germany, where they all died in concentration camps. In the end, Truman supported recognition and the Soviet Union was a quick second. Had the United States not recognized Israel, such a decision would have given the Soviet Union an entrée into the Middle East and the history of that region of the world might have followed a different course with the Soviets the principal supporter of a homeland for Jews. It would have placed

American Jewry in a difficult position since David Ben-Gurion and the other leaders of the Zionist movement in Israel would have accepted military and economic aid from any country, no matter what its political philosophy.

Three separate but closely related events further ensured the development of the Cold War and changed the course of America's post-war history. The United States would learn that Soviet scientists and engineers had mastered the technology of the atom bomb, and America's monopoly on the most powerful weapon in the world had been broken. That was in August 1949, when an American patrol plane in the Pacific Ocean spotted traces of radiation in the air coming from the direction of Siberia. Three months later, the last of Chiang Kai-Shek's army embarked for the island of Formosa, leaving mainland China in the hands of the Chinese Communists. Seven months later, North Korean troops crossed the 38th parallel and invaded South Korea.

Occurring less than five years after the end of the Second World War, these events sent the American public into a state of shock. It seemed like only yesterday that the war had ended; the dead had been buried; the maimed were trying to adjust; and the majority of Americans were looking forward to a peaceful future. Instead, the country seemed to be facing one crisis after another. Making it more difficult to comprehend was the fact that the US economy appeared to be doing fine. What preyed on people's minds was not the loss of China to the Communists but the fact that the Soviet Union now possessed the same deadly weapon we had. The two oceans that had served to secure the United States from the ravages of previous World Wars no longer provided the security once taken for granted. This was only the beginning of a long and bumpy ride that would last for another half a century. As bad and as frightening as events might appear at times, there was one major compensation — a prosperity that would alter the lives of the majority of the American population. Or, so it seemed.

By 1949, the first appearance of a slowdown in the US economy emerged. Truman's upset election victory in 1948 was because the US economy was enjoying the biggest boom in its entire history. Revenues from taxes were so large that the federal budget showed a surplus of nearly $12 billion, by far the largest ever. But by 1949 it had declined to $850 million, and by 1950, the federal budget was back in the red. Stalin's prediction seemed about to be realized. The civilian pipelines had been filled. The growth in the basic heavy industries, a result of orders for the Marshall Plan, was winding down. There were layoffs in major industries as well as strikes, and the vaunted US economy seemed to be on the skids. The economic indicators pointed in the direction of a recession, or maybe a recession was already in progress.

At that moment in history, irony took over. Instead of the United States initiating hostilities, Stalin would fulfill his own prophecy. By giving the go-ahead to Communist North Korea to invade its southern neighbor, it set in motion the wheels of a permanent wartime economy in the United States. In one of history's greatest ironies, it would be a planned Communist aggression that would alter the very concept of capitalism and move it in a direction contrary to its core beliefs. In place of a balanced budget, deemed a necessity in order to maintain the value of its national currency, deficit spending on a scale unimaginable in 1950 would become the linchpin to the growth of the US economy. The much-reviled Stalin had saved the capitalist system that he expected to replace with a Socialist economy.

When the army of North Korea crossed into South Korea in June 1950 and set in motion the Korean War, few Americans even knew where Korea was located — except for the scant troops that had been left stationed there. Following the surrender of the Japanese, and its pacification, most of the US troops stationed in Korea had been withdrawn. Even the administration in Washington did not consider that country vital to America's interests in the Pacific.

Until the very end of the nineteenth century, Korea had been an independent nation under the protection of the Manchu dynasty. As that kingdom began to crumble, factionalism within the Korean regime resulted in one side inviting the Japanese to help bolster their efforts to dominate the opposition. This fatal error allowed the Japanese to gain a foothold, and the Japanese never left. In effect, Korea became Japan's first colony on the Chinese mainland and a steppingstone for its further conquests in Manchuria and mainland China. During the Japanese invasion of mainland China in the 1930s, a Korean government in exile was formed under the protection of Chiang Kai-shek in Shanghai. When that city fell into the hands of the Japanese, the Korean government in exile followed Chiang to Chunking.

On the way to their first meeting with Stalin at Tehran, Roosevelt and Churchill stopped in Cairo, where Chiang met them, and the decision was made that following Japan's defeat Korea would be granted its independence. At Yalta, the topic of Korea was brought up again and Stalin evinced no objection to a free Korea. In fact, it was decided that a four-power trusteeship should be established in Korea until such time as the country would become independent. The designated four trustees were Nationalist China, the Soviet Union, the United States and Great Britain. In 1945, the Chinese Foreign Minister flew to Moscow to confirm with Stalin that a trusteeship would be set up after the war. Since the Russians had entered the war against Japan by invading Manchuria, the Big Three agreed that following the surrender of Japan, the Soviet Union would disarm and repatriate the Japanese troops in the northern sector of Korea; and the United States would perform the same function in the southern half of the peninsula. An arbitrary line was drawn at the 38th parallel to distinguish the North from the South.

Syngman Rhee was an anomaly in many ways. An ardent nationalist from the beginning of his career, he was imprisoned by the Japanese. Ultimately, he made his way to the United States, where he was the first Korean to obtain a doctorate at a US university, Princeton. Totally fluent in English and a convert to Christianity, he had journeyed to Versailles in 1919 to plead for the independence of Korea. Since Japan had fought on the side of the Allies during the First World War, his plea fell on deaf ears. He spent the next 30 years in America, lobbying Congress for Korean independence. While he had contacts with the Korean government in exile in China, he was unable to assume the leadership of the movement. On the other hand, during his years in America, he had cultivated many friends in high places. In the United States, it was assumed that he would be an advocate for a democratic regime.

The American delegation had in mind Syngman Rhee as the first president of Korea once the trusteeship ended. But when the four powers originally met to set up a trusteeship for Korea, Rhee was convinced that under such an arrangement he would be pushed aside by the majority of Korean appointees as an outsider; he had sat the war out in America. The four powers had agreed to such a preliminary government, and the Soviet Union was opposed to seating any delegate who did not accept those terms; the US insisted that Rhee be included in any provisional government. As a result of this impasse, the trusteeship went by the boards and Korea was divided into two nation states, each with its own Constitution, and each ruled by one man. In the North, Kim Il-sung, who had led a brigade of North Koreans in defense of the Soviet Union during the Nazi invasion of Russia and had received the Order of Lenin for his bravery at the battle of Stalingrad, was installed as head of state. He would establish a Communist state analogous to that of the Soviet Union. A majority of the delegates from the Korean government in exile desired to establish a Socialist regime in the South. Since the US military controlled the country, that outcome was out of the question. Instead, Syngman Rhee was appointed the first president of South Korea. To prevent the formation of a leftist leaning government, the United States had placed its own man in power. Dissidents were either murdered or imprisoned. While the United States provided military and financial assistance to the Rhee government, America had withdrawn all of its troops and most of its military advisors for South Korea, much as the Soviet Union had done in the North. The brutal policy used by Rhee to crush any dissidents was overlooked by American foreign policy makers. He was virulently anti-Communist, and at that moment in American history this stance was sufficient reason to supply his regime with financial support.

Early in 1950, Stalin invited Mao Tse-tung, Chou En-lai and other leaders of the Chinese Communist party to Moscow to celebrate their victory over the Nationalists. It was an awkward moment for Stalin. Mao was well aware that until it became obvious that the Chinese Communists would win the Civil War, Stalin had backed Chiang and the Nationalist government. Nothing Stalin did was without a reason. After the treachery of the kulaks in the Soviet Union Stalin's hatred of the peasants as a class knew no bounds. Mao's successful revolution was made possible by promoting the Chinese peasant into his army. Mao's basic appeal to the Chinese peasant was reformation of the feudal agricultural system in China. By destroying the landlord class and turning over their land to the peasants, he had won the loyalty of the peasants. To Stalin, indoctrinated in Marxist theory, the peasants as a class were counter-revolutionaries. Nevertheless, a Communist regime had been established in the largest nation in the world, and that feat overrode any of Stalin's inherent opposition to a peasant-dominated Socialist state.

To Mao, Stalin's duplicity was meaningless in the long term. For a Communist regime to succeed, China would have to be industrialized. The Soviet Union could be of enormous help. Mao also was aware of the growing hostility between the Soviet Union and the United States.

Perhaps he could play one off against the other for the benefit of China. To accomplish that would require recognition of the Peoples Republic of China by the United States. An important step would be to have the Nationalists' seat on the Security Council of the United Nations turned over to the Peoples Republic of China, since his regime now was the *de facto* government in China. But it would be impossible for the Truman administration to even contemplate taking such a step. While logic might dictate that it would be in the best interest of the United States to recognize the *de facto* government of the largest nation in the world, domestic considerations took precedence: the hue and cry of the Republican minority in Congress blaming the Democrats for the loss of China to the Communists was reinforced by the conviction of Alger Hiss as a Russian spy; the confession of Klaus Fuchs (in Britain) that he had passed secrets from the atom bomb project to the Soviet Union; the incarceration of Julius and Ethel Rosenberg, American citizens also convicted of passing on atomic secrets to the Soviet Union; as well as the strength of Nationalist China lobby. Mao's chances were doomed before Andrei Gromyko, the Russian delegate to the Security Council, brought up the subject. The United States used the power of its veto to squash the Soviet demand. Stalin had lost face not only with Mao but also in the Communist world at large. He recalled his delegate back to Moscow. Stalin would have his revenge, and the United States would pay dearly for its rejection of Communist China. When the US Ambassador to South Korea placed a frenzied call to Washington in early June 1950, informing his superiors that North Korean forces had crossed the 38th parallel and were marching on Seoul, the South Korean capital, the Truman administration was dumbstruck. The news only got worse. The North Koreans had captured South Korea's capital; the army of the Republic of Korea (ROK) was disorganized and in panic; and civilians were jamming the roads, hindering the South Korean army from establishing defensive positions.

Truman was facing the second crisis of his administration. With China now in the hands of the Communists, only the US was capable of preventing South Korea from being swallowed up by its northern neighbor. As the situation on the ground continued to deteriorate, the President was left with two alternatives, neither one very palatable. Since South Korea was not deemed to be part of America's national interests, it could go to the United Nations and ask that body to intercede, or the

United States could stand by and allow North Korea to swallow up its weaker neighbor. Asking Congress to declare a state of war was out of the question. The administration already had stated that Korea was not part of America's national interest. On the other hand, to stand by and do nothing might well lead to further Communist aggression in other parts of the world.

Before making any decisions it was necessary to prevent the armed forces of the ROK from collapsing. Using his authority as Commander-in-Chief, he ordered General Douglas MacArthur, the commanding General in the Pacific, to dispatch troops stationed in Japan to aid the besieged forces of the ROK. Without taking into account that these peacetime occupation forces were ill prepared for combat duty, MacArthur dutifully complied. Truman's next step was to bring the subject of the illegal invasion before the Security Council of the United Nations. With the Russian delegate still in Moscow, the Security Council unanimously condemned North Korea's action, and called on its membership to send troops to support the US effort to repel the North Koreans. It was a brilliant move. Instead of having to go before Congress and asking them to declare a state of war, as prescribed in the Constitution, at best a difficult and time-consuming process, Truman had invoked the UN Charter. The history of the Korean War (or "Police Action" as it was called) became America's first military disaster. In many ways Korea was the first signal of the inadequacy of America's military forces. It was only during and after the Korean conflict that the Defense Department would come to dominate all federal expenditures. In 1950, defense expenditures accounted for 32.2% of the federal budget. Three years later that percentage would grow to 69.4%. While that percentage would continue to decline as the national economy expanded, even during the height of the war in Vietnam, national defense still remained the nation's top priority as long as the Cold War lasted. In the beginning of the conflict in Korea, the unprepared US troops dispatched from Japan were unable to withstand the impact of the North Korean army and were forced to retreat until defensive lines had been established in front of the port city of Pusan. Then, with neither side able to advance, a war of attrition set in.

MacArthur, the overall Commander of the US and UN forces in Korea, remains the most enigmatic general in US military history. As a strategist he had no equal. Mocked as "Dugout Doug" by the troops who served under him in the Pacific during the Second World War, his army had fewer casualties than any other during the war. His aloofness even among close associates was similar to that of Generals De Gaulle and Washington. Even among close associates he expected to be referred to as General. He was brave, daring, and above all, a showman. He was easily recognizable by his crushed military cap and the long corncob pipe in his mouth. He and his associates created the Constitution that turned Japan into a democracy.

When MacArthur assumed command of the US and UN forces, Congress had established a different chain of command. Military strategy now passed through the Secretary of Defense and the Joint Chiefs of Staff, representing all three branches of the Service. In addition the President, as Commander-in-Chief, had to sign off on whatever plans were approved. Put simply, any major decision MacArthur might undertake would have to be approved by these five men. Under these conditions the general unveiled a plan so bold and fraught with potential failure that it was immediately rejected. In place of the US-led forces remaining bogged down on the narrow, southern tip of the Korean peninsula, with no room to maneuver, MacArthur proposed an amphibious landing behind the enemy lines at the small port of Inchon, which would place the North Korean forces in a vise. The only timing feasible before winter set in was a few days in October when the tides would be right, and the Marines would be able to land beyond the breakwater. The immediate reaction of the Secretary of Defense and the Joint Chiefs was negative. The leaders of the Navy and Marine Corps, who shared the command with him during the war in the Pacific, as well as those representing the Army and the Air Force, held no love for the preening general. However, there was no real alternative other than for the armed forces to remain trapped in this narrow space, with casualties mounting every day.

Finally, with great reluctance and trepidation, the Joint Chiefs, the Secretary of Defense and the President signed off on MacArthur's plan. The Inchon landing went off exactly as conceived by MacArthur. The Marines were able to establish a beachhead, and US troops followed. Overnight, the fortunes of war had been reversed. Caught between two armies, the North Koreans panicked and retreated northward. For a frustrated and loudly criticized President, MacArthur had produced a miracle. Truman's popularity soared. Weeks later, the US-led forces had succeeded in fighting their way up the peninsular and recapturing Seoul, arriving at the 38th parallel, the original dividing line between the two Koreas.

The mandate issued by the United Nations was not to destroy North Korea but to restore the government of South Korea. If US-led troops invaded North Korea, the United States would be exceeding its mandate. Syngman Rhee viewed the defeat of the North Koreans as an opportunity to unify the country under his rule. His ROK troops first crossed the 38th parallel and invaded North Korea. MacArthur wired Truman requesting permission to pursue the now retreating North Korean forces. By this time, winter was approaching and the US-led forces moved forward. As they approached the border of Manchuria, the UN army would be butting up against the border of the Peoples Republic of China. Great Britain, quick to recognize the new government of China because of the British lease on Hong Kong, sent a message to Washington informing the administration that the Chinese government looked with disfavor on an enemy army approaching its border. Truman, perhaps not fully realizing the import of that warning, cabled MacArthur to avoid approaching the Yalu River that separated North Korea from Manchuria. In turn, MacArthur kept his forces clear of the border area. At the same time, he ordered the head of US military intelligence to estimate the number of Chinese troops amassed on the other side of the border. The report indicated that the number of Chinese troops on the border was insignificant. With that information in hand, MacArthur ordered the field general to continue his pursuit of the remaining North Korean army, while still staying clear of the Yalu River.

The US military command was caught off guard by a Chinese army of 300,000 men. What had been a mopping-up operation now had become a major counter offensive led by the Chinese. Because of the sheer size of their numbers, there was no way to halt the Chinese army's progress. No military strategy had yet been invented to cope with this situation. The onset of winter further added to the plight of the US-led armed forces. Gun turrets froze, as well as the oil in tanks and motor vehicles. The soldiers also suffered from the artic weather, not being equipped with the proper clothing. MacArthur flew in from Tokyo to assess the situation on the ground. With no possibility of stemming the Chinese advance, in desperation he called on the President to use atomic weapons. Truman categorically refused, fearing that Russia might enter the conflict and use its own supply of atomic weapons, unleashing a possible Third World War.

MacArthur, frustrated by his newly discovered impotence, took out his anger on Truman, openly criticizing him and his handling of the war.

MacArthur finally overstepped his bounds in a letter to the Republican Minority Leader of the House, Joseph Martin, criticizing Truman. Instead of keeping the letter confidential, he read it before the House. It was one thing to openly taunt the Chinese when the administration was attempting to enter into negotiations with Communist China to negotiate a truce; quite another for a military man on active duty to enter American politics. Either the President was the duly elected Commander-in-Chief, or MacArthur was. Despite the public uproar that was sure to ensue, Truman fired the general. MacArthur and his wife and son returned to America after an absence from this country of almost 15 years. Greeted by a huge and enthusiastic crowd when he debarked in San Francisco, he was given the same reception everywhere he went. Called upon to address both houses of Congress, he left some of the audience in tears with his concluding remark, "Old soldiers never die; they just fade away." Some Republicans believed he would make an ideal presidential candidate in 1952, and efforts were made in that direction, but the very idea of the general stooping down to the level of American politics was insane. MacArthur was his own man, not a servant of the people. As he promised in his farewell speech, he faded away in the luxury of an apartment in the Waldorf Astoria towers.

Historians later on would make him the scapegoat for the rout of the US-led forces in Korea and for the numerous casualties that followed in the wake of the Chinese attack. It was more than a counteroffensive. If one side in a conflict, even with inferior weaponry, is convinced that it faces a threat to its very existence, it is likely to be more willing to sacrifice the lives of its men; and then, it is mighty hard to stop them. Yet with reinforcements arriving from America and with discipline, the morale of the Eighth Army was revitalized. Over the next two years, the Chinese and North Koreans were driven back to the starting point of the conflict, the 38th parallel. While the blame for the disaster was placed on MacArthur's shoulders, as it should have been from a strictly military point of view, an equal degree of culpability could be ascribed to the President and the Joint Chiefs. It was their decision, not MacArthur's, to cross the 38th parallel and invade North Korea. It was Truman's decision not to recognize the Peoples Republic of China as the legitimate representative of the Chinese people, leaving Mao with the belief that the long-range goal of US foreign policy was the overthrow of his regime. Under those circumstances, having a hostile regime on its Manchurian border was unacceptable. Those responsible for US foreign policy had a view of the world limited to black and white. Yet America had to accommodate itself to the Soviet presence because Russia now possessed the ultimate weapon. The decision by Truman to repel the North Korean invasion of South Korea signified that America's original policy of containing the spread of communism to Western Europe now had been extended to include the rest of the world, including those nations not considered to be vital to US interests. Without realizing the long-range consequences, America's anti-Communist hysteria, provoked by the loss of Nationalist China to the Communists, would alter its foreign policy to the point where emotions replaced rational behavior.

Until 1948, for most Americans the concept of a Communist state was viewed as an abstraction rather than something concrete. They believed that the United States was the best of all possible worlds. The idea that some Americans would think otherwise was unimaginable to most of the public; and, if there were a few who disagreed, these few must be foreigners who had never attempted to integrate themselves into American society. The House Un-American Activities Committee (HUAC) was originally established to ferret out sympathizers of Germany, Italy and Japan. However, once the war had ended and the Republicans had captured both houses of Congress, HUAC focused its attention on Communist sympathizers or actual members of the Communist party who had infiltrated the US government.

This soon led to the phenomenon known as McCarthyism. Over a period of three years, Senator Joseph McCarthy convinced half of the American public that subversion within the State Department had led to the fall of China to the Communists and the resulting military disaster that was occurring in Korea. Without the failed Korean War, he never could have acquired the power and fame that terrorized liberals, State Department employees, the Democratic Party and the Army. The senator launched fabricated attacks against individuals and the State Department that eventually collapsed when he failed to supply evidence to support his allegations and when the horror of the Korean War ended with a truce.

McCarthy would be the least of the problems that Truman would pass on to his successor, Eisenhower. The two most serious were the Korean War, which had yet to be resolved, and the Cold War, which seemed to be intensifying now that Communist China appeared to be in partnership with the Soviet Union. Another situation — one that threatened US oil interests in the Middle East, involving Iran — had to be dealt with immediately. The modern history of Iran begins in 1906 when a seemingly spontaneous revolution broke out against the Shah and the ruling elite, resulting in the passage of a constitution and the creation of a parliament of elected representatives. With Iran in political disarray, Britain and Russia took the opportunity for each nation to expand its colonial interests. A year later, the two nations signed the Anglo-Russian agreement carving Iran into two spheres of influence. The Russians took control of the north, and the British took control of the east and the south, with control of the center of the country left undecided.

In 1908, Iran would take on foreseen importance. British archaeologists digging for ancient artifacts struck a small layer of oil near the surface. British geologists followed up this discovery and uncovered the first of many huge oil fields that existed in the Middle East. The Anglo-Persian Oil Company was formed, with Russia granted the rights to the oil fields in the north and the Anglo-Persian Oil Company granted the rights throughout the rest of the country. During the First World War the British Navy, in order to insure a steady flow of oil for its fleet, purchased a majority interest in the Anglo-Persian Oil Company. With the newly formed Soviet Union involved in a revolution and the new Russian government having annulled all previous agreements made by the tsarist government, the Anglo-Persian Oil Company gained control over all the oil in Iran. (The Anglo-Persian Oil Company changed its name to the Anglo-Iranian Oil Company in 1935, and became the British Petroleum Company in 1954.)

In 1921, with most of the world in the throes of an economic recession that followed the end of the war, Britain would engage the military services of Reza Khan, the leader of a Persian Cossacks Brigade, to protect British oil interests. Khan seized control of the entire country putting down whatever pockets of resistance that remained. Two years later, Khan secured the post of Prime Minister of the country, with a little financial help from Britain. In 1925, again with backing from the British, he deposed the royal Qajar dynasty and had himself crowned as His Imperial Majesty Reza Shah Pahlavi, the following year. It was under these circumstances that the Pahlavi regime came to power. The new Shah, again with British support and counsel, not only would modernize

Iran's political and social systems and reduce the power of the clergy and the tribal leaders but would ensure his power-base by expanding the military to serve as his watch dog and crush any signs of dissidence. In effect, the Shah had become a dictator with all the trappings of a Constitution and a Parliament. The Shah revolutionized Iranian society and dragged it into the twentieth century. The educational system was secularized, and in 1935 the first European-style university was established. The transportation system was expanded, and industrial production was encouraged with state subsidies. But this progressive Shah did not stop there. The legal system was revamped and secularized, and was removed from the control of the clerics. As in the case of Turkey, women were liberated, European dress codes were imposed on the population, and the women's veil was outlawed.

With the collapse of prices on the New York Stock Exchange in 1929 and the onset of the worldwide Depression, followed two years later by Britain abandoning the gold standard, the price of crude oil on the world market plunged. In 1933, desperate for revenue to support the large army which maintained him in power, and which consumed a large percentage of the government's revenues, the Shah annulled the old contract the government held with the Anglo-Persian Oil Company and negotiated a new one. Under the new agreement, the areas under exploitation were reduced, and the Iranian government would receive a larger share of the oil profits. After 60 years, all the oil fields and the refinery would revert to the Iranian government. In no way did this agreement ameliorate the plight of the majority of the country's residents, its rural folk.

With the rise to power of Hitler and his focus on the purity of the Aryan race, and since the Persians considered themselves the fountainhead of Aryanism, the Shah's regime began to take on all the trappings of the Nazi party. Anti-Semitic slogans surfaced; the largely successful Jewish population was harassed, and the army adopted the goose step of the German army. In 1938, the Tudeh, Iran's Communist party, was banned. As Hitler became more successful, the foreign policy of Iran switched away from Britain and toward Nazi Germany. Although Iran declared its neutrality with the outbreak of the Second World War, the sympathy of the Shah was pro-German. With the German invasion of Russia in 1941, and the newly forged alliance between Britain and the Soviet Union, it became necessary to have a friendly regime in Iran, given that its northern border touched one of the southern borders of the

Soviet Union. In August 1941, a combined force of British and Russian troops invaded Iran, crushed the Shah's army, deposed the Shah in favor of his son, Reza Shah Pahlavi, and reinstalled the Iranian Parliament as the center of power of the government.

In 1951, on *Time* magazine's Man of the Year cover, appeared the elongated, shaven head of Mohammad Mossadegh, the Prime Minister of Iran. Newly elected, he had done the unthinkable. He had nationalized the interests of the Anglo-Iranian Oil Company, breaking the original 1933 contract signed by the father of the current Shah. The background to this radical move by the government of Iran dates back to the end of the Second World War. In 1945, the Russian troops in northern Iran refused to evacuate the region, contending that the original agreement between tsarist Russia and Britain, whereby Russia had the rights to exploit the northern oil fields of Iran, still remained in effect. Despite pressure from the United States and Great Britain, Russian troops refused to evacuate Iran until the Soviet Union was granted that concession. Iran initially granted that concession, but pressure from the United States forced the Parliament to revoke the agreement by an overwhelming vote of 102 to 2, with Mossadegh in the forefront of the repeal. The Parliament then passed a bill that disallowed any future oil concessions to foreign nations and called on the government to develop new oil fields. The United States was instrumental in forcing the Soviet Union to vacate Iranian territory, so the Parliament entered into an agreement with the United States to provide military aid and training. In that same year, the Anglo-Iranian Oil Company reported an after-tax profit of $112-million, of which only $19.6 million was disbursed to the Iranian government.

In 1949, under the leadership of Mossadegh, the Parliament demanded to renegotiate its contract with Anglo-Iranian in order to attain a more equitable share of the profits. Mossadegh's hard line position with Anglo-Iranian, and his role as leader of the National Front party, catapulted him to chairman of the government's Oil Committee. Anglo-Iranian refused to meet the 50-50 split that had become the standard for the other oil-producing states in the Persian Gulf area; and the newly elected prime minister of the Iranian government took the unprecedented step of nationalizing the Anglo-Iranian Oil Company, in which the British government held a majority interest. As a first step, the government took control of the world's largest oil refinery, which supplied Western Europe with 43% of its oil needs.

If Iran should be successful in breaking a contract, what was to stop the other nations in the Persian Gulf area — in which US oil companies held the dominant interest — from following in Iran's footsteps? The British government reacted immediately. It called for a worldwide boycott of Iranian oil and asked its allies to follow suit. It continued its pressure by freezing the Sterling assets of Iran and placing a ban on exports to that country. The Truman administration supported it wartime ally and refused to lend Iran any money until the dispute was settled. Britain took its case to the Security Council of the United Nations in New York and to the International Court of Justice in The Hague. In turn, Mossadegh, who had a doctorate in law from the University of Lausanne, flew to New York and from there to The Hague to present Iran's case to the court. Mossadegh successfully defended Iran's action by proving that it is outside the Court's jurisdiction and the case had no standing. Mossadegh then returned to Iran by way of Egypt; in Cairo, he was greeted by an enormous and enthusiastic crowd. He was the first leader in the Middle East to have twisted the British Lion's tail successfully. Back in Tehran, an even larger crowd greeted him at the airport. He had become the hero of the Iranian people. But once the enthusiasm faded away, reality stepped in. The worldwide embargo on Iranian oil threatened to choke the economy of the nation, despite Italy's and Japan's non-participation.

Given the weakened economy and fearing a putsch led by the Shah, Mossadegh sought control of the Ministry of Defense in 1952. When the Shah refused his request, Mossadegh resigned from his office. The result was a general strike and three days of rioting throughout the capital, led by nationalists and Communists. Two days later the Shah conceded, reappointed Mossadegh to head the country, and allowed him to appoint a new Minister of Defense. Mossadegh appointed himself, and began the process of purging the high command of officers loyal to the Shah and replacing them with Nationalists. A few weeks later, the Parliament granted him total power over the nation's affairs for a six-month period, extending it for an additional six months. Mossadegh then set in motion a reformation of Iran's tax and revenue structures and assumed control over the government's expenditures. He had the Assembly pass a law reducing the term of senators from six years to two years, and all the members of the Senate resigned. At the same time, Mossadegh offered to enter into negotiations with the Anglo-Iranian Oil Company over the amount of money owed the company as a result of its nationalization. There were two provisos. The company was to release the $1.4 billion it held in a contingency account, and Britain was to lift the worldwide embargo on Iranian oil. Britain and the United States presented a counter offer. Both countries were prepared to recognize the nationalization of Iranian oil if Mossadegh agreed to allow the International Court at The Hague to decide the amount of compensation due the Anglo-Iranian Oil Company. Since neither side was willing to accept the offer of the other side, the talks broke down.

With the Conservative party now controlling the British Parliament, the old warhorse, Winston Churchill, once again Prime Minister, believed it was time to revert to a modern version of nineteenth century gunboat diplomacy. He ordered the British Secret Service to set in motion plans for the assassination of Mossadegh. Churchill notified Truman of the plan, entitled Operation Ajax. It would be a British operation. Mossadegh discovered the plot against him. Without hesitation, the Iranian Prime Minister ordered the British embassy closed and threw out all the British diplomats. Once again, the British government was left with no alternative but to call on the Americans to come to its aid. With Eisenhower elected President, the soon-to-be-departing Truman administration refused to step in. It would be up to Eisenhower to salvage Britain's pride. Truman's main legacy to the former general was the Cold War and the necessity for the United States to retain and increase it arms superiority in the event of future Soviet aggression whether by one of its surrogates or by Russia, itself. It was the beginning of the arms race and its concomitants, the military-industrial complex and the huge federal budget deficits that would change the face of capitalism and lead the country into a prosperity never before imagined. In 1953, the American people had no idea of their future. They were sick and tired of wars and they had elected a general to bring wars to an end.

Chapter 6. The Cold War in Neutral: The Eisenhower Presidency

Once the liberal wing of the Republican Party had secured the presidential nomination for General Dwight Eisenhower, it was a foregone conclusion that he would be elected, given the inability of the Truman administration to resolve the war in Korea. And even those party members who had been instrumental in convincing him to seek the nomination — lead by twice-defeated presidential candidate Thomas Dewey and recently defeated Senator Henry Cabot Lodge — failed to appreciate or understand the political skills of their selected nominee. Eisenhower's elevation from a lieutenant colonel attached to General Douglas MacArthur in the Philippines, to the leader of the Normandy invasion, the largest seaborne landing in the history of warfare, had not been the result of mere chance.

Having made his peace with the right wing of the party by selecting Richard Nixon as his running mate, the General now began to plan his election strategy. Ignoring the advice of all the political pundits of the party, he was determined to show the American public his independence of all party affiliations by launching his campaign on a whistle-stop tour of the solid Democratic South. Wherever the train stopped, he was greeted by huge crowds, including many soldiers and officers who had fought under his campaigns in North Africa and Europe. To these former GIs he was Ike, who had led them to victory. This was the posture he planned to assume throughout his campaign. He was more than the

Republican nominee for President; he was running for the presidency to unite the American people. He was above the partisanship associated with political campaigns. He would leave whatever dirty work was necessary to his running mate, Nixon. Eisenhower's unique approach paid off. For the first time since Reconstruction, a Republican presidential candidate carried five Southern states. On the strength of his popular vote, the Republicans gained control of both Houses of Congress, albeit just barely.

Eisenhower's previous experience as an executive was limited to his years in the military, as Commander-in-Chief of the allied invasion forces and as head of NATO. In the case of the former, his role was to delegate authority and oversee that his instructions were carried out. In the case of the latter, while he exercised control over the military aspects of the alliance, he had less control over the individual politicians from the diverse 14 nations that were part of the alliance. Therefore, his approach to his new role as chief executive of the nation would be that which he had used as commander of the allied forces. Once having signed off on policy and strategy, he would delegate authority to the various members of his cabinet and expect his decisions to be carried out. As President, he had another role to play in which he had no previous experience to call upon. He was titular head of the Republican Party, and in that position, he was to coalesce the various divisions within the party and unify them behind his programs. Since the Republican members of Congress were sharply divided between its conservative isolationist wing and its liberal internationalist segment, he discovered the limitations of his power as head of the party. In addition, because of the small majority the Republicans held in both the House and Senate, he had to take into consideration the leadership of the minority party, the Democrats. Unused to politicians who were more concerned with serving the interests of their own constituents than with the overall good of the nation, he focused his attention on foreign affairs.

Eisenhower first offered the post of Secretary of State to Thomas Dewey, who had been instrumental in Ike's attaining the nomination. Dewey demurred and recommended his own foreign policy advisor, John Foster Dulles, who possessed the broad range of experience requisite for that position. The close relationship that developed between Dulles and Eisenhower enabled the president to direct his energies to the subject he considered to be most important for the future of the nation — namely preventing the spread of communism, while at the same time curbing the arms race with the Soviet Union, and if possible, arriving at some form of *modus vivendi* with that country.

Given the different backgrounds of the two men, it seemed an unlikely fit. Ike was convivial, with that famous smile that entranced people; Dulles was dour-faced, with his pronounced tight lips that never seemed to open. Eisenhower was a mediocre student at West Point; Dulles was first in his class at Princeton, and completed his studies in law school in two years instead of the usual three. Ike was a poor boy, who owed his success in life to his service in the military; Dulles was to the manor born. He was fluent in French and had a passable knowledge of Spanish and German. In 1950, President Truman had called upon him to negotiate the successful peace treaty with Japan. Like Eisenhower, Dulles was a dedicated internationalist but an even more dedicated opponent of the spread of communism any place in the world. As a result, he viewed every nation in the world in terms of black and white. He rejected out of hand those nations that contended they would remain neutral in the Cold War. To Dulles, either you were with us or against us in the struggle against the Soviet Union. However, he was unable to convince the President to commit military forces in pursuit of his objectives.

The first item on Eisenhower's agenda was to fulfill his election campaign promise to go to Korea. After conferring with the generals in the field, all of whom he knew personally, he was convinced that the major roadblock to negotiating a truce at the 38th parallel were the two heads of state of North and South Korea. Both of them were in favor of continuing the war until Korea was unified by one or the other. In March 1953, with the announcement of Stalin's sudden and unexpected death, the situation changed dramatically. The members of the Politburo were involved in a personal struggle to determine who would succeed him. The decision to attack South Korea had been made by Stalin. There was no reason to continue supporting the war. Kim Il-sung, the leader of North Korea, was notified by the Kremlin to enter into negotiations to end the hostilities and arrive at a truce. Mao Tse-tung, the leader of the Chinese Communists, received the same notification. Later that spring, it appeared that negotiations had been completed. The two Koreas would return to their pre-war status, divided at the 38uth parallel as called for in the original UN mandate. A demilitarized zone would be established between the two Koreas, and there would be the all-important exchange of prisoners of war. It was at that moment that Syngman Rhee, president of South Korea, still seeking to continue the war until the two Koreas were unified, made the arbitrary decision to release the 25,000 North Korean and Chinese prisoners in his custody, who evinced no desire to be repatriated. The American High Command was furious. The fighting was over, but there could be no return of prisoners held in North Korea until those held in the South were returned. It wasn't until July that the prisoner exchange was completed and the final papers signed.

With Eisenhower's attention focused almost exclusively on foreign affairs during the first two years of his administration, a sufficient number of opportunities would arise to create the need for action on his part. With the Korean conflict resolved, the only other subject to warrant Eisenhower's immediate attention was that of Iran. The failure of the famed MI-6, the secret intelligence arm of the British government, to overthrow the regime of Mohammed Mossadegh by an attempted assassination, had resulted in the closure of the British Embassy. This bungled attempt had been followed by another, organized this time by the Shah, with the same failed results. With the Conservative party back in power and with Churchill as Prime Minister, it was time to call on his wartime friend and ally to come to Britain's aid once again. Britain's Foreign Minister Anthony Eden was dispatched to Washington. Eden stressed, in his conversations with Dulles, the fact that Mossadegh's National Front Party was supported by the Tudeh, Iran's Communist Party. Dulles was well prepared to accept Eden's thesis that the Communists were behind Mossadegh's nationalism. The fact that Mossadegh had been instrumental in forcing the Soviet Union to vacate northern oil fields in Iran in 1946 counted for naught. The Secretary of State was convinced that Mossadegh was not to be trusted because of his insistence that Iran remain neutral in the Cold War. Dulles advised the President that the CIA be allowed to instigate a plot that would topple the Mossadegh regime. There was another factor that played a role as well. Ever since the Mossadegh government had nationalized the assets of the Anglo-Iranian Oil Company and had refused to agree to a decision by the World Court at The Hague to determine the amount of compensation due to the company, the Seven Sisters had joined Anglo-Iranian in imposing an embargo on oil shipments coming out of Iran. As a result the largest oil refinery in the world, located in Iran, and which had once supplied Western Europe with 43% of its oil needs, now lay idle. In 1951, the economies of Western Europe were still recovering from the after-effects of the war. But by 1953, their economies had recovered sufficiently to create a greater demand for refined oil than other facilities were able to provide. Dulles, in his previous role as senior partner at Sullivan and Cromwell, knew many of the top executives of these major US oil corporations. This certainly added to his rationale for removing Mossadegh from power. Although his brother, Allen W. Dulles, was head of the CIA, no action was possible unless Eisenhower signed off on it. Any attempt by the agency to overthrow a sovereign nation required the President's signature. When Congress established the agency in 1947, it was the only way of insuring that the executive branch had some control over its activities.

While the CIA was formulating its plans to remove Mossadegh, the economic situation in Iran continued to deteriorate. The two-year loss of revenue from its oil exports was placing a strain on government expenditures. The Iranian clerics, the mullahs, dependent upon state subsidies, were getting restless. Along with other factions within the National Front Party, they were in favor of settling the dispute with Anglo-Iranian on the last terms offered by the company — an equal split in the company's profits. They refused to understand that the terms were not quite that simple. Anglo-Iranian insisted on compensation for the two years when the embargo had been in place, and no was oil shipped, as well as the loss of revenue from the idled refinery. It was at this time, before the CIA's plans had been finalized and submitted for presidential approval, that General Fazlollah Zahedi presented himself at the American Embassy in Tehran and asked to see the Ambassador. Zahedi informed the Ambassador that the military, under his command, was prepared to stage a coup and remove Mossadegh from office, provided the general had the backing of the US government. When the Ambassador cabled this information to the State Department, Zahedi was seen as the missing link to a successful coup. The agency then selected Zahedi as Mossadegh's replacement. By July 1953, the final stages of the plan designed by the CIA had been put in place, and the logistics were approved by Churchill and Eisenhower.

The plan consisted of four stages. First, with one million dollars in cash from the CIA's slush fund, a propaganda campaign was to be launched with the dual purpose of undermining Mossadegh's popularity and raising the threat of a Communist takeover of the government. This was to be followed by the Shah's dismissal of Mossadegh as Prime Minister. Next would come the organized and funded street riots. Finally, the Shah would appoint Zahedi as Prime Minister. On paper, it appeared to be fool proof. Unfortunately, the agency underestimated Mossadegh. As Minister of Defense, he replaced those officers he believed to be loyal to the Shah with those who would be loyal to him. As a result, the bare outlines of the agency's plot emerged. Knowing that under the Constitution no Prime Minister could be appointed without the full approval of the Majlis, he organized a referendum in which the voters were to choose between the dissolution of the Majlis or the resignation of his Cabinet. The results of the referendum showed an overwhelming support for Mossadegh's cabinet. Once the results had been certified, he dissolved the Majlis.

Since the first three stages of the agency's fool proof plan had backfired, the only one left was the fourth — for the Shah to appoint Zahedi as Prime Minister, which the Shah did. But Mossadegh's ploy had worked. Without the approval of the now dissolved Majlis, the appointment of Zahedi couldn't be confirmed. Despite this further setback, following the original plan, a colonel from the Royal Guard attempted to serve Mossadegh with a royal decree from the Shah, ordering his dismissal. With the plot within the army now laid bare, the colonel was arrested and the majority of the military remained loyal to Mossadegh. The following day, a spontaneous massive turnout took place in the streets of Tehran. Fearing for his life and that of his family, the Shah and his entourage fled first to Baghdad and then on to Rome. Those officers known to be involved in the conspiracy were arrested, but not Zahedi, who had fled the capital. It was at this moment, when his rule over the country had never been so secure, that Mossadegh committed a massive blunder. Instead of having the troops loyal to him scour the countryside and arrest Zahedi, he sent them back to their barracks. Only Zahedi could salvage the amateur plan concocted by the CIA. He waited four days, until he was certain that the officers and troops loyal to Mossadegh were in their barracks and out of immediate reach of the capital. Then, accompanied by a few officers and troops still loyal to him, he surrounded the well fortified house of Mossadegh and attempted to arrest him. In the ensuing melee, Mossadegh managed to escape. When the people of Tehran learned that Mossadegh's house was being besieged, they poured into the streets to come to his rescue. Zahedi then gave the order for his troops to fire indiscriminately on the crowds. Within a short time, 300 civilians were murdered and hundreds of others were wounded. Realizing that without the presence of officers and troops loyal to him the slaughter of innocent civilians would continue unabated, Mossadegh agreed to surrender to Zahedi.

Zahedi, afraid that Mossadegh would go free in a civilian court, decided to use a military tribunal. Although the Prime Minister acted as his own defense attorney, the military court proceedings were predictable. Mossadegh was sentenced to three years in prison in solitary confinement. Following the completion of his term, he was under house arrest at his country estate.

With $5 million in loans from the US government, Zahedi was able to form a temporary government. Once the streets of Tehran had been secured, the Shah returned from his brief exile. Since the senators in the Mossadegh government had resigned rather than see their term in office reduced from six years to two, he saw no reason to revive that institution. The same applied to the Majlis, which Mossadegh had dissolved after the referendum. From here on the Shah would rule without the previous restraints that had been provided by the Constitution. In effect, he established a monarchical dictatorship, complete with a secret police force. He also realized his indebtedness to the United States, which had saved his throne. He would reciprocate by breaking the monopoly held by the Anglo-Iranian Oil Company and awarding half of Iran's oil production to United States oil corporations. Iran would be the only Muslim country in the Middle East to establish normal commercial relations with Israel. He would support US foreign policy throughout the turbulent 1970s and use the huge profits he amassed as a member of OPEC to acquire the latest in US military equipment. His secret police, SAVAK, would infiltrate Iran's Communist party, eliminate its leadership and drive its existing members underground. His efforts to further westernize Iran at the expense of the religious community served to alienate the mullahs. Efforts by students to restore the Constitution and the return of the Majlis were dismissed by the Shah. The collapse of his regime in 1979 is discussed in a later chapter.

In 1953, however, the age of colonialism of one sort or another was still flourishing; or so it seemed to Europe's colonial powers. To Britain, France, Holland and Belgium, their colonial possessions represented the last vestige of their one-time economic and political power. Should they be stripped of all their possessions, these European countries would have to depend upon their limited national resources to grow their economies. Until the advent of the Cold War, the policy of the United States was to oppose colonialism on the grounds that it closed markets to US business. However, with the advent of the Cold War and the threat of Communist infiltration and subjection of these newly born nations, the Eisenhower administration and Dulles revised US policies. Nations newly liberated from European colonialism might be swayed into the Communist camp. The lure of state socialism was strong. The success of the Soviet Union, once the most backward nation in Europe, was impressive to these nations. The Cominform had replaced the pre-war Comintern now that the wartime alliance had ended. The name may have changed, but its goals remained the same — the overthrow of existing governments and their replacement by regimes that would take their orders from Moscow. American intervention in Iran had been predicated on avoiding such a calamity.

At the beginning of 1954, the threat of a Communist takeover of governments had spread from Southeast Asia to Egypt and from there to Central America. In February of that year, the French government dispatched an urgent appeal to Eisenhower asking for American military intervention in Vietnam to prevent a Communist regime from taking over that country. It was not the first time that the French had called for military aid for its army engaged in a war against Communist insurgents. During the Korean War, when French troops had participated along with those from other nations as part of the UN force under US military command, US cargo planes had ferried supplies to the French forces in Vietnam. Now the French request involved direct US involvement with military personnel. The French army was trapped in a valley, Dien Bien Phu, and was faced with either annihilation or an abject surrender. Dulles believed it was in America's interest to prevent Vietnam from becoming a Communist nation.

This was the first time that the "domino theory" would surface. Dulles wanted a joint force of American and British troops to come to the relief of General Henri Navarre and his entrapped French army. The British wanted no part of it. The British military explained the difference between their successful campaign against the Communist insurgents in Malaya and the situation in Vietnam — the absence of a common border with China. Without access to new war materiel, the Communist insurgents in Malaya were eventually defeated in a war of attrition. That had been the case in Vietnam until the Chinese Communists drove the nationalists out of China.

The year before, Eisenhower had sent US military advisors to Vietnam to assess the ability of the French command in that country. Their reports had come back negative. As the Americans later on would learn to their dismay, the use of air power to destroy an enemy was useless in jungle warfare. That is how Navarre had managed to get the French army entrapped in the valley of Dien Bien Phu. Even though the French air force controlled the skies, the modern artillery pieces of General Vo Nguyen Giap, hidden in the jungle and continually moved from one spot to another, were able to rain down a continual barrage of devastating artillery shells. In May 1954, with no US relief in the offing, and with French casualties increasing every day, Navarre was forced to surrender unconditionally to Giap. The news of Navarre's surrender struck the French public like a tidal wave. It had been 14 years before, almost to the exact date, that a French army had unconditionally surrendered to the German army. In that instance, the French army had faced the most powerful army in the world. Now they had been defeated by a bunch of half clad, illiterate peasants.

Shortly after, a peace conference was held at Geneva. While the terms of the peace were resolved between the Vietminh, the Communist government of North Vietnam, and the Republic of France, also present were observers from the major interested parties, Great Britain, the United States, the Soviet Union and the Peoples Republic of China. Under the terms of the treaty, the French were to evacuate all their military and civilian personnel from Vietnam, Laos and Cambodia. Vietnam was to be divided in two, with the Vietminh recognized as the official government from the 17th parallel to its northern border with China. Temporarily, that area of the country below the 17th parallel would revert to its former emperor, Bao Dai. In two years, a referendum would take place below the 17th parallel, allowing that population the choice of joining the government of the Vietminh and unifying the country or remaining independent. Free movement of the Vietnamese population above and below the 17th parallel would be allowed over the next six months. Of the major powers present during the negotiations, only the United States refused to be a signatory to the peace treaty. Dulles, who was representing the United States, was so furious that when another delegate offered to introduce him to Chou En-lai, who represented the Chinese, he deliberately turned his back upon him. As for France, Vietnam was only the beginning of the end of its colonial empire. Dulles would have much better luck when it came to Guatemala.

The Monroe Doctrine, designed to prevent Britain and France from taking advantage of the weak governments and rapid turnover of ruling cliques in Central and South America, allowed the United States to have a free hand in this hemisphere. While America pictured itself as a kind of big brother to the smaller and less developed nations, they viewed the US as Yankee imperialists. This was particularly true in Central America, where the Boston-based United Fruit Company dominated the national economies by acquiring huge tracts of lands and becoming the largest employer in many of these countries, which earned them the name of Banana Republics. During the late nineteenth century and throughout the twentieth century, the influence of this company became more pronounced. Governments would rise and fall — some republics, others dictatorships — but as long as US business interests were unaffected by these changes, Washington showed little or no interest. In 1931, Jorge Ubico was elected president of Guatemala with the usual promise of reforming the government. At the outset of his administration, he kept his promises. He expanded the construction of roads and enforced fiscal discipline to the point where year after year there was a surplus in the federal budget. However, in the meantime no schools were constructed; secondary education was practically eliminated; and teachers' salaries were kept to a bare minimum. His attitude was that education could be used to foment rebellion and disturb the status quo. He also did nothing for the large native population. Although he believed that with his secret police he had control of the population, in 1944 the working class, upset with the rising inflation, called for a general strike. Everything came to a halt. Fearing for his life, he submitted his resignation and fled the country with all the wealth he had accumulated.

The vacuum was immediately filled by General Federico Ponce Vaides and his supporters in the military. His reign was brief. The growing inflation in the Guatemalan economy led to the organization of labor. A general strike orchestrated by labor now led to the formation of political parties, including the Communist, each with a different political message. As a result, on October 30, 1944, the interim government of Vaides was overthrown by a military junta of young officers. Working with the leadership of the recently formed political parties, a new Constitution was drafted that called for an elected body of representatives and the election of a president through a popular vote by the people. In the balloting that followed, Jose Juan Alevaro was elected on a platform to reform Guatemalan society. Education now became a priority. The Social Security system was reformed, and initial steps were taken for land reform. But the principal beneficiary of his administration was labor, which had been his major supporter during the election. A new labor code was enacted, and pressure was put on foreign corporations to raise salaries and benefits. Alevaro's determination to improve the lot of labor enabled the Guatemalan Communist party to emerge into the open. It was the leadership of this party that had been in the forefront of organizing the general strike that led to the overthrow of the Ubico dictatorship and the emergence of the reform parties. Highly disciplined, the party soon took control of the rank and file of the large working class. Alevaro, who was anti-Communist, refused them participation in his administration.

In 1951, at the conclusion of his single six-year term, Alevaro stepped down and new elections were held. The candidate for the popular, labor dominated party was Jacobo Arbenz Guzman, the son of a Swiss pharmacist, who had immigrated to Guatemala. Guzman had attended the National Military Academy and had been one of the Young Turk officers responsible for overthrowing the interim government of Vaides. He had been named Minister of War in the Alevaro government. His opponent, representing the more conservative elements in Guatemalan society, was General Miguel Fuentes. Backed by the Communist-dominated labor movement, Guzman was elected in a landslide. The focus of his administration would not be on labor or the educational system but on the plight of the landless, native Indian population, abused for centuries. As in the other republics in Central America, most of the land was owned by a small coterie of wealthy Guatemalans, foreign speculators or by the ubiquitous United Fruit Company. The bulk of the arable land owned by these three groups of investors remained unused. At the time the land was acquired, the cost to these buyers was next to nothing. Guzman believed he could solve the economic hardships of the Indians by expropriating some of these vacant lands for their personal use. For his government to undertake such a radical step would require the passage of legislation by the National Assembly. Guzman was steering his administration into dangerous waters. His land reform would be opposed not only by the Guatemalan establishment but by the all-powerful United Fruit Company.

In order for this legislation to be passed by the National Assembly, it would require the full support of the left wing representatives of labor. Since they had no interest at all in the plight of the Indians, a quid pro quo would be required to gain their support. Guzman acceded to their demands for positions in the various government ministries. From the outside, it appeared that he was in the process of establishing the first Communist government in Central America. Lobbyists for the United Fruit Company were quick to bring the expropriation of its lands to the attention of the State Department and the Secretary of State. The decision was made to use the CIA once again, this time to remove the Guzman regime. The old days of sending in the Marines and ignoring the other Latin American republics were over. Dulles would use the meeting of the Inter-American Conference, scheduled for March 1954 at Caracas, to put forward the US point of view. Given the need of many of the nations gathered there for US financial aid, it was not difficult to convince the overwhelming majority to pass a resolution condemning the Guatemalan government as a Communist regime. The two exceptions were Mexico and Argentina, both of which abstained from casting a ballot. With that document in his pocket, Eisenhower now would sign off on a CIA coup to topple the Guzman government.

Guzman was not ready to concede. He invoked the Charter of the United Nations, which called for non-interference in the affairs of a sovereign nation. When his petition was placed before the Security Council, Dulles was appalled to learn that America's two allies, Britain and France, supported Guzman's position. While the United States still intended to use the power of its veto, the very idea that France and Britain would take a position other than the one adopted by the United States was intolerable. Henry Cabot Lodge, US Ambassador to the UN, was instructed to have his French and British counterparts reverse their original vote. The implications were made clear. America's junior partners adhered to the line taken by the senior partner. Both delegates quickly reversed their vote.

Meanwhile the CIA's plans for removing the Guzman government were being finalized for Eisenhower's signature. As in Iran, the operation would begin with a propaganda campaign, followed by funded street riots against Guzman's Communist regime. To replace Guzman, the agency engaged the service of a colonel in the Guatemalan army, Carlos Castillo Armas. Funded by the CIA, Armas planned to launch an invasion of Guatemala from neighboring Honduras. At the same time, agents hired by the agency made generous donations to the officers in the Guatemalan army. Guzman was counting on these officers, who owed their ranks to him when he was Minister of War in Alevaro's government, to remain loyal to his government. Up until the end, he remained confident that the Guatemalan army easily could defeat Armas. But when Armas's mercenaries entered Guatemalan territory, the key officers Guzman had been depending upon informed him it was time to resign and flee the country. He finally understood the power of the Yankee behemoth in the North. Once again the CIA had pulled the coals out of the fire at a minimal cost while preserving America's stance of not visibly interfering with the sovereignty of another government. Eisenhower began to believe in the agency's infallibility.

The third effort by Dulles to stem the advance of communism in a Third World country, Egypt, had the opposite outcome. As a result of his actions, the Soviet Union was able to penetrate a Muslim state in the all-important Middle East. The modern history of Egypt begins with the rise to power of Colonel Gamal Abdel Nasser. Following the end of the Arab-Israeli wars of 1948-49 and the defeats suffered by the far larger Egyptian armies, a group of officers formed the Free Officers Association. Their original goal was to determine what had gone wrong on the battlefield. Most of them voiced complaints about the inferiority and malfunction of the war materials supplied by the Egyptian Ministry of Defense. Out of this initial discussion there emerged an overview of the Egyptian government and the corruption that pervaded every element of society, from its ruler, King Farouk and his entourage, to the Wafd, Egypt's national assembly. As is often the case with a conspiracy, one of the officers defected and informed King Farouk, without naming any names. Farouk reacted immediately. He removed the current Minister of Defense and replaced him with his brother-in-law. His instruction was to seek out those officers involved and crush the insurgency before it could spread. Nasser, correctly reading the significance of the appointment, convinced his fellow conspirators that the time was now or never. On July 23, 1952, the conspirators entered the private quarters of Farouk and announced his deposition and the appointment of his infant son to replace him under their regency. Farouk and his entourage were sent into exile.

Nasser was astute enough to recognize that the rank of colonel lacked the necessary prestige to head up a government. He enlisted the support of General Mohammed Naguib and elevated him to the role of leader of the Revolutionary Command Council. It didn't take long for the current Egyptian establishment to recognize that Nasser was intent on overturning the legitimate government of Egypt. His first step in dismantling the government was to appoint Naguib as Prime Minister. This was followed by his issuing a decree to reform the nation's agrarian laws. The large privately-owned landed estates were to be broken up and the owners compensated for the loss of their property. Estates of the royal family were confiscated and appropriated by the state. Confiscated lands were distributed to the landless rural population in parcel of 100 acres each. Three months later, the Constitution of 1922 was abolished. A month later, all political parties were dissolved and their treasuries confiscated for use by the new governing body. They were replaced by a single party, the Liberation Rally, with Nasser at its head.

It now became clear that Nasser and his fellow officers were determined to alter the very foundations of Egyptian society. But the revolution had more in mind then simply that goal. High on its agenda was to rid Egypt of the presence of the British and take control of the Suez Canal. As a corollary, it was determined that the Sudan should be returned to Egypt. By February 1953, Nasser had worked out an agreement with the British authorities in Egypt, and they had received the approval from London. Sudan would establish it own traditional government and after three years, it could opt for total independence or to become part of Egypt once again. Britain also agreed to withdraw its troops from the Suez Canal by 1955.

By June 1953, less than a year after King Farouk was deposed, the Revolutionary Command Council would announce the creation of a new republic. Naguib would assume the dual role of president and prime minister. Nasser would be named his deputy, as well as minister of interior. With the old political parties dissolved and some of their leaders facing trial for corruption, the only remaining organization with a large following was the Brotherhood of Muslims. The Brotherhood was founded in Egypt in 1923 by a primary school teacher who preached a return to the fundamental tenets of the Muslim faith. In its early stages of development, it had been apolitical, but when it expanded into Palestine, that changed. As a result of its strong opposition to the creation of a Zionist state, its membership increased not only in Palestine but in Egypt as well. Its basic theme now became that religion should be the dominant force in the nation.

With the other political parties completely discredited and their leaders in prison, the Brotherhood viewed this as an opportune moment to seize the government and impose a religious state on the population. Moreover, some of the leading members of the Revolutionary Command Council subscribed to their philosophy. Nasser viewed the organization as counter-revolutionary, and as Minister of the Interior he had the organization proscribed. Those members of the Council who supported the Brotherhood and who had allied themselves with Naguib saw in Nasser's challenge to the Brotherhood the first step towards a personal dictatorship. By April 1954, having consolidated his leadership among those officers on the Council who sought a secular society, Nasser was prepared to challenge those members who supported the Brotherhood. Seeking a counterweight to the growing power of Nasser, they rallied around Naguib. A temporary compromise was reached. Naguib would remain president, and Nasser would be elevated to the position of Prime Minister. In October, the truce was broken when a member of the Brotherhood made a failed attempt to assassinate Nasser. This incident provided Nasser and his loyalists with the opportunity they sought. In November, Naguib was placed under house arrest; the leadership of the Brotherhood assassinated; and 18,000 of its known members arrested and thrown into prison. Nasser now was in command of Egypt. In less than two years, this unknown colonel had become the leader of the largest Arab nation in the world. As in the case of Mossadegh in 1951, *Time* magazine would name Nasser Man of the Year. There were certainly good reasons for the editors' choice. In that brief period of time, he had expunged Egyptian society of the layers of corruption that had been built up ever since the Constitution was passed in 1922. He had eased the condition of the Fedayeen by turning over to them the vast landed estates of the wealthy and the royal family. He committed some errors as well. His anti-Zionist stance morphed into anti-Semitism as well. He forced the departure of an important segment of the Egyptian economy, its Jewish population, which had played a notable role in the development of Egyptian industry. Their worldwide contacts with other Jewish communities could not be replaced. But his major blunder was to take for granted United States support for his new regime. Nasser's first priority, once he had consolidated his power, was to acquire funds for the construction of the High Aswan dam. While a small dam had been constructed in 1902 under the then British Protectorate, it only controlled the tail end of the Nile River when the annual flooding took place. Of far greater importance to the Egyptian economy was to be able to control the headwaters of the Nile, where its annual floods devastated Egyptian agriculture. The plans for such a dam had been in place for years, but under Farouk and the Nationalist party nothing had been done to implement its actual construction.

Nasser turned to the United States for a loan to begin construction of the dam. As head of the State Department, Dulles personally approved the loan. He viewed the loan as the first step toward better relations with nations in the Arab world and as a counterweight to America's early recognition of the State of Israel. The $274 million for the first stage of construction was approved. When completed the High Aswan's reservoir would hold a capacity of 133 million cubic feet of water, compared to the four million of the lower dam. Not only would it generate an enormous amount of electrical power, but it would resolve the problem that had haunted the nation since time immemorial, the annual flooding of the Nile. When news of the loan was released, Nasser's popularity among the Egyptian populace was insured. During his brief period in office, he had addressed the needs of the people. It reinforced his reputation in the Arab world, already established by forcing Britain to remove its troops from the Suez Canal and to cede control of the Sudan. Nasser had become a major figure on the world's stage. He also had raised his stature among those nations that had recently gained their independence from Britain and the Netherlands in Southeast Asia. In 1955, a conference was scheduled at Bandung, Indonesia, to take up the subject of anti-colonialism, specifically aimed at the French in North Africa. Its sponsors were the five nations that had recently gained their independence from Britain and the Netherlands — India, Pakistan, Burma, Ceylon and Indonesia. Invitations were extended to 24 other nations, including Nasser in Egypt and Tito in Yugoslavia, which no longer followed in lockstep with Moscow's foreign policy. Also high on the agenda was the growing friction between the United States and the Peoples Republic of China, over the disposition of the small islands of Quemoy and Matsu; there was also a great deal of concern over what role the new leadership of China expected to play in that region of the world. The featured speaker at the conference was Chou En-lai, second to Mao Tse-tung in the leadership of China. At the conclusion of the conference, a document was issued condemning colonialism anywhere in the world, but it failed to include the Soviet Union in Eastern Europe. Nasser was one of the signatories. In addition, the document included a statement that socialism was the only viable economic system, and that most of those nations present had adopted it for their economies

When Dulles was made aware of the agenda and outcome of the Bandung conference, it appeared to him that the United States was subsidizing a regime hostile to the interests of the United States. The State Department informed Nasser that the United States was canceling the loan. Nasser had failed to recognize that every nation, whether they liked it or not, was a participant in the Cold War. He would take out his anger by canceling whatever time remained on Britain's 99-year lease on the Suez Canal. He defended this action on the grounds that those funds had become necessary now in order to finance the construction of the High Aswan dam. Feeling that Egypt now was cut off from the West, Nasser would orient the nation's future towards the Soviet Union. The rural law was revised again, reducing the size of a plot any individual could own. He promised the Fedayeen that their income would double over the next five years. Following the example set by the Soviet Union, he would institute Egypt's first Five Year Plan, designed to further industrialize the nation. In order to cement his control over the nation, the press now would come under government control. A secret police would be established to eliminate the possibility of any opposition to the regime being formed. Having now aligned his foreign policy to conform to that of the Soviet Union, a steady stream of armaments and subsidies would follow. The Soviet Union later on would provide the loans for the completion of the Aswan dam. Dulles's decision had backfired. By his un-nuanced and inflexible attitude he had opened the door for the Soviet Union to enter the Middle East. Unwittingly, he had changed the balance of power in that region of the world. Russian influence soon would extend from Egypt to include Syria and Iraq as well. Dulles failed to comprehend that in this post-colonial era, when the former possessions of Western Europe were determined to be masters of their own destinies, the US was not the only arbiter. The Cold War might be in neutral but the Soviet Union represented an alternative to US dictates. Moreover, for the majority of the world's population, the leadership of the Third World nations, socialism appeared to be the best road to economic independence.

The eight-year presidency of Eisenhower has been treated rather cavalierly by historians. They point to his indifference to civil rights legislation as a black mark against his administration. Yet they fail to take into account what he was able to accomplish or sought to accomplish. A president is judged by his deeds and actions while in office; thus emanated the severe judgment laid upon him by liberals, because of his seeming indifference to civil rights for the Negro. He understood that it would take time for the South to adjust to the Supreme Court's decision banning separate but equal facilities. Yet he could not be painted as a racist. To understand his attitude toward the plight of the Negro, a different factor has to be taken into account. Eisenhower viewed his role as President differently than any of his predecessors or successors. He was courted by both parties and could have attained the Democratic nomination far easier than he did the Republican. With the exception of George Washington, there is no previous example in American history. The Korean War, coming just five years after the greatest armed struggle in our history, was difficult for the public to digest, not only because of the brief time span between the two wars but because it was the first war in which we obviously did not emerge victorious. With his large majority in the Electoral College, Eisenhower assumed that he had been given a mandate by the entire country to govern as he saw fit. FDR had made the same assumption following his landslide victory in his second term. The major difference, however, was that Roosevelt had been active in Democratic politics all of his life, while Eisenhower had spent his life in the apolitical military.

Eisenhower's basic agenda when he entered the White House focused on four major subjects — to maintain America's military superiority over the Soviet Union, which would act as a deterrent to any possible Soviet aggression; to contain the spread of communism in any part of the world; to arrive at some kind of *modus vivendi* with the new Soviet leadership; and as a corollary, to bring a halt to the arms race, thereby reducing military expenditures and balancing the budget. If he could achieve these four objectives, then he believed he had fulfilled his role as President. Any other subjects, such as race relations or the antics of Senator Joseph McCarthy, only would distract him from attaining his sought-after goals. Judging him from this point of view, he came close to attaining his goals. However, he was unable to achieve a comprehensive test ban treaty on atomic weapons with the Soviet Union, a result of the U-2 over flight, and he failed to control government spending on defense. Throughout his tenure in office and in his parting speech to the American public, he continually warned against the growing power of the "military-industrial complex," which he viewed as the major culprit in increasing government expenditures.

On that subject, his views were no different than those of the late Senator Robert Taft. Neither one understood that the federal budget deficits had been subsidizing the US economy since 1931, two years before Roosevelt took office and three years before he could introduce his own budget. Despite the views of many Republicans and most of the Democrats, who believed that the good old days of the 1920s would return once the war was over, the reality was that capitalism had entered a new stage of development that required federal deficits. Members of Congress, whose districts and states had profited from these subsidies, might give lip service to balancing the federal budget but at the same time, they wanted and expected support from federally funded projects.

The rapid growth in defense expenditures, from $13.7 billion in 1950 to $49.2 billion in 1954, a direct result of the Korean War, had opened up a new avenue for government expenditures on products related to the military. Even more important to the growth of the US economy was Truman's decision to use the United Nations as the vehicle for conducting the war. By using the UN, not only was he able to avoid going to Congress for a declaration of war but this conflict was fought without the imposition of rationing or wage and price controls. As a result, the gross domestic product of the country expanded by almost $100 billion, a figure until then unmatched in the history of this country. Almost all of this increase in the GDP took place while the war was still being waged. From 1953 to 1954, the GDP increased by only $5 billion. Although defense expenditures showed a sharp decline in 1955, from $49 billion to $42 billion, income from tax receipts fell as well, and the government showed a larger deficit than it had the previous year. There was a direct correlation between government spending and economic prosperity at that time. In 1956 and 1957, the federal budget showed a healthy surplus, a result of an increase in tax receipts despite an increase in government expenditures. In the previous year, 1955, both receipts and expenditures had declined, the latter caused by a decrease in defense expenditures. But by 1958, government revenue failed to show an increase while expenditures continued grow.

As a result of the Eisenhower programs of fiscal austerity, in 1958 the economy would experience its first recession since the end of the Second World War. Once again, inadvertently, the Soviet Union would come to the rescue. The first time, it had been the Korean War manufactured by Stalin. This time it would be the launching of Sputnik into space, indicating that Russia was far in advance of the United States in rocket technology. On October 4, 1957, Americans learned that Sputnik, the first of a series of satellites, was orbiting the earth. The other launches would carry animals and check temperatures and radiation in outer space. For years, the President whom they trusted implicitly had informed the American people that the United States defenses were far superior to those of the Soviet Union. If they couldn't believe Eisenhower, whom could they believe? For the Democrats, it was the political opening they had been seeking. Still defending themselves from McCarthy's charges that the party had lost China to the Communists and from the error the party's leading officials made in defending Alger Hiss, they were quick to go on the attack. The President's response — that the country's defenses were more than well secured by our advanced technology in intercontinental ballistic missiles — satisfied no one, not the press, not the public, and for certain not the Democrats.

For the Joint Chiefs of Staff and Eisenhower, the Sputnik launch was a black eye. It was not that the United States lacked the technology or the scientific know-how to launch a rocket into space. Rather the US found itself behind the eight ball because of internal wrangling among the Joint Chiefs of Staff over the allocation of defense funds between the Army and Navy. With the Army allocated the funds for the development of the Redstone intercontinental ballistic missile, the Navy was selected to develop the space program — despite the fact that the Navy had no previous experience in the development of rocketry and would be starting from square one. The space project should have gone to the Army, which had in its employ Werner von Braun, the German scientist who had created and developed the V-I and V-II rockets that had terrorized Great Britain in the closing days of the war. The rationale used by the Secretary of Defense for his decision was that von Braun was currently helping the Army in its perfection of the Redstone. Now it was time to play catch-up with the Russians, and the job was turned over to von Braun. By early 1958, when work commenced on America's space program, the United States was three years behind the Russians. By the time that von Braun and his scientists and engineers were capable of launching a 3-pound object into space, the Russians had advanced their technology to the point they were able to launch a 3,000-pound object into space.

The competition between the services had created a serious gap in America's ability to collect intelligence. The advantages inherent in space technology suddenly became clear to the military. In place of Lockheed's U-2 spy plane, which could reach an altitude of 70,000 feet above the earth and photograph Soviet military installations, satellites circling the earth every 96 minutes and equipped with sensitive photographic equipment would enhance one-hundred fold the ability of United States intelligence to maintain surveillance over Soviet military operations. It became obvious that the Sputnik program was fulfilling that role for the Soviet Union. It was time for Congress to allocate the funds to develop a crash program in order to gain superiority over the Russians in space technology. Eisenhower, fixated as he was on maintaining a balanced budget, viewed the creation of a separate agency devoted to space exploration as another example of the self-interested power and influence of the military-industrial complex. He favored the use of satellites for military intelligence but, beyond that, he considered space exploration to be a waste of the taxpayer's money. With the Democrats now in control of both Houses of Congress with huge majorities, and the public calling for action, there was nothing he could do to prevent the creation and funding of the National Aeronautics and Space Administration, NASA. Since Speaker of the House Sam Rayburn and Majority Leader of the Senate Lyndon Johnson both represented Texas, the facility to house NASA would be located in their state. As a result of the recession of 1958, the federal budget was once again showing a deficit as revenues from taxes were less than outlays. By 1959, thanks to the financing of NASA, the previous year's deficit of $2.7 billion had increased to $12 billion. But the additional federal monies being poured into the economy were taking effect. By 1960, government income from tax receipts, which had remained relatively constant at $79 billion from 1957 through 1959, now advanced to $92 billion, reflecting the increase in the budget deficit of 1959.

Eisenhower was not alone in calling for fiscal austerity on the part of Congress. Both of his Secretaries of the Treasury, first George Humphrey, who served during the first term, and then Robert B. Anderson, during the second, pushed for fiscal responsibility on the part of the legislative branch of government. Both men, devout believers in private enterprise, were either unwilling or unable to recognize the financial support that government spending was contributing to America's basic industries. Military contracts extended to the airline industry enabled it to develop aircraft for commercial usage. The Big Three automakers in Detroit also profited from defense department contracts, as did the steel and aluminum industries. The agricultural sector was dependent upon government hand outs. All of these government programs, some a continuation of policies inaugurated during the New Deal, others now a part of the Cold War, provided the additional growth to the economy that the private sector was unable to achieve. But Eisenhower and both of his treasury secretaries sought a return to pre-Depression capitalism, which had resulted in the Great Depression. Because the US dollar was redeemable for gold, they concluded that the pre-World War I gold standard had been restored. All three men were living in a time capsule that the Cold War had made irrelevant. Nor could they foresee the applications to the civilian sector that research and development in defense would bring. The Cold War was still in its infancy. Over the next two decades, major breakthroughs would take place in military technology that would revolutionize the civilian sector as well.

From the very outset of his administration, Eisenhower believed that the best way to reduce government expenditures on defense and bring the budget into balance was to put a cap on the arms race with the Soviet Union. Now that Stalin was dead and a new leadership had emerged, the President decided to take a first step in that direction. Using a meeting of the General Assembly of the United Nations as a backdrop for his address, Eisenhower made his first appeal to the Soviet Union to enter into some kind of agreement with the United States. He realized that with the new Soviet leadership only in power for a little more than a year, to call for a dramatic change in relations between the two countries was out of the question. His proposed Atoms for Peace program was so innocuous and non-threatening that he believed it would be adopted. He proposed that each of the three nations possessing atomic weaponry — Great Britain having joined that exclusive club — contribute from their stockpile of isotopes to a new organization developed by the United Nations, to be used solely for peaceful purposes. This organization, composed of scientists and engineers from every country in the world, would act independently of any of the three atomic powers. To prove its good intentions and since the United States had been the first nation to develop the bomb, it would contribute its isotopes at a ratio of 5-to-1. When he had finished his speech, all members of the General Assembly, including the delegate from the Soviet Union, rose to their feet and greeted his proposal with a deafening applause. Had he confined his speech solely to Atoms for Peace and left it there, the Kremlin might have taken up his proposal. But the President insisted on adding the potential threat that an atomic war posed by emphasizing the destructive power currently in America's arsenal of atomic weapons. By comparing America's greatly enhanced destructive power with the two novice bombs it had dropped on Hiroshima and Nagasaki, he terrified the Soviet leaders. Axiomatically, they assumed that Atoms for Peace was some kind of a trap to ensnare the Russians. Not only was the proposal rejected, but the Soviet Union now accelerated its efforts to catch up with the United States. In his effort to slow down the arms race, Eisenhower pressed the accelerator.

Early in 1955, the ongoing negotiations between the United States and the Soviet Union finally resulted in a peace treaty with Austria. The motivating force that convinced the Russians to withdraw their troops and end the four-power occupation of that country was the realization that Austria lacked the major industries to develop war material that might threaten the Soviet satellite countries in Eastern Europe. Convinced that this was the first real break in the Cold War, Eisenhower scheduled a summit meeting with the Russians. Ever the optimist, Eisenhower believed that the Soviet leadership now was prepared to enter into serious negotiations with the United States on a host of topics. The first thing on Eisenhower's agenda was the reunification of the two Germanys. Once that had been resolved, the next subject would be a mutual reduction in the arms race, followed by the liberation of all the nations of Eastern Europe.

Dulles had more realistic goals. Prior to their departure for Geneva, he informed the President that nothing would come from the negotiations. Dulles was firmly convinced that although Stalin was gone, the attitude of the new leadership would be no different. Instead of addressing the far more controversial subject of the two Germanys, the President decided that the first item on the agenda was to allay whatever mistrust existed between the two countries. To prove that the United States harbored no hostile intentions to its former ally, he proposed a joint program of open air inspections. Nikita Khrushchev, who by now had consolidated his power in the Politburo, was stunned at the audacity of the President's proposal. The Soviet Union, which since Stalin's time in office had closed its borders to any unauthorized foreign inspection, under Eisenhower's proposal would allow the stationing of US aircraft on its territory, with permission to observe every part of the Soviet Union. In exchange, the Soviet Union would enjoy the same privileges in the United States. As Dulles had predicted, Khrushchev rejected the proposal immediately. Eisenhower, determined to reach some kind of agreement with the Soviet leadership that would put a brake on the arms race, would have to bide his time. Over the next two years, Khrushchev's attention would be occupied by events taking place in Moscow and then among the Soviet satellite nations of Eastern Europe. Eventually, these events would lead to a second Berlin crisis and the potential threat of a major confrontation between the two nations.

Ever since the sudden and unexpected death of Stalin, a struggle had taken place within the confines of the Politburo for his successor. The only major opponent Khrushchev faced, early on, was Lavrenty Beria, former head of the NKVD, the old secret police, and the man who had been responsible for overseeing the development of the Russian atom bomb. The Khrushchev faction disposed of Beria — by having him shot. While his death eliminated Khrushchev's most dangerous rival, there remained other members of the Politburo who were not prepared to accept him as First Secretary of the Soviet Communist party. Over the next two years, he would weed them out gradually and replace them with people loyal to him. By February 1956, at the Twentieth Congress of the world's Communist parties, held in Moscow, Khrushchev felt secure enough to assume his new role as leader of the world's Communist movement. In an address to the delegates, he would denounce the excesses of Stalin's purges and invoke a new era of tolerance. The political prisoners that Stalin had sent to gulags in Siberia would be released and returned to Soviet society. Khrushchev believed that by softening the tone set by his predecessor, he would usher in a new age of cooperation between Russia and its satellite Eastern European nations.

There is a law in physics that states: for every action, there is an equal and opposite reaction. Following the refusal of Stalin to hold free elections in Poland in 1945, a hard-line Communist regime had been established in that country. Wladyslaw Gomulka, an old-time Communist trade union leader, was named vice president of the new government. As a trade unionist, Gomulka resisted the head of the government's efforts to impose Soviet style communism on Poland, which would eliminate the bargaining power of trade unions. In 1948, he supported Marshall Josip Tito's efforts to work independently of the Soviet's foreign policy, and was dismissed from office. Three years later he was arrested, and but for Stalin's death, would have been executed.

As a result of Khrushchev's speech announcing a relaxation from Stalin's previous policies, a surge of nationalism was seen in all the Eastern European nations under Soviet domination. In June 1956, there was a spontaneous anti-government and anti-Soviet demonstration in the Polish city of Poznan. The issues that provoked the outburst were universal throughout Poland. The standard of living in Poland continued to regress, a direct result of low wages and high taxes. The Russian army, still stationed in Poland, reacted immediately. Russian tanks rolled into Poznan; the protestors were dispersed, and order was restored. The use of military force was not a solution to an underlying problem. Khrushchev realized this, and in October of the same year, on a personal visit to Poland, he offered the post of First Secretary of the Polish Communist party to Gomulka, provided the Polish government continued to support Soviet foreign policy. In domestic affairs, Khrushchev gave Gomulka a free hand to develop Poland's economic policies. The result was a dramatic change in Poland's economy. Only 10% of Poland's farmland remained collectivized, and Poland now geared its trade to nations in Western Europe seeking low-cost labor for labor-intensive industries, such as apparel and agricultural products. As a result, Poland now would have access to dollar-backed currencies.

It was this decision to relax the controls on the Polish economy that would set in motion the Hungarian revolution which occurred a few weeks after Khrushchev's return from Poland. News of Khrushchev's decision to allow Gomulka greater freedom to manage Poland's economy, soon reached Budapest, the capital of Hungary. Feeling that this was the initial stage in the liberation of Eastern European nations, on October 23, 1956, students and workers in Budapest took to the streets demanding the removal of Soviet troops from the country and calling for the independence of Hungary. That night, Imre Nagy, a Hungarian trained in Moscow, was appointed Prime Minister. What first appeared to be a minor uprising continued to grow with each passing day. Officers and troops from the Hungarian army joined the students and workers. For the first few days of the rebellion, Nagy appeared to be immobilized, not knowing which side to take. As the rebellion continued to expand, Nagy made the decision to join the majority of the nation. He called for social and political reform, the establishment of alternative political parties within Hungary, and the withdrawal of all Soviet troops. As head of state, he announced Hungary's withdrawal from the Warsaw pact and appealed to the United Nations to support Hungary's independence and neutrality. On October 31, the rebellion seemed to be succeeding following a statement in *Pravda*, the Soviet government's official newspaper, promising greater equality between the Soviet Union and its Eastern European satellite nations. The most telling statement in the article was the sentence that read: "The Soviet government is prepared to enter into the appropriate negotiations with the government of the People's Republic of Hungary."

That same day, Khrushchev would dispatch Aleksey Kosygin, a member of the Politburo, to assess the situation. Meanwhile, on October 29, Khrushchev had received an urgent call from Nasser of Egypt, now a client state of the Soviet Union, calling for immediate aid. A combined force of Israeli troops and British and French warships were moving in on the Suez Canal, with the intention of overthrowing his regime. At the same time, Eisenhower was made aware of the same facts. Eisenhower was furious on two counts. First, that America's closest allies would act independently of Washington; second, when the eyes of the world were focused on the Hungarian people fighting for their independence, now the attention of the unaligned countries was shifted to the sight of British and French naked imperialism. The Soviet delegate to the United Nations called for an emergency session of the Security Council, and Moscow informed the British and French ambassadors that it would not sit by and watch an innocent nation invaded by outside forces. It called on Israel to withdraw its armed forces from Egyptian territory and return to its natural borders. Eisenhower's action was similar. He called the British and Israeli prime ministers, ordering them to withdraw their forces. None of the three conspirators seemed to recognize the gravity of the situation. Although the United States had voted with the Soviet Union in the UN, condemning the three nations and calling for their immediate withdrawal, the plan conceived by the three partners followed its natural progression. The now motorized Israeli army, backed by recently acquired French fighters, bombers and tanks, easily overran the Egyptian armed forces and were soon sitting on the opposite bank facing the Suez Canal. At the same time, British and French paratroopers landed on the Suez Canal and seized it. Nasser ordered a cement-loaded ship to be sunk into the Canal, blocking it.

Meanwhile, back in Budapest and in the Hungarian countryside, the rebellion appeared to be succeeding as more and more of the population adopted the cause. Buoyed by the information emanating from Radio Free Europe, the propaganda arm of the CIA, listeners were given the impression that the United States and its allies were going to intercede on their part. Instructions came over the air waves on how to booby trap tanks and harass Soviet soldiers. Back in the Kremlin, Khrushchev was waiting for Kosygin's assessment of the situation on the ground. Kosygin reported that if action was not taken at once in the capital, the countryside would be difficult to handle. Furthermore, if the rebellion was allowed to continue, it could spread to the other Eastern European satellite nations. In addition, the Soviet Union needed a free hand to deal with the Egyptian problem. Two days later, Nagy's replacement, Janos Kadar, was sent to a small town 60 miles from Budapest. On November 4, Russian tanks backed by motorized infantry and artillery invaded Budapest. Nagy made a brief radio address to the Hungarian people, calling on them to resist the invaders. He then fled to the safety of the Yugoslav Embassy. Three days later, on November 7, the anniversary of the Russian Revolution, order was restored in the capital and in the countryside. In the process, thousands of Hungarian freedom fighters were killed or wounded. More than 125,000 fled the country into neighboring Austria. Western intellectuals who had previously supported the Soviet Union now witnessed the brutality of the regime and became disillusioned. The Iron Curtain had been replaced by one of steel. The French and British paratroops were forced to withdraw from the Suez Canal; Israeli troops returned to their natural borders. And in March 1957, British Prime Minister Anthony Eden, thoroughly disgraced, retired from politics and was replaced by Harold Macmillan. Nagy, promised safe passage to Yugoslavia, was taken away by Soviet agents and ultimately executed; Janos Kadar replaced Nagy as head of state. Nasser was even more indebted to the Soviet Union than he had been before the Suez incident.

The greatest fear of the Eisenhower administration had come to fruition. The Soviet Union had planted itself firmly in the Arab world. With the announcement that the governments of Egypt and Syria had merged to form the United Arab Republic, Soviet influence in the region now included Syria as well. Nasser soon called on the other Arab nations in the region to join the new government in expelling Western influence in the Middle East. Terrified of the growing power and influence of Nasser in the region, Britain put together an alliance of Jordan and Iraq as a counterweight. A few days later, a coup organized by the Iraqi military overthrew the King and slaughtered all the members of his family. On the surface, it appeared that Nasser soon would unite all the nations in the Middle East under his control. The rulers of Saudi Arabia, the largest oil producing nation in the world, through its US partner, Aramco, placed pressure on the State Department to intervene. Eisenhower was reluctant to move, until he received a call from the President Camille Chamoun of Lebanon, the smallest country in the region. Fearful of Syrian aggression, he asked for the presence of US troops. Eisenhower reacted quickly. A large contingent of Marines were landed in Lebanon, ready to be backed up by more Marines if necessary, and he instructed British Prime Minister Macmillan to land paratroopers in its former mandate, Jordan. Nasser received the message, and his rhetoric cooled down. Nor did the Soviet Union react to the presence of US troops in the region. A far more serious problem was that of Berlin. As the economy of the Federal Republic of Germany continued to grow and flourish, so too did that of the allied sector in Berlin. The result was a stark difference in the living standards between those Germans living in East Berlin and those in the western sections of the city. In the allied sector, stores had modern fronts and featured merchandise from all over the world. There were plentiful supplies and varieties of foods. Modern high-rise buildings either were under construction or had been completed. The invidious comparison between the western and eastern sections of the same city was dramatic and devastating. Little wonder why there was a continuous flow of emigrants from the eastern city and from East Germany to the western sector and to West Germany. Moreover, those leaving the East for the West often were the best and brightest of that sector's citizens — i.e., scientists, engineers, professionals and artists, not only seeking freedom but in search of a better and more prosperous life. Unable to stem the flow of emigrants, the Communist leaders of East Germany called on Khrushchev for relief.

On November 18, 1958, in an address to allied powers occupying West Berlin and in a formal document delivered to them on November 27, Moscow notified the three allied powers that since they had violated the original agreement made at Potsdam in August 1945, of not rearming the Germans, the former Soviet authority over the city would be turned over to the Democratic Republic of Germany. Berlin would become a demilitarized city under the rule of the East German government. Unlike Stalin, who always used surrogates to confront the United States, Khrushchev employed a style of direct confrontation between the Soviet Union and the United States. In essence, Khrushchev's actions were those of a cunning peasant. He was not prepared to engage the Soviet Union in an all-out war with the United States, but if he could buy something on the cheap, he would try. Following the release of the official document, a meeting of the four foreign ministers was scheduled for May in Geneva. The conference ended without any agreement, but the six-month deadline passed without any action being taken either by the Soviet Union or the East German government.

Once the Berlin question had been set aside for the moment, Eisenhower, the inveterate bridge player, arrived at the conclusion that Khrushchev was playing his cards from a suit of weakness rather than from one of strength. When Khrushchev announced that he would appear at the opening session of the United Nations in September 1959, the President extended him a personal invitation for a 10-day visit of the United States. Anxious to demonstrate the hospitality of the Soviet Union, Khrushchev in turn invited the President and his family to visit Moscow the following year. Eisenhower thought that by showing Khrushchev the lifestyle of the average American working man, he could be convinced of the opportunities that capitalism offered to its citizens. It was an exercise in futility. When Eisenhower took Khrushchev for a helicopter tour and pointed out the thousands of homes occupied by working people, along with their cars, the response of the First Secretary was that cars were a waste of precious energy and that Soviet citizens preferred to live side by side with their fellow citizens in huge apartment houses. He viewed this ostentatious display of material wealth as the last gasp of a failing capitalist system. When he informed the President that his grandchildren would live under a Socialist economic system, not only did Khrushchev believe the statement, but he cited statistics to back up his contention. He could point out that over the past two years the Soviet economy had been growing at an annual rate of 6% while that of America was sputtering between 1.5 and 2%. In fact, this extraordinary growth rate was a direct result of reconstructing the country's infrastructure to its pre-war status. Once Russia had attained that goal, the growth would come to an end.

The President's effort to extract a non-proliferation treaty that would ban all future tests of atomic weapons in the atmosphere came to naught, but on the positive side of the visit, no reference was made to Berlin. Despite his dismissal of the higher living standards enjoyed by the average US worker, Khrushchev came away from his visit deeply impressed by the wealth and dynamism of American society. The highlight of his trip was a visit paid to a farmer in Iowa. Viewing with his own eyes the huge combines that the independent farmer used to harvest his crop of corn, the former Minister of Agriculture was overwhelmed by the degree of productivity these combines could obtain. Their purpose was to reduce the cost of labor and increase the profitability of the farm. A bank would lend the farmer the capital with which to acquire the combine, and he in turn would repay the principal on the loan, along with interest. None of these basic facts of US capitalism were possible under the constitution of the Soviet Union. Since the state owned and controlled the means of production, there were no profits for individuals; no individuals were engaged in their own enterprise; therefore there was no necessity for loans or for interest on them. And there was no possibility of cutting jobs. The fundamental concepts that underlay the two economic systems were at odds. . During his 10-day sojourn in the United States, once Khrushchev left Washington, his host was Henry Cabot Lodge, US Ambassador to the UN. He suggested that before departing, the Russian leader visit Disneyland in southern California. For the leader of the second most powerful nation in the world, this diversion was the highlight of his trip. As was the case with the Soviet soldiers and officers in Berlin, who were exploited by their US counterparts through the sale of Mickey Mouse watches, the cartoon characters developed by Walt Disney transcended all ideologies.

In spite of his inability to reach any kind of accord with the new leader of the Soviet Union, Eisenhower refused to give up his effort to reach some kind of agreement before he left office. Early in 1960, his last year in office, he sent a proposal to Khrushchev calling for a moratorium on all atomic testing in the atmosphere and in the oceans, and high-kiloton testing underground. To Eisenhower's pleasant surprise, a month later he received a communication from the Russian leader accepting the proposal, provided there was a moratorium on low-kiloton underground tests as well. Once again the President was hopeful enough to believe that such an agreement would lead the Soviet Union to open its borders to US inspection teams. He didn't expect the opposition of the Joint Chiefs of Staff, the scientific community, the military-industrial complex and above all the Democratic majority in both houses of Congress. In addition to any other qualms they might have had, in their political minds, should a major breakthrough be made with the Soviet leadership and the potential for bringing to an end the Cold War, it would be attributed to the Republican party. In all likelihood, that would ensure the election of Richard Nixon, their number one nemesis now that Senator McCarthy was dead.

With Dulles dead, Eisenhower planned the agenda for the forthcoming summit meeting by himself. He notified America's allies that since this was the first step towards bringing the Cold War to closure, neither the issue of a final peace treaty with Germany nor the future status of Berlin would be brought up for discussion. Following a successful conclusion to the summit, he would take up Khrushchev's invitation to visit Russia with his family. In order to avoid any unpleasantness with the Soviet leadership prior to the summit, he put a hold on all U-2 flights over Russia. For years, the U-2 spy aircraft had penetrated Soviet air space, photographing Russian military installations. The Soviet Union had lodged vigorous protests with the US government over this violation of its air space but to no avail. Since Russian anti-aircraft guns were incapable of reaching the plane's altitude, the United States denied the plane's existence, and the Soviet Union was loath to admit that it was possible to violate its air space with impunity. Such was the situation when the head of the CIA, who had control over the U-2 flights, asked the President for permission to make one more flight over the Soviet Union prior to the summit. His rationale made perfect sense. One of the conditions Khrushchev would demand for the moratorium on testing would be the cessation of all over flights over the Soviet Union. Eisenhower reluctantly agreed. But for the following two weeks, the clouds over Russia were too thick for a camera to penetrate.

There was a touch of irony in the scenario that followed. The first day possible for the last successful over flight was the first day of May, a day celebrated in Europe by Communist and Socialist parties alike. In Russia, it was a national holiday, and members of the Politburo and other dignitaries would review a parade of the Soviet's military forces. On that day in 1960, a U-2 spy plane was shot down 1,300 miles within the borders of the Soviet Union. The only information that the CIA possessed about the condition of the plane was a last-minute message from its pilot, Gary Powers, who had reported that the engine of the aircraft had been hit and was on fire. Following that message, there was no further communication. The assumption at CIA headquarters was that the pilot and the plane had been blown up. On May 5, that assumption was found to be short of accurate. In an address to the Russian people, and disseminated over the air waves to people throughout the world in their native tongues, Khrushchev announced that a US spy plane had been shot down, violating Soviet air space, and that the pilot and the remains of the aircraft now were in Russian custody. He also made it clear that it was not Eisenhower who had authorized the flight, but men within the administration determined to break up the peaceful relationship between the United States and the Soviet Union. The Soviet leader had provided the President with a graceful way to continue their relationship and allow the summit and the disarmament proceedings to continue.

There was no way that the US government could deny that the U-2 over flights had been taking place since 1956. Not only were the Russians privy to this fact and had protested, but America's allies along with the Turkish and Norwegian governments were aware of these flights since the spy aircraft took off from the territory of the former and landed on the territory of the latter. Khrushchev had provided Eisenhower with a perfect way out of this terrible embarrassment: find a logical fall guy and throw him to the wolves. The only possible choice was the head of the CIA, who could be replaced easily and would understand it was in the national interest that he resign. Instead Eisenhower, who prided himself on his honesty, would resort to a number of fairy tales that assured Khrushchev of his complicity in the over flights. The first was the biggest whopper of them all. He had NASA issue a report that a weather plane flying over Turkey may have accidentally strayed into Soviet territory and disappeared. Khrushchev now knew that the flight had been authorized by the President. The trust Eisenhower had built up with the leader of the Soviet Union was shattered. Moreover, Khrushchev had sold a bill of goods to the other members of the Politburo. Now, his own credibility as First Secretary was at stake. Had Khrushchev entered into negotiations now that the Powers incident had been revealed, he would have been deposed. But the President was so determined to achieve his legacy of a non-proliferation treaty that he blinded himself to reality. The cunning peasant was determined to make a fool out of Eisenhower. First he released a photo of a damaged aircraft that bore no resemblance to the U-2. The President fell for the bait, publicly declaring America's innocence. The following day he released the actual photo of the U-2 aircraft along with its pilot, Gary Powers. The wily Russian had one more salvo he intended to aim at the President. Since Khrushchev gave no indication that the summit was off, Eisenhower had an unexpected surprise waiting for him when he arrived in Paris where the negotiations were to be held. France was the host nation and French President Charles De Gaulle chaired the meeting. Khrushchev had been waiting for this opportunity. With the attention of the entire world riveted on them, before De Gaulle could establish the agenda to be discussed, Khrushchev rose to his feet and launched into a tirade, accusing Eisenhower of duplicity and attempting to sabotage the summit before it could get underway. He brandished the photos of Powers and the remains of the U-2 spy plane and called on the world to witness the perfidy of the US government. Finally, Khrushchev and his entourage rose to their feet and left the room. The summit was over.

Eisenhower did leave a legacy, albeit not the one he sought. He left to his successor a Communist nation, Cuba, 90 miles off the coast of Florida, headed by Fidel Castro. Today, it is difficult to understand what Eisenhower, the skilled military commander who had planned and led the largest military invasion in history, intended to do with the rag-tag band of Cuban exiles that the CIA had assembled in Guatemala for the invasion of Cuba by the sea. Castro's own earlier attempt to invade Cuba by sea had resulted in a catastrophe, with only 12 out of the original 82 escaping with their lives. Fidel, his brother Raul and Che Guevara had been among the survivors, fleeing to safety in the mountains of Sierra Maestra. It was from the safety of these mountains that he had built up the revolutionary force that led eventually to the departure of Cuban dictator Fulgencio Batista and his entourage of sycophants.

From the very beginning, Eisenhower was ill-informed about Castro and his force of rebels. He was aware that Che Guevara, an Argentinean doctor, was an avowed Communist, but the reports published in *The New York Times* by its correspondents portrayed Castro and his supporters as modern-day Robin Hoods, whose intention was to reform the abuse of Cuban labor in agriculture. Those who were exploiting these illiterate workers were foreign-owned corporations, largely American. At the same time, America historically exhibited an affinity for Cuba and it was the US military that had liberated the island from the tyrannical rule of Spain. A special quota on imported sugar had been set aside to support its economy. Castro's armed forces entered Havana on January 8, 1959; a few days later, Jose Miro Cardona, a leading Cuban liberal, announced the formation of the Revolutionary Government of Cuba. Shortly after, the United States officially recognized the new government in Cuba. Six weeks later came the first of many surprises. Cardona stepped down, and Fidel Castro became the head of the new government and reserved for himself the role of Commander of the Cuban armed forces.

Although the State Department had recognized the new government, Eisenhower in particular was disturbed by its name. To him, the word revolutionary carried all the connotations of a Communist government. This initial distrust was compounded by Castro's unofficial 12-day visit to the United States. Castro went out of his way to show his disdain for the written and unwritten policies of America towards its Negro population. Instead of staying at a midtown hotel, he and his entourage settled in at the Hotel Theresa in Harlem to indicate his repugnance for the unspoken policy of not renting rooms to American Negroes. He also went out of his way to hold a well-publicized meeting with Malcolm X, the Black Muslim revolutionary. At the United Nations, which was in session, he appeared to align Cuba's future foreign policy with those of Jawaharlal Nehru's India and Nasser's Egypt. In turn, when he paid a call on the White House, Eisenhower was out on the golf course and had Vice President Nixon substitute for him. Already suspicious of Castro's intentions, the administration was waiting to see the political direction that Castro intended to follow. Shortly after his return to Cuba, the Cuban government began the process of nationalizing US-owned corporations. Singled out immediately was the ubiquitous United Fruit Company, one of the largest in Cuba. As had been the case in Guatemala and every other Latin American country, United Fruit deliberately undervalued the actual worth of its corporation in order to reduce the amount of taxes it paid. When the Castro regime offered compensation based on its listed valuation, UFC balked and called for negotiation. The response of the Cuban government was: take or leave it. When UFC continued to insist on negotiations, their land holdings in Cuba were confiscated by the Cuban government. The company's lobbyists were able to convince the administration to reduce the quota of sugar imports allocated to Cuba. Castro's answer was to nationalize the remaining US corporations on the island, whose valuation was estimated at $850 million.

That was only the beginning. His next step was to nationalize all the corporations on the island, whether foreign-owned or in Cuban hands. He then initiated a program to collectivize all Cuban agriculture. Had John Foster Dulles still been alive, the reaction of the US government might have been different. His replacement, Christian Herter, was far more cautious. He advocated a program of "watch and wait" to determine whether or not the Soviet Union had become involved in Cuban affairs. As for Castro, he had yet to decide what Cuba's policy should be with regard to the United States, Cuba's major customer. First he wanted to be certain that he had consolidated his power. By July 1959, he had forced out of office the provisional President Manuel Lleo and replaced him with one of his ardent supporters, Osvaldo Torrado.

The mass exodus of Cubans to the United States had grown from the original supporters of Batista to the upper-middle and middle class of Cubans whose businesses had been nationalized. The liberal business community that had once supported Castro's revolution now viewed him with intense hatred. In their minds, he had betrayed them. Their lives and careers had been ruined. They would have to begin a new life and establish new businesses in a country where Spanish was a second language, and where business was conducted differently than it had been in pre-Castro Cuba. The Eisenhower administration had yet to come up with a policy *vis-à-vis* Castro. Reducing the quota on sugar imports had not altered Castro's policies. Meanwhile, Castro had negotiated an agreement with the Soviet Union to purchase their crude oil. When the US-owned refineries in Cuba refused to process the oil, Castro expropriated them. The administration reacted by placing an embargo on all merchandise shipped from Cuba. The die had been cast. The door now was wide open for the Soviet Union to make its entrance into the western hemisphere. A series of agreements between the two nations followed, calling for economic and military aid to Cuba. The greatest fear of the United States now was a reality; the Soviet Union had a satellite nation in the Americas, and only 90 miles off the shores of Florida.

The reaction of the Congress, the media and the American public was outrage. Throughout the country, there was a clamor to send in the Marines before it was too late. Within days, the Joint Chiefs of Staff had drawn up plans and informed the President that the Navy would be ready to execute them within a brief period of time. Eisenhower still hesitated to give the go-ahead order for an invasion. The major drawback was the effect on America's relations with other Latin American countries. Yankee imperialism always was foremost in their minds. On the other hand, to stand by and do nothing was to concede our impotence. Eisenhower's solution was to use the CIA to try to overthrow Castro's regime. The agency had been successful in Iran and Guatemala. By using its covert services, it would be less obvious that the hand on the trigger was that of Uncle Sam. Richard Bissell, now the head of covert operations, was called in to draw up a plan. He pulled from the files of the organization the standard plan it had used in Iran and Guatemala. Establish a government in exile; flood the country with anti-Castro leaflets; make contact with anti-Castro people on the island; and develop a paramilitary group prepared to lead an invasion of Cuba. Two problems immediately surfaced. Not only was there a fundamental conflict between those who had supported Batista and those who had opposed him, but within those who had opposed him, factions had developed as well. Training a paramilitary group on the outskirts of Miami was no way to operate a covert mission. As a result, first the trainees would be moved to the Panama Canal Zone and later to Guatemala. But the cat was out of the bag. Castro now knew that the United States was planning an invasion of the island with Cuban exiles. It would be no problem for one or two of his supporters to infiltrate the paramilitary forces. The obvious fact, which no one would admit, least of all the CIA, was that its plan had no chance for success without the direct support of the United States military. Cuba was not Guatemala. There was no neighboring Honduras in which an army of mercenaries could be assembled prior to the invasion. It would have to be a well-coordinated attack, with total control of the air space above the landing site. The man who had led the largest seaborne invasion in history now realized he had committed a terrible blunder in assuming that the agency was the proper vehicle for overthrowing the Castro regime. He could see a disaster ahead, unless the United States military participated in the invasion. He was caught in his own trap. He had foresworn the use of the military publicly, so he couldn't go back on his word. He took the easy way out. By contending that the CIA had yet to establish a legitimate Cuban government in exile, he could pass the Cuban problem on to his successor. His military reputation would remain intact. His name would not be associated with the forthcoming Bay of Pigs disaster.

CHAPTER 7. EXPANDING THE COLD WAR: THE KENNEDY PRESIDENCY

During the 45 years that the Cold War lasted, nine presidents from diverse backgrounds attempted to cope with the Soviet Union with varying degrees of success and failure. Once the Soviet Union had acquired the technology to develop its own arsenal of atomic weaponry, the actions of these nine men and their counterparts in Russia were constrained by the simple fact of the potential threat to both nations in the event these weapons should ever be used again. As a result, during that time span, whatever conflicts the United States was engaged in were fought in defense of its surrogate allies, South Korea and South Vietnam. In each instance, the United States had neither an immediate strategic nor a vested interest in the country. Both wars were fought ostensibly to prevent the spread of communism, a strategy originally designed to protect Western Europe.

John Fitzgerald Kennedy, the thirty-fifth President of the United States, came from an ambitious, newly wealthy family of Irish Catholics. Only one of the other eight presidents who presided over the destiny of this country during the period of the Cold War, George Herbert Walker Bush, was born to wealth and in his case, it was old-line, Protestant Anglo-Saxon money. His family's attitude toward money was quite different than that of the nouveau riche. There was nothing unseemly about the sons of the old-line wealthy entering into the crass world of business. Thus, George Herbert Walker Bush, once he had graduated Yale, made the decision to enter the potentially lucrative oil industry before turning to seeking political office. Of course, he didn't start from scratch. There were family contacts and funds when required.

John F. Kennedy was the youngest man ever elected to the presidency and the only "poster boy" President in American history. A touch of glamour surrounded him. Elected at age 43, he was tall, handsome, intelligent, highly articulate, married to a very attractive woman, with two beautiful children, and whose natural wit and charm appealed equally to men and women. He was the author of two works of non-fiction, *Why England Slept* and *Profiles in Courage*. For the latter, he had been awarded the Pulitzer Prize. Even these two significant accomplishments had been orchestrated by his father, Joseph P. Kennedy. In the case of the former work, based on his senior thesis while at Harvard, his father had enlisted the services of Arthur Krock, the senior columnist at the prestigious *New York Times*, who had rewritten it and had it placed with a publisher. In the case of the latter, the writing and organization of the text had been the efforts of Ted Sorenson, Kennedy's major speech writer and political consultant before and during his administration. Once again, Arthur Krock, who sat on the Pulitzer Prize committee, had been instrumental in steering the award to Kennedy. The respected columnist must have been deeply indebted to JFK's father in order to provide these services to his son. When JFK entered the White House, the same Arthur Krock tendered his personal, Negro man-servant to cater to the personal needs of the newly elected President.

It was also Kennedy's father who had made up his mind that his son John should be the first Catholic to be elected President, following the untimely death of his older brother in World War II. With unlimited money and political connections on his mother's side of the family, the second son moved easily from Congressman to Senator, abetted by his personal charm and the support of his immediate family. JFK was a young man in a hurry. Under his father's guidance, in 1956 the young Senator made a bid for the vice-presidential nomination. It was a clever, if obvious, move. Knowing full well that Adlai Stevenson, running for a second time, had no chance of defeating the popular Eisenhower for the presidency, it would put JFK in a prime position to be the leading Democratic candidate for the job in 1960. While he came close to achieving his objective, the liberal wing of the party still viewed him as the son of his arch-conservative father, and he lost that vote. Nevertheless, now that

JFK had become somewhat of a national figure, he took the opportunity to campaign for the ticket in more than 20 states. On the advice of his father, he also cultivated the local politicians in key states in preparation for the 1960 presidential nomination. The strategy paid off. Kennedy now was postured as being in the vanguard of the liberal movement. His father, who had long-term political connections with the big city bosses of the Democratic party, would devote his efforts to convincing them of his son's ability to be elected.

With Stevenson playing coy about seeking a third try for the presidency and with Estes Kefauver representing a Southern border state, the major opponent Kennedy faced for 1960 was the liberal senator from Minnesota, Hubert Humphrey. Unlike Kennedy, Humphrey's liberal credentials were impeccable. He had been in the forefront of the fight for civil rights legislation. As the Mayor of Minneapolis, he had advanced progressive programs. He had been an ardent supporter of the New Deal and Truman's Fair Deal. If Stevenson was out of the running, then the dyed-in-the-wool liberals would throw their support to Humphrey. The only other candidate was Lyndon Johnson, majority leader of the Senate and a representative of the Southern wing of the party. Since the liberal wing of the party rejected Johnson's candidacy out of hand, his only chance was a deadlocked convention, where in desperation the party faithful would turn to him as a compromise candidate. The major objection to Kennedy's candidacy was his Catholic religion. The only Catholic candidate that the party had nominated for the presidency was Alfred E. Smith, the Governor of New York, and in 1928, the solid Democratic South had deserted the party because of his religion. The old war cry that had resonated then — that with the election of a Catholic president the Pope would be sitting in the White House — was revived. But in World War II, men of all religious faiths had fought side by side against a common enemy and that old shibboleth no longer resonated as it had then. Having defeated his only liberal opponent, Humphrey, in three primaries by large margins, nothing could stop Kennedy from attaining the nomination other than a last minute entrance by Stevenson. But the party's twice defeated nominee continued to play coy. Unwilling to challenge Kennedy for fear of suffering an ignominious defeat, Stevenson preferred to sit on the sidelines, waiting for a draft movement that never materialized.

Kennedy's decision to offer the vice presidency to his opponent, Johnson of Texas, was a prime example of the political astuteness that had been drilled into him by his father — winning took precedence over everything else. The fact that Johnson's barbs running up to the nomination were often vicious was set aside. Without Johnson on the ticket, Kennedy could never be elected. Kennedy's slim victory in the popular vote and his questionable win in the Electoral College — which he owed to the Texas Board of Elections and to Chicago Mayor Richard J. Daley resurrecting the dead in Cook County, Illinois — did not faze him at all. Johnson had been put on the ticket to help carry Texas and some of the Southern states, and he had come through. As for Illinois, Kennedy knew that Nixon would not challenge him by demanding a recount. It would take months to sift through the names, and the nation would be without a President. More important, JFK had won the popular vote, and that was enough to indicate that he was the choice of the American people. After all, in his lexicon, winning was everything. How it was accomplished was immaterial. With the election behind him, his next job was to select a Cabinet that would help him govern. Kennedy's choice of his brother Bobby for Attorney General may have been outlandish, given his lack of legal experience, but it turned out to be the best choice he made. In times of crisis, and he experienced more than his share during his three years in office, he required someone he could implicitly trust and who could hold his hand when necessary. He also decided to emulate Franklin Roosevelt by surrounding himself with a coterie of professors and intellectuals drawn largely from his alma mater, Harvard.

In January, the day before Kennedy was to be sworn into office, Eisenhower invited him to a final meeting to brief him on the major foreign problems facing the US. Also present were the new Cabinet appointees, Secretary of State Dean Rusk, Secretary of Defense Robert McNamara and Treasury Secretary Douglas Dillon, and their departing counterparts, Christian Herter, Thomas Gates, and Robert Anderson. Kennedy needed and wanted the backing of the former President once he made decisions in the area of foreign policy. He was well aware of the influence and popularity of the former President with the public. Berlin, Cuba and Laos were discussed as the potential sources for serious problems, but no mention was made of Vietnam as requiring immediate attention. Rather it was the small country of Laos, where Communist insurgents were making headway. And Cuba was a high priority. As for

Berlin, all that could be reported was that the outflow from East Berlin to the West continued unabated. Kennedy would have to wait for the next move by the Soviet leader, Nikita Khrushchev.

The following day Kennedy would deliver his famous inaugural speech, culminating in that famous phrase: "Ask not what your country can do for you; ask what you can do for your country." Kennedy's mode of governance differed dramatically from that of Eisenhower. Since he possessed no previous executive experience he was terrified of delegating authority to others. Yet, he would never be a hands-on president. Insecure in his new role as chief executive of the nation, in almost every instance he would seek a consensus from his advisors before making a decision, and even then, always sought a last minute chance to change his mind. It was this inability to take a firm stand and abide by his initial judgment that would lead to the Bay of Pigs disaster, the Cuban missile crisis and America's involvement in Vietnam. Nor was this approach to decision-making out of keeping with his background and upbringing. Up until he entered the White House his father had made every decision for him.

During JFK's first days in office the subject of Vietnam emerged. He was leafing through the last report filed by the CIA on the situation in Vietnam with his Deputy National Security Advisor Walt Rostow. Brigadier General Edward Lansdale had stated in his report that Vietnam was in a state of crisis and required immediate attention or the government, headed by Ngo Dinh Diem, might collapse. Lansdale had returned from Vietnam only a few days before, and he was summoned to meet with the President and the members of his Cabinet and advisors. Lansdale had earned his general's star in the Air Force as an intelligence officer, but he had started his career during World War II in the Office of Strategic Services (OSS) and transferred to the CIA when it was organized after the war. He had served in the Philippines, helping to defeat the Communist-led Huks and developed a personal relationship with Ramon Magsaysay, then the Philippines' minister of defense, who later became president. Subsequently, Lansdale established a similar rapport with Diem since he had been the CIA's station chief in Saigon in 1954. Like most CIA operatives overseas, he had utter contempt for the striped-pants boys in the State Department. He viewed himself as one of the few men who understood the Asiatic mind. He had been the subject of caricature in two successful novels, *The Ugly American* and *The Quiet American*. His view of the world was as simplistic as that of most Americans, including Eisenhower and Kennedy. Americans were the good guys, and the Communists the bad ones. Kennedy suggested that Rusk name him ambassador to Vietnam. Rusk ignored the suggestion, and since it wasn't an order, chose his own man for the post, Fred Nolting. But Rusk and others soon would discover that Lansdale was about to play a far larger role in Vietnam than ambassador. Before leaving office, the Eisenhower administration had allocated funds to support the Diem regime, and Kennedy immediately ordered the release of these funds, along with monies to be used for propaganda. This, too, was part of the American approach to fighting communism: convince the illiterate, exploited Vietnamese peasant that democratic values were superior to those espoused by communism. What other approach was available? The tactics used by the Viet Cong — the insurrection forces of the Viet Minh — were those of terror and intimidation. Not only was this assessment of the enemy naïve; it was absurd. The success of the Vietcong among the peasants of South Vietnam was a direct result of their being exploited by the US-backed government of Diem. It would take three years for Kennedy and his advisors to recognize this basic fact and by then it was too late. Kennedy had committed this country to prevent the spread of communism in Vietnam.

It was Eisenhower, not Kennedy, who had promulgated the "domino theory" at the January meeting with Kennedy and his leading Cabinet members. Eisenhower had warned them that if Laos was taken over by the Communists, the rest of Southeast Asia soon would follow, including Thailand, a member SEATO. Although Britain and France also were members of this Southeast Asian counterpart to NATO, along with Pakistan, the Philippines, Australia and New Zealand, none of these countries were prepared to send in troops to fight on the Asian mainland. Since Eisenhower had stated that Laos was more critical than the other problems in Asia, Kennedy called in the US Ambassador to that country for an assessment of the situation. The Pathet Lao, the Popular Front Communist party, controlled almost half of the country. The Laotian army was worthless; their commanding general had never witnessed a battle. The only person in the government who wasn't corrupt was Prince Souvanna Phouma. The only reason that the French had maintained the colony was to foster their national pride. Kennedy was stunned. He queried the Defense Department to provide him with an estimate of how many soldiers it would take to keep Laos from falling into the hands of the Communists. Since Defense had no knowledge of the situation on the ground, the answer was as fuzzy as the question: anywhere from 10,000 to 60,000 ground troops.

Meanwhile, there was the more important question of what to do with the approximately 1,500 armed and trained Cuban exiles sitting in Guatemala, prepared for the invasion of the island and the overthrow of the Castro regime. Allen Dulles, head of the CIA, had shown Kennedy the plan he had submitted to Eisenhower. Dulles was convinced it was foolproof. He went so far as to exaggerate that it was easier than the plan the agency had used to topple the government of Jacopo Arbenz Guzman in Guatemala. Despite his confidence, there was one major difference that made the plan risky. The invasion would be coming from the sea and not from neighboring Honduras. Kennedy showed the proposed plan to the Joint Chiefs of Staff, and they informed him it had a 30% chance for success. Kennedy returned the plan and told Richard Bissell, head of the operation, to submit another.

Kennedy was firm on one condition. There had to be no trace of any US involvement. Had Bissell or Dulles been candid with the President they would have informed him that such an idea was impossible. The 1,500 Cuban exiles that the CIA had organized into a paramilitary army now stationed in Guatemala would require support from the air if a successful landing was to be achieved. Each of the two men had a reason for the operation to continue. First and foremost, covert operations accounted for 60% of the agency's budget. Its previous successful operations in Iran and Guatemala had served to reinforce the importance of covert activity. It was vital for the new President to understand the agency's role in the fight against Communist regimes. The CIA's attempts to assassinate Castro, under Eisenhower, had failed. The only way his regime could be toppled, according to the agency, was with an invasion of the island. According to Cuban agents that the CIA had sent to Cuba, once the invasion force had landed, the majority of Cubans would rise up and the Castro regime would collapse. Still missing from the equation is how Kennedy could have believed that an invasion of Cuba was possible without the full complicity and backing of the US government. Not only was the presence of the Cubans in Guatemala known to the entire world but Castro had infiltrated the organization with his own men.

Despite these obvious facts, Kennedy continued to insist that before he would give the go-ahead to an invasion, it had to appear that the US had no part in it planning or execution. He had a very good reason to minimize the publicity that would surround this effort to overthrow Castro's regime. One month before the invasion was planned, on March 16, he had invited to the White House the heads of state of every Latin American country except Cuba and the Dominican Republic, which was still under the control of Rafael Trujillo, to unveil what he considered would be the *piece de resistance* of his administration, the Alliance for Progress. The goal of this program was to establish in the Western hemisphere an economic alliance similar to the proposed European Common Market. But the 10-point program he would present would go further than mere economics. It was designed to raise the living standards in all of these countries through land reform, education and improved health facilities. The plan called for the United States to contribute $20 billion over a period of 10 years, divided between government grants and private investments; as the program advanced, the wealthier nations of Latin America would contribute an additional $60 billion. The fundamental motive for the Alliance was the recognition by the Eisenhower and Kennedy administrations, couched in diplomatic language, that the best way to prevent the spread of communism in this hemisphere was to offer a good alternative — in other words, to raise the standard of living of these nations. In no way did Kennedy want the proposed invasion of Cuba to change the new image of the United States. The Alliance for Progress was meant to destroy the age-old perception of Yankee imperialism.

The Alliance for Progress did not emerge from thin air. In a speech in 1956 Premier Nikolai Bulganin of the Soviet Union spoke of the failure of the Soviet Union to expand its commercial ties with the nations of Central and South America. At the present time, he informed the committee, the only business relations the Soviet Union had were with Mexico, Argentina and Uruguay. In other words, the infiltration by Communists into the government of Guzman, which had led to the coup that overthrew his regime, could not be blamed on outside Soviet agents but was the work of indigenous Communists. President Eisenhower had already sent his brother, Milton, president of Penn State University, to make informal tours to get a reading on Latin American attitudes towards the United States. In every instance, the reports he brought back to the President indicated a negative attitude towards US policies in the region. And in 1957, Rostow and Max Millikan published the book *A Proposal: Key to an Effective Foreign Policy*. While the two professors did not mention Latin America, their thesis of economic aid as a deterrent to the spread of communism could easily have been applied to the countries of Latin America as well as the rest of the world.

Two unrelated events then shook the Eisenhower administration out of its lethargy with regard to Latin America. The first took place in 1958, when the President sent Vice President Richard Nixon on a good will tour of South America. Everything seemed to be going smoothly until Nixon and his wife landed in the airport at the capital city of Caracas, Venezuela. At the airport, Nixon and his wife were spat upon by an angry crowd of students, led by Communist organizers, and on the motor trip to the capital, they barely made it to the safety of the American Embassy. Even though it was an organized protest, the number of people in the streets shouting "Yankee go home" left a vivid impression on Nixon and on Eisenhower. They realized that changes in United States policy towards the region were necessary. But it was the emergence of Fidel Castro and his expropriation of US business properties without compensation that propelled the Eisenhower administration into taking action. Under the leadership of Milton Eisenhower and Douglas Dillon, then Under Secretary of State for Economic Development, a Pan-American organization was established, and an Inter-American investment bank was created. A few months later, the Act of Bogota was approved by the council of the Organization of American States; it called for the development of measures to improve economic and social conditions in Latin America, under the framework of the Pan-American agreement. A special inter-active fund was established, with the United States Congress appropriating $500 million for that purpose. When Eisenhower made a tour of Latin America before leaving office, he was greeted everywhere by enthusiastic crowds. It was upon this groundwork, laid out by the Eisenhower administration, that the expanded program of the Alliance for Progress program was created. Both Dillon, now Treasury Secretary in the Kennedy administration, and Rostow, deputy to Bundy, head of the National Security Council, played a major role in its formulation.

During the first 60 days of Kennedy's administration, his actions appeared to live up to the rhetoric of his inaugural speech. Early on, he had adopted Humphrey's suggestion to create a Peace Corps. In place of young men performing their mandatory two years of service in the military, they could volunteer to spend their two years as ambassadors of good will by relocating to Third World countries, living under the same conditions as the native inhabitants, and instructing them in such practical matters as crop rotation, healthful living practices, and where it was possible, education. This program would show the world America at its best. Americans had always been generous with their money, both in foreign aid and in supplying help when a natural disaster struck; now the US would be sending its youth to work side by side with the impoverished. The formation of both the Peace Corps and the Alliance for Progress was indicative of the basic thrust underpinning Kennedy's view of the world and of his responsibility. He was the prime example of those young men who had gone off to war, seen its horrors and were determined to avoid the pitfalls that had plagued the previous generation. Nor was his image and popularity confined to the United States. As he would soon learn when he visited Paris, Vienna and London, the Kennedy mystique transcended borders. Wherever he traveled, he was the man of the hour.

Even with this sterling early record, the problem of Castro and Cuba had to be tackled. Bissell and Dulles had returned with an alternative plan after Kennedy had vetoed the original that called for a landing on the major city of Trinidad. Although it was logical to choose a large city, since the landing force could count on support from the local population, Kennedy vetoed it. Choosing a well-populated city would only call attention to the invasion and the role the US would play. Instead the CIA had chosen an obscure site on the coast of southwestern Cuba known as the Bay of Pigs. On the right side of the landing site was a large impassable swamp. As designed, the plan called for two days of initial bombing of the air fields where Castro's air force was located, to be followed by the actual invading force. All the B-26 bombers used would bear the insignia of the Cuban air force in order to mask American involvement. No one paid much attention to the negative side. Given the distance between Guatemala, where the B-26 bombers would take off, and the Bay of Pigs, the pilots would have only enough fuel in their tanks to cover the landing site for a little more than an hour. But the major blind spot in the plan was that no consideration had been given to the possibility that men loyal to the Castro regime had infiltrated the paramilitary group of the Cuban exiles and would report to Castro the exact site for the landing. On the positive side, information gathered from recent exiles from Cuba indicated that a massive uprising would take place once the paramilitary group came ashore and established a beachhead. Even though Kennedy had stressed to those in the final meeting that he would not use US forces to aid the Cubans, most of his advisors believed that in the end, if the invasion ran into trouble, the President would make use of US aircraft to come to the rescue of the invading force.

In his desire to lower the visibility of the upcoming attack, Kennedy called off the second bombing of the Cuban airfields where Castro's small air force was located, and reduced the number of B-26 bombers designed to support the landing from sixteen to eight. Bissell protested that the president was jeopardizing the success of the invasion, but Kennedy could not be swayed. Of course, everyone in Havana, as well as the American press, was aware of the forthcoming invasion. In trying to cover his tracks he fooled no one, while at the same time defeating the purpose of the invasion. Castro's forces were waiting for the invasion with 20,000 troops backed up by tanks. The spies he had placed with the Cuban exiles had kept him informed. The uprising on the island, which recent Cuban exiles had predicted, never materialized. At the United Nations the Cuban delegate denounced the United States for plotting the invasion. He asked: where had the exiles acquired the ships for the invasion; where did they get the aircraft and the communications equipment? The invasion was a disaster, and Kennedy had no one to blame but himself.

Even after the failed invasion, Kennedy's poll ratings remained consistently high. He possessed that rare quality of being able to project optimism and confidence. Television was made for him, and he used it skillfully. Even more important was Kennedy's close relationship with the national media.

Kennedy had set the stage for the forthcoming missile crisis. When he met with Nixon shortly after the Cuban disaster in an effort to enlist his support, Nixon reportedly empathized with Kennedy but at the same time told him he should get rid of Castro now with the use of US force. Of course, that is easy to say without pondering the consequences; but Nixon believed it was more important to show the Soviet Union that the US was determined to keep the USSR out of the Western hemisphere than to worry about the world's reaction. There is no doubt that the leadership in the Kremlin looked upon Kennedy's unwillingness to use American force as a sign of weakness. When it came to the Hungarian rebellion, Khrushchev had no qualms about sending in Soviet tanks and artillery to put the insurgency down. Throughout his tenure in office,

Kennedy was able to rationalize his unwillingness to use force by contending that this was the difference between a democracy and a totalitarian government. At the same time, he never gave a second thought to the use of napalm and poisonous defoliants used by US forces in Vietnam.

Kennedy had little time to dwell upon that subject. He was still faced with the Laotian problem. This time, he intended to be more cautious. He arrived at the conclusion that he would have to engineer some kind of compromise that would leave Laos with its present status quo. Ambassador-at-Large Averill Harriman contacted Prime Minister Jawaharlal Nehru of India, who would forward the message to Moscow. The United States would leave Laos with its present mixed government of Communists and Prince Souvanna Phouma, if Khrushchev could convince North Vietnam to cease its open support for the Pathet Lao. To Kennedy's delight and surprise Ho Chi Minh, the head of state of North Vietnam, agreed. He was winning the war in South Vietnam, which was necessary to achieve his primary goal — the eventual reunification of Vietnam. Laos was not part of his plan. The introduction of US troops into Southeast Asia, and right next to the border of his country, could only bode trouble in the foreseeable future. Laos would remain neutral. But if Kennedy, Khrushchev and Ho Chi Minh were satisfied with the new arrangement, the hard-line anti-Communists in the United States were not. The old charge that the Democrats continued to be soft on communism was resurrected. It was at that moment in time that Kennedy arrived at the conclusion that South Vietnam must be defended at all costs. He immediately increased the number of military advisors to that country but insisted that they arrive in civilian dress. As had been the case with Cuba, he continued to play games.

Secretary of State Rusk might have believed that he had end-played the President by sending Nolting as Ambassador to South Vietnam instead of General Lansdale, but he was mistaken. Kennedy had become intrigued by the ideas the General had put forth at their initial meeting. He was in agreement with Lansdale that the only way to fight the Communist insurgents was through counter-insurgency forces. Moreover, having made the personal decision that South Vietnam was the place to halt Communist aggression in Southeast Asia, Kennedy wanted a man in place with hands-on experience in fighting insurgents. Lansdale had been successful in combating the Communist-led Huks in the Philippines.

Why not apply the same tactics in Vietnam? After all, one jungle was the same as another. Thus, he created a team to lay out a strategy to be used in Vietnam. Their initial report called for an increase in the number of military advisors, if the United States agreed to fund South Vietnamese President Diem's request for funds to pay the cost of adding 20,000 new troops to the already existing 150,000 men in the Vietnamese army. While it was a violation of the original accords reached at Geneva in 1954, it was certainly far less of a violation than the failure of both the North and South to hold a referendum in 1956 to determine the future status of South Vietnam. But the gist of Lansdale's report was the increasing strength of the Viet Cong over the previous year. To back up his thesis, he presented figures that were based on pure speculation about the number of Viet Cong in action. In 1960, he claimed, there were about 4,400. In just 15 months, he continued, that figure had grown to over 12,000. He went on to state that the Viet Cong, either directly or indirectly, now controlled over 58% of the countryside, and that the casualties on both sides numbered 4,500. Nobody sitting in that room challenged him about the source of these statistics or the basis for his assertion that the Viet Cong were predicting victory by the end of 1961. The President signed off on Lansdale's proposal and shortly thereafter he sent Vice President Johnson to deliver a personal letter to President Diem, assuring him that he could count on the full cooperation of the United States in fighting the Communist insurgency. This would include economic as well as military aid. The Bay of Pigs and Laos still haunted Kennedy. He would not regain his confidence until later, when he resolved successfully the Cuban missile crisis. By then, it was too late; US policy in regard to Vietnam had been set in stone.

Following his initial enthusiasm generated by General Lansdale's pep talk, Kennedy wondered if he was getting into something that would eventually lead to a disaster. He asked John Galbraith, his Ambassador to India, to stop by Saigon on his way to India. Galbraith, after spending a few days and consulting with Ambassador Nolting, reported back to the President that the Ambassador was certain that the problem was Diem. This contradicted what Lansdale had told him. Moreover, if not Diem, then who was to replace him and how was that to be effected? Nolting may or may not have been accurate in his judgment, but at the moment the problem was of a military rather than an economic nature. Meanwhile Diem, knowing there was no alternative to him on the immediate horizon, could use Kennedy's letter that had been delivered by Johnson, to play on the President's insecurities to his own advantage. Having received the funds and the additional military advisors to expand his army by 20,000 men, Diem upped the ante by informing the White House that he would require an additional 80,000 men, for a total of 250,000, men to wage war. He also requested additional military advisors to train the troops as well as some US combat units. The Vietnamese game was about to become serious. But before that happened, Rusk and McNamara decided to dispense with the services of Lansdale. Robert Kennedy would inform Lansdale that he was to be operating head of a new group designed to dispose of Fidel Castro.

Seven months before Kennedy had to deal with this new phase of Vietnam, he had to contend with Khrushchev on the matter of Berlin. Since Eisenhower had left office, discussions regarding the future status of US forces in Berlin had been on hold. Now Khrushchev once again was threatening to sign a peace treaty with the East German government and leave the status of Berlin in East German hands. A private meeting was set up for JFK and Khrushchev to meet alone in Vienna. Since the British and French had a vested interest in Berlin, being part of the initial agreement made with Stalin in 1945 that called for a joint occupation of the capital, Kennedy notified them of the proposed meeting. Before going to Vienna, Kennedy planned to stop in Paris and accept the invitation that had been tendered by French President Charles de Gaulle. On the way home, Kennedy would stop in London to meet with British Prime Minister Harold Macmillan. The reception that Kennedy and his wife received upon landing in Paris was beyond belief. De Gaulle met them personally at the airport and on the drive into Paris huge crowds lined the streets to welcome the President and his wife. The Second World War and the German occupation were still fresh in the memory of all generations, and it was the French way of saying thanks to the Americans for having liberated their nation. They also were paying their respects to the leader of the United States, the nation that was protecting the free world from Russian domination. In a private conversation, the French president counseled Kennedy on two subjects. As far as his dealings with the Soviets were concerned, France would back him all the way. As for Southeast Asia, De Gaulle cautioned Kennedy not to get trapped in a land war in Asia. Unlike in the West, de Gaulle said, human lives in that part of the world were considered expendable. It was exactly the same advice

JFK had received from General Douglas MacArthur. Kennedy understood the logic of their message. But the two generals were oblivious to American politics, and to Kennedy's obsession with his historical legacy. The latter was always foremost in his mind and transcended all other considerations; should Vietnam fall to the Communists, his reputation would be that of the President who had lost all of Southeast Asia to the Communists. No future historian would inscribe his name in a book illustrating courage in the face of adversity.

When Kennedy met with Khrushchev in Vienna in June 1961 to discuss the future of Berlin and possibly Laos, American intelligence was unable to provide the President with any information about the extent of Khrushchev's power within the Politburo. While Stalin was alive, both Roosevelt and Truman knew that the dictatorship of the proletariat meant one man. Before launching his attack to put down the Hungarian rebellion, Khrushchev sent Aleksei Kosygin to Budapest, upon the insistence of the other members of the Politburo, to determine whether armed force was necessary. It was only when Kosygin returned and gave his approval that the Russian tanks and armored vehicles were unleashed. Of course, at the time, the United States was unaware of these facts. Nor did Khrushchev, when he met with Eisenhower, give any intimation that his position in the Politburo was not analogous to that of Stalin. Thus when Kennedy met with Khrushchev in Vienna, he made the assumption that Khrushchev exercised absolute power in the Soviet Union. Nor did Kennedy understand that his charm, so effective in dealing with people from both parties in the United States, would get lost in the translation into Russian. Khrushchev had come to Vienna with one purpose in mind. He was going to intimidate Kennedy, whom he believed, after the Bay of Pigs fiasco, to be over his head in his role as President. For two days, Khrushchev flooded JFK with a verbal barrage to which the President had no effective response. It was the first time in his life that he had been brow beaten by another man, and he just sat there and took the abuse. The summit meeting that was supposed to lead to détente between the two nations now appeared to be heading for war over the issue of Berlin. Khrushchev appeared to be adamant. He was going to sign a peace treaty with the German Democratic Republic because the United States had violated the Potsdam agreement by rearming the Federal Republic of West Germany. After visiting with Macmillan, before returning home, Kennedy was prepared to face the worst, a war with the Soviet Union.

The United States and its allies, Britain and France, had no intention of evacuating the city.

As had been the case with Eisenhower in 1958, Khrushchev was bluffing. But the inexperienced Kennedy could not be sure. He increased the number of draftees called up for service and expanded the Navy and the Marine Corps. He sent General Lucius Clay, who had commanded US forces during the Berlin Blockade, back to the city to reassure the Berlin public, some of whom already were exiting for the Federal Republic of West Germany. The United States possessed the weaponry to destroy the Soviet Union, and the other members of the Politburo were not about to allow Khrushchev to undertake a war that could annihilate their country. In short, Khrushchev was playing a weak hand and could only succeed by a successful bluff. But bluffing was as far as he could go. The Politburo's answer to the brain drain of East Germany would be the construction of the Berlin Wall. Over the next few years, there were threats and even some incidents that might make it appear that the East German government was prepared to exercise its sovereignty over the entire city, but in the end the status quo remained. The twelve-foot stone wall with its barbed wire and its searchlights came to represent an addition to the original Iron Curtain.

During his first year in office, almost all of Kennedy's time and energy had been devoted to foreign affairs crises. But in 1962 there were Congressional elections coming up, and historically the party in power lost seats to the opposition party in mid-term elections. If he was to maintain a sizeable majority in both houses of Congress, he would have to devote a considerable amount of his time to the economy. The head of his Council of Economic Advisors, Walter Heller, was a Keynesian and wanted an across-the-board tax cut to stimulate the economy. Treasury Secretary Dillon, a Republican, insisted on a change in the tax code before addressing a reduction in taxes. Meanwhile, Labor Secretary Arthur Goldberg was attempting to negotiate an agreement between the major steel producers and their union, the United Steel Workers, in order to restrain any increase in the price of steel, which could lead to inflation. On March 31, 1962, he informed Kennedy that United States Steel, which manufactured one-fourth of the steel produced in the country, had arrived at an agreement with the union. It would grant the union workers a 10-cent an hour increase in wages and benefits without raising the price of steel. The following day, the other major steel producers followed suit.

Kennedy viewed this agreement as a major victory since it would satisfy the Democratic party's core base of labor while at the same time restraining inflation. On April 6, the contract was signed. Four days later, Roger Blough, head of US Steel, reneged on the contract and personally handed the President a four-page mimeographed statement that was being delivered to the press at the same time. Actually, the statement required only one sentence: As of tomorrow United States Steel is increasing prices an average of 3.5% on its entire line of products. US Steel, and the other five steel companies that followed the increases set by Blough, discovered all too soon what it meant when someone tried to double cross the Kennedy brothers, especially Robert. He viewed the action by US Steel as a deliberate attempt to embarrass his brother. Within hours, Robert marshaled the powers of J. Edgar Hoover's FBI and the phone lines of all the executives of these companies were tapped. Agents made phone calls late at night telling them they might be required to supply information to the Justice Department on a variety of subjects including their expense records for a possible investigation by the IRS. The following day, Clark Clifford, the notorious Washington lawyer and one of the leading lobbyists in the country, held a meeting attended by the head of Inland Steel. Later that afternoon, the head of Inland Steel announced that the company was withdrawing its price increases; the other steel companies followed suit.

Forcing the rollback of steel price increases was unquestionably a victory for Kennedy, albeit accomplished by illegal means. However, the greatest moment of the Kennedy presidency, upon which his fame is built, was the peaceful resolution of the Cuban missile crisis. During this spine-tingling drama when the world appeared to be headed towards the Armageddon of atomic war, he is pictured as the fearless and resolute leader of the Free World who stood up to the Russians and forced them to back down and remove the offensive missiles from Cuba. The facts are that he had no alternative. As he himself remarked: had he done nothing, he would have been impeached. To give him credit, there were two alternatives on the table. There was the one proposed by the military and the hawks — a massive bombing of the missile sites under construction or already completed, followed by a large-scale invasion by US troops. The other, proposed by cooler heads, was to place a blockade around the island and turn back any Soviet ships attempting to land their military cargoes. According to international law, the latter also constituted an act of war. Kennedy chose the blockade. However, he determined if the blockade failed to force the removal of the missiles and their sites, attaining that goal would be put in the hands of the military. All of the logistics necessary to carry out the military option were in place at the moment when Khrushchev backed down. It was not Khrushchev who made the decision but the other members of the Politburo. Khrushchev had violated a central canon of Stalin: never challenge the United States directly; use only surrogates to avoid losing face. To salvage his own career he would have to get some quid pro quo. Through an intermediary who had maintained contact with Robert Kennedy, he proposed to withdraw all the missile sites from Cuba in exchange for the United States dismantling its Jupiter missile sites located in Turkey. Since American Polaris submarines outfitted with their own missiles now were capable of reaching the Soviet Union, Kennedy and his advisors accepted Khrushchev's proposal on one condition. He could use the quid pro quo to salvage his own reputation within the Politburo but he was not to make it public immediately. Six months after the crisis had passed the missile sites in Turkey and Italy would be dismantled.

Lost in the midst of this euphoria and the kudos Kennedy received from the press as well as from both political parties was a question nobody bothered to ask. Why had it taken the administration 18 months to discover what was taking place in Cuba? It wasn't until August 6, 1962, a year and a half after the failed invasion at the Bay of Pigs, that John McCone, the new head of the CIA, determined that there was sufficient evidence on hand to investigate the significance of the increasing number of Russian military advisors on the island and the large quantity of freight that was being off-loaded at obscure ports in Cuba. How could the CIA and military intelligence not realize that Castro would turn to the Soviet Union for military equipment to defend the Cuban revolution against a military attack led by US armed forces? On the floors of the House and Senate, legislators from both parties were calling for military action against this Communist dictatorship off the coast of Florida. Even more inexplicable is that Robert Kennedy had assembled a task force headed up by General Lansdale, named Operation Mongoose, whose avowed purpose was to eliminate Castro by fair or foul means. Obviously, in order to accomplish that task, Lansdale would have had to engage Cubans living on the island. In other words, the Kennedy administration had been living in a dream world.

Therein lay the fundamental weakness of the Kennedy presidency. No one was in charge or responsible. Robert Kennedy and his group were more concerned with revenge than with keeping tabs on what was taking place in Castro's Cuba. The various intelligence agencies, which should have been monitoring what was taking place in Cuba, were asleep on the job. The President, whose role in government was to make the decisions, relied on a consensus instead. During the height of the missile crisis, with two dozen of his advisors in the Oval Office, the President called for a vote on whether or not to launch a preemptive strike on Cuba. Robert Kennedy, who had no qualms about organizing a team to assassinate Castro, believed such an attack to be morally wrong. The President appeared to agree with him, while the Joint Chiefs sat there dumbfounded. It was the members of the Politburo who solved the dilemma facing Kennedy and his advisors.

Meanwhile, the situation in Vietnam was deteriorating or improving, depending upon who was releasing the information. By 1962, the US presence in Vietnam had grown from about 2,500 to 11,500. There were American casualties as well. The strategic hamlet program had been established in a large number of villages and was believed to be successful, although some contended that they were nothing more than concentration camps. Of the 2,350 villages in South Vietnam, 1,617 were under the control of the Vietnamese government and 793 were under the Viet Cong, a gain of 27 villages for the Viet Cong and 25 for the government. The number of Viet Cong killed during the year and the number still operational were at best guesstimates. The Viet Cong fighters no longer feared the US helicopters and were now shooting them down. The only thing everyone agreed upon was that Ngo Dinh Diem had to go. Kennedy, following his usual pattern, straddled the middle. His response to the situation was to dispatch more advisors, each of whom returned with a different solution to the problem but none of whom could come up with a satisfactory answer. If he pulled the US troops and advisors out of the country, all of his advisors concurred that the Viet Cong would seize power in less than three months. If Kennedy remained and attempted to win the war by increasing the number of Americans involved, the deaths and casualties would continue to mount. So he made the only decision with which he was comfortable — he complained.

On the domestic front, he hedged on all legislation. He could have enforced the Federal Fair Housing Act through an executive order, but if he did that it would alienate the Southern senators he might need for more important legislation. On civil rights, his record was no better than that of Eisenhower, even though his brother Robert was Attorney General. Robert's attitude was to protect JFK's legacy by not rocking the boat. On the economy, Kennedy's chairman of the Council of Economic Advisors continued to badger him for a tax cut in order to stimulate the sluggish economy, and while the president finally was able to get it through the House in the fall of 1963, its chances for passage in the Senate were meager.

While national defense continued to be the single largest outlay, as a percentage of the total budget it continued to decline. From a defense-expenditure high of almost 70% in 1955, it had declined to 48% by 1963. The major increases in spending were coming from the space program, supporting JFK's desire to beat the Russians in placing a man on the moon, and in agricultural benefits, which provided pork for the legislators from every state. Meanwhile the budget deficit continued to mount. During Kennedy's three years in office, it would increase by $17 billion or almost equal to the $20 billion deficit during the 16 years of the Truman and Eisenhower presidencies. The Eisenhower recession of 1958 had ended before Kennedy took office. The problem could be laid at his doorstep. Part of the cause was his deep involvement in foreign affairs, which allowed him little time for those on the domestic front. He viewed his role as President to be the leader of the free world in the struggle to contain the threat of communism rather than a master of the intricacies of pushing through legislation in a legislative body jealous of its own prerogatives. Moreover, as the titular head of the Democratic party, he was expected to support his fellow Democrats in the pursuit of their objectives. In the same way he was expected to attend Democratic fundraising events and promote favorite-son judges to higher courts, the Democratic majority in both houses of Congress assumed he would accept some of the necessary pork they wanted for their constituents.

In foreign affairs, he was more or less free to act without Congressional interference, but if he wanted to increase the funding of the space agency, he had to give way in other areas. In Europe, there was de Gaulle, who had blocked Britain's entry into the Common Market and was determined that France should pursue its own foreign policy rather than be a lackey of the United States. In Laos, there was a resurgence by the Pathet Lao and a possibility that government might fall under Communist rule. And, Kennedy still had his hopes for an atomic test ban treaty with the Soviet Union. Last but not least, he had to decide what to do about Vietnam and the intransigence of Diem.

The first success the Kennedy administration achieved, a test ban treaty on the use of atomic weapons in the atmosphere, in space and under water, was a result of sending the so-called elder statesman of the Democratic party, Averill Harriman, to negotiate with Khrushchev. Harriman had handled Lend-Lease for FDR and had been his Ambassador to Russia during the Second World War. Harriman understood from his dealings with Stalin and Molotov that any on-site inspections within the Soviet Union were out of the question. Instead of seeking an overall ban on atomic explosions, which would include underground tests as well, he kept his focus on those that could be verified without any inspections — namely the atmosphere, space and under water. As a result, he obtained an agreement that could be ratified by the necessary two-thirds majority required in the Senate. Having delivered an important victory for the President, he was now appointed Under Secretary of State for Far Eastern Affairs in the hope he would be able to untangle the mess in Vietnam. Kennedy also decided to replace Nolting, whom many considered to be too close to Diem, with former Senator Henry Cabot Lodge of Massachusetts, whom Kennedy had defeated in his first run for the Senate. By appointing a Republican, the President hoped that whatever blame might be placed on his administration for failure could be shared equally by the Republicans.

The political situation in Vietnam had taken a sharp turn for the worse. The US military claimed it was winning the war against the Viet Cong; the State Department and recently appointed Ambassador Lodge called for the removal of Nhu and Diem; the CIA was certain that the hamlet program was working; and Diem contended that everything was under control. In such an atmosphere, rumors were the order of the day. The most prevalent one was that Diem or Nhu was collaborating with the French to make a deal with Ho Chi Minh and expel the American presence in the country. Only the American correspondents on the ground had a partially accurate picture of what was taking place. The Vietnamese peasants were in a vise, caught between the government's tax collectors and the forced unpaid labor to construct the hamlets, and the extortion from the Viet Cong guerillas who despite the protection of the hamlets were able to infiltrate these compounds at night. In Saigon, corruption was rampant. The influx of dollars for economic and military aid was being siphoned off into the general economy. Nhu had used some of funds for the army to create his own Praetorian guard of 1,100 dedicated men. Some of the generals in the Vietnamese army were planning to overthrow the Diem regime but were waiting for the approval and silent support of the US authorities in Saigon. Despite the claims of General Paul Harkin, the American military commander in Vietnam, that the war against the Viet Cong was being won and that by 1965 almost all of the now 17,000 US soldiers would be withdrawn, it was more wishful thinking than reality. No matter how many Viet Cong that the Vietnamese army reported killed, there appeared to be more reported alive every year. Kennedy felt trapped. On the one hand, the military informed him that the war against the Viet Cong insurgency was advancing favorably, even with Diem and Nhu in power, and the people from the State Department, along with Lodge, were telling him that as long as Diem and Nhu remained in power, especially Nhu, there was no hope that the campaign could be successful.

Kennedy decided that the only men who could give him a clear assessment of what was taking place in Vietnam were Secretary of Defense McNamara and General Maxwell Taylor, the head of the Joint Chiefs. These two men, along with Lodge, held a long meeting with Diem.

Accompanying Harkin, McNamara and Taylor visited some of the battle sites. Taylor was impressed by the way the war was being conducted, but McNamara was beginning to get disillusioned with the rule of Diem. The more he saw and heard, the more he began to swing over to the side of Lodge and those in the State Department who were convinced the war never could be won as long as Diem and Nhu ruled the country and did not have the support of the Buddhists, who represented 80% of the population. The basic fallacy in their assessment was that both US Military and the State Department viewed the situation in Vietnam as an ideological struggle between the forces of communism and those of democracy, whereas the insurrection was more a matter of the South Vietnamese peasantry revolting against their ongoing economic exploitation. Even though the French military and civil government had departed, French Colons still remained in control of the vast rubber plantations. The Vietcong was an indigenous insurrection. Most of its arms came from peasants who had been conscripted into Diem's growing Vietnamese army and had deserted. The intense antipathy to the rule of Diem and Nhu was concentrated in those members of the military who were excluded from the ruling clique.

Shortly after McNamara and Taylor had returned to Washington, Lt Colonel Lucien Conein, employed by the CIA in Saigon, was contacted by General "Big" Duong Van Minh. It was not the first time that the Minh had approached Conein. During the summer of 1963, Minh had approached the Colonel to get feedback on how the Americans would react in the event the military engineered a coup. At that time, the general did not receive a straight answer. He had no idea how the Kennedy White House functioned. The opposite of a dictatorship, it was a debating society, with the President refusing to commit himself one way or the other. While Roger Hillsman and Harriman at State, as well as Lodge in Saigon, were pushing the President to get rid of Diem and Nhu, Kennedy insisted on some guarantee that whatever government replaced them would be better than the current one. Since no one could be certain which general would emerge as the new head of state, the situation in Vietnam continued to drag on, going from bad to worse. Moreover, President Ngo Dinh Diem and his brother, Ngo Dinh Nhu, were unwilling to have the Americans dictate their policy. By spreading the rumor that a negotiation with the government of Ho Chi Minh was an alternative to the current situation, the brothers caught the attention of the Americans.

For Kennedy, Vietnam had become an albatross around his neck. By expanding the number of US military advisors to that country from a few hundred to 17,500 he had made success or failure in Vietnam a central point of his foreign policy. Even worse, it had become the focus of a debate within Congress and the media. If he abandoned Vietnam and all of Southeast Asia should fall to the Communists, that would be his presidential legacy. If he remained and continued to support a corrupt regime, he would be forced to support it with additional troops, and the quagmire he was already in would swallow him up. Of more immediate concern was the 1964 presidential campaign. He told his brother and other intimates he would wait until he was reelected and then in 1965 he would disengage America from Vietnam and allow events to follow their natural course; but this was the myth that was developed to preserve the Kennedy image. In fact, there was no way the President could leave Vietnam to its fate without bearing the responsibility for it loss and America's loss of face. His conduct of the war might have differed from the approach Johnson took, but no matter what JFK's apologists contend, it was Kennedy who had expanded America's presence in Vietnam to the point where the United States would have to see it through to the bitter end.

General Minh met with Colonel Conein in the beginning of October to inform him that the members of the coup were determined to take action within a short period of time. He sketched out an outline of the plan, including the intention to assassinate Nhu and Ngo Din Can, but to leave Diem in office. The decision was finally made to allow the coup to go ahead.

While the Kennedy and his brother Bobby were concerned about the coup's potential failure, less attention was paid to the implications if it succeeded. Once the administration recognized the new government and backed it both militarily and economically, it would be obliged to ensure its future success. The United States inadvertently had committed itself to winning the war now that it had given silent support for the overthrow of the legitimate government. The military coup turned out to be successful, although the assassination of Diem was unforeseen. General Minh was named President and former vice president Nguyen Ngoc Tho was named Premier. The National Assembly was dissolved and the Constitution suspended. On November 8, 1963, the new government was formally recognized by the United States. Lodge was quick to reassure the new government that military and economic aid would be forthcoming in order to continue the war.

With the coup now a *fait accompli*, Kennedy could pursue that part of the presidency he truly enjoyed, hitting the campaign trail. In place of facing one crisis after another on the domestic and foreign fronts, he could bathe himself in the cheers of the crowds like a performer in show business. In the midst of this glory and fanfare came the shots that were heard around the world. On November 22, 1963, while the President was riding in an open car with his wife at this side, a bullet killed him. The reaction of the public was shock, followed by grief and mourning. Leaders from all over the world came to honor the man and his presidency at the state funeral. Some in the media compared his tragic death to that of Lincoln. But while Lincoln had steered the government to the successful conclusion of a Civil War that had threatened to divide the nation, Kennedy had steered the government into a foreign war that eventually would divide the country. And inadvertently he had expanded the Cold War.

CHAPTER 8. THE GREAT SOCIETY: THE LYNDON JOHNSON PRESIDENCY

Any assessment of Lyndon Johnson's presidency is immediately distorted by the question of his responsibility for the expansion of the Vietnam War. Some historians and biographers refer to his role in that war as a tragedy that marred an otherwise perfect record devoted to alleviating the plight of the poor, the aged and the Blacks. But Johnson inherited an ongoing war on coming to office. It was not his decision to expand the several hundred military advisors attached to Vietnam to a military force of 16,000 men. It was not Johnson who gave his approval to the military coup that overthrew the legitimate government of Diem in the desperate hope that a new government would take orders from the US and attain the sought-after victory on the battlefield. It was Kennedy, not Johnson, who by his actions converted Vietnam into an American war. Despite these facts, the Vietnam War is seen as if it belonged exclusively to Johnson. The motivation for this historical distortion was Johnson, himself. This oversized man, with his oversized ego, his Texas roots, complete with the heavy southern drawl, his previous association with Southern bigotry, his lack of culture, and the general assumption that he was a wheeler-dealer were in sharp comparison with the urbane, cultivated, and charming Kennedy. With Johnson there were no pretensions; what you saw or heard was the man. Whether he picked a dog up by its ears or slapped a woman on her fanny, he was the same crude Texan who on his travels to other countries would hand out tie clips and other souvenirs with his Vice Presidential insignia. In every aspect of his life he was the direct opposite of those people Kennedy had brought to Washington to help him run the government. Yet when Johnson asked the Kennedy clique to stay on and serve in his Cabinet, all of them except Arthur Schlesinger, Jr. and Ted Sorenson agreed. Even Robert Kennedy remained, although he and Johnson shared a more than mutual dislike. As Henry Kissinger, later would remark: power is a great aphrodisiac.

A number of myths about Johnson and his expansion of the Vietnamese war are being played out again today in the current war in Iraq. The first is the Gulf of Tonkin Resolution, enacted almost unanimously by Congress on August 7, 1964, which gave Johnson the authority to increase America's presence in the war. For four years prior to its passage, the dirty little war in Vietnam had been off the radar screen of the overwhelming majority of Americans. The number of US casualties among the military personnel Kennedy had sent to Vietnam was too small to elicit any public interest. The new Vietnamese regime — which seized power after Kennedy ordered Diem overthrown — had proved no better at stemming the growing strength of the Vietcong insurgency. Thus, in June 1964, Secretary of Defense Robert McNamara, along with the Joint Chiefs of Staff, decided to replace General Paul Harkins with General William Westmoreland, in the hope that a new commander might find the solution to the deteriorating situation on the ground. Westmoreland, who had not received his stars sitting behind a desk, immediately recognized the problem. The Vietnamese army of 250,000 men — which Kennedy had sent US military advisors to train — was incapable of coping with the enemy. The corruption among the senior officers extended down to the junior officers; and the peasants conscripted into the army often deserted to join the ranks of the Vietcong. If Vietnam was to be salvaged, it would take an increase in the number of US forces on the ground. As had been the case in Korea, the commanding general could request additional forces, but without the approval of the Secretary of Defense, the Joint Chiefs and the President his request was meaningless. In other words, the policies initiated by the Kennedy administration would be continued. Instead of 16,000 US military serving, the number would be augmented in an effort to quell the insurrection and maintain the Vietnamese government in power. The number of bombing raids against North Vietnamese targets, begun under Kennedy, would be stepped up. The same strategy used by the French, which led to their eventual defeat, would be augmented in the hope that it would cut off supplies coming down from the Communist North. This was the first myth: that without support from the North, the Vietcong insurrection would collapse.

The basic tragedy of the Vietnamese war and America's participation was not only the more than 58,000 US servicemen who lost their lives, but the war's inevitability. The decision by Kennedy to sustain initially and then to dispose of the corrupt Diem regime was part of America's overall strategy to prevent the expansion of communism in the Far East. This effort began with Truman's refusal to recognize the de facto government of the Peoples Republic of China after it had expelled the nationalist forces of Chiang Kai-shek from mainland China, and continued with Eisenhower's defense of the small islands of Quemoy and Matsu off the coast of China. The next phase saw the creation of SEATO, a military alliance between the US, Britain, France, Australia, New Zealand, the Philippines, Thailand and Pakistan, which was designed to protect Thailand from a possible Communist takeover. South Vietnam was not a member state. That being the case, why did Kennedy decide it was in America's interest to defend the corrupt Vietnamese regime? Some historians contend it was the "domino theory" first advanced by Eisenhower, which claimed that if South Vietnam should fall to the Communists, the rest of Southeast Asia, including Laos, Cambodia and Thailand would soon follow. Since Thailand was a member of SEATO, the other member nations would have to come to its rescue. According to that logic, it was best to defend South Vietnam before the conflict led to a major war that might involve Communist China. There was another theory that is equally relevant. Truman and the Democratic party had been accused by Senator Joseph McCarthy of being responsible for the loss of China to the Communists. If Kennedy and Johnson had allowed South Vietnam to fall to the Communists, it would only reinforce McCarthy's charges that the Democrats were soft on communism. In order to prevent the Republicans from resorting to this charge, both Kennedy and Johnson found it in the national interest to maintain the government of South Vietnam.

Following the Tonkin Resolution the number of US troops sent to Vietnam would continue to grow as it became more apparent to Westmoreland that the bulk of the Vietnamese army was incapable of defeating the Vietcong. Moreover, this was jungle warfare where the US superiority in military equipment was meaningless. The cadres of the Vietcong had to be searched out and destroyed. In 1966, as the number of draftees being called to service increased, Johnson committed his one fatal error. He was going to institute changes in the draft laws in order to make them more equitable: young men from all walks of life could be called up to serve their country. The system in use at that time first targeted 26-year-old men and worked down to a minimum age of 19. There were 4,100 draft boards spread throughout the country, and the men who made the decisions as to who should be drafted and who should be deferred were almost all white and part of the establishment. In order to develop a more equitable system, Johnson created an 18 member commission, which included prominent Blacks, educators, businessmen, two women and a priest along with two men from his administration. By a vote of 11 to 7, the commission made the following recommendations: establish a lottery system of random selection, starting with 19 year olds and working up to 26 year olds; reorganize draft boards and limit their discretionary power; and finally, end college deferments. This was exactly what Johnson had in mind.

Before he could implement the findings of the commission, he would have to consult with the head of Selective Service, General Lewis Hershey, who had occupied that post since the first draft in 1940. Hershey voiced no objection to random selection or calling up the 19 year olds first, but he insisted that the discretionary power of the draft boards remain intact. A compromise was reached between Johnson and Hershey. It called for the appointment of 200 blacks, 10 Hispanics and 16 Native Americans to be added to existing draft boards.

With the Selective Service system coming up for its quadrennial approval by Congress in July 1967, Johnson proposed the following changes for Congressional approval: a random selection system starting with 19 year olds; the elimination of draft deferments for students in graduate school, with the exception of medicine and dentistry; and a national debate on college deferments before any action was taken. Congress agreed to broaden the age pool and to eliminate deferments for graduate schools. But it refused to accept random selection and insisted on college deferments. The basic recommendations of the commission were ignored. The addition of Blacks, Hispanics and Native Americans was meaningless since they would be in the minority. The new standards for induction caused panic among college seniors and recent college graduates, and those in graduate school.. In his effort to make the draft more equitable, Johnson was alienating the most important and influential group in American society — the establishment. He was also terrifying their children, who up until then had assumed they were immune from being called up.

By 1968 the protests had spread to college campuses throughout the nation. The dirty little war 10,000 miles away now was the top of the evening news broadcasts. Pictures of dead or wounded GIs became a staple. Protest marches were organized to descend on Washington. Outside the White House students were chanting: "Hey, hey, LBJ, how many kids have you kill today?" Johnson personalized everything, and these attacks on him were the last straw. In February 1968, he retaliated by eliminating the remaining deferment for graduate school and back-dated the order to 1967. He was determined that every graduating college student should be first in line for the draft. In the end, Johnson was defeated in this effort.

Meanwhile, the actual war in Vietnam was being accelerated by Westmoreland. In the year and a half since he had taken command, he had discovered that without an increased number of US troops there was no possibility of controlling the Vietcong insurrection. Thus began the buildup of US forces. To accomplish his goal meant expanding the number of draftees needed from 17,000 a month to more than 35,000. By the beginning of 1968, the number of Americans serving in Vietnam had reached 525, 000 and as a result the Vietcong was gradually losing ground to the superior US-led forces.

Faced with increased bombing attacks and the continuing build up of US ground troops the North Vietnamese decided to change its strategy and launch a major offensive against major cities, including Saigon, where the US military, civilian headquarters and media were stationed. At the same time a major offensive was launched against the Marines' base of Khe Sanh. While US intelligence arm was prepared to meet the attack at Khe Sanh, it overlooked the possibility of an attack on the cities. Up until then all the military activities of the Vietcong had been focused on the countryside. The surprise attack on Saigon enabled the media to record and report the actual fighting; this was the prime factor that led the media to believe that the US military had exaggerated the effectiveness of its policies. The temporary seizure of the national radio station, and the penetration of the outer walls of the US Embassy compound, seemed to contradict Westmoreland's optimistic reports that the war being waged by the Americans was proceeding according to plan. In fact, the surprise Tet offensive launched by the forces of the Vietcong and two divisions of the Vietminh, when they had previously signaled a seven-day truce for a national holiday, proved to be a total disaster for both the Vietcong and the Vietminh. With the enemy forces now out in the open, once the Americans had recovered from the initial shock their superior fire power took a devastating toll on the armed forces of both the insurgents and the North Vietnamese divisions that had been used for the first time in the war. It was because those forces had been decimated, first at Khe Sanh, and later in the battle for the ancient capital of Hue, that over the next four years Nixon was able to draw down the number of US troops and finally end the war.

Vietnam was and wasn't a war. If that sounds absurd to the relatives of the more than 58,000 servicemen who died there, or to those permanently maimed, this contradiction deserves an explanation. It was a war in the sense that it was part of the Cold War, which had evolved into a war to block the spread of communism into those countries thought to be still independent of Moscow. It wasn't a war because the presumed enemy was the Communist regime of North Vietnam, which the US believed was sponsoring the insurrection of the Vietcong. If such was the case, then to win the war it would be necessary to defeat North Vietnam. Only that was impossible. If North Vietnam should be invaded it might bring the Chinese Communists into the war, such as happened when the UN forces approached its northern border during the Korean conflict. Instead the military resorted to massive bombing of the countryside but avoided bombing either its capital, Hanoi, or its major port city, Haiphong. These self-imposed restrictions made the war last as long as it did. The war that wasn't a war only was concluded when Nixon recognized Communist China.

If Johnson has been pilloried for having expanded the Vietnam War, at the same time he has been almost beatified for the two major achievements of his presidency — the passage of the civil rights and voting rights acts, which for the first time since Reconstruction removed the artificial strictures that had been placed on the American Negro, especially in the South, and restored his dignity as an American; and the passage of the legislation which came to be known as the Great Society, which encompassed almost every facet of American life.

The first item on Johnson's agenda, after being sworn in as President, was to establish his credentials with the liberal wing of the Democratic Party. He had to demonstrate to them that he was capable of pushing through the Senate the legislation that was on the party's platform, or he would face a challenge for the Democratic nomination for the presidency in 1964. Initially he tackled s the Kennedy tax cut, which had been bottled up in a Senate finance committee, chaired by Senator Robert Byrd. In dealing with the Senate, Johnson as former majority leader was on his home turf. When Byrd insisted that the proposed 1965 federal budget total less than $100 billion, Johnson got the proposed budget reduced to $97.4 billion, and the measure already adopted by the House was approved in committee. At the last minute Senator Everett Dirksen, Republican minority leader, attempted to add an amendment that would reduce the excise tax on a number of luxury items. If Dirksen's amendment was added, other amendments would be tacked on by the House and the effect of the tax cut would be diminished. Johnson had kept his promise to Byrd, and the Senator now reciprocated. The vote against the Dirksen amendment was nine to eight, with Byrd supplying the necessary majority. Once brought to the full Senate, the bill passed overwhelmingly. Johnson's intimate knowledge of the Senate and its members paid off. Ironically, as was the case with all proposed federal budgets, the final budget had increased to $118 billion. There was no way any administration could control the spending habits of Congress, especially in an election year.

Getting the tax bill though the Senate was the easiest part of Johnson's job. Getting the Southern and border state Senators to approve a civil rights bill that would eliminate discrimination in all public facilities, including restaurants and hotels, faced a far greater challenge. Johnson was well aware that the only method open to the South to block passage of this legislation was a filibuster on the floor of the Senate. First, he had to be assured that he would have the necessary support of Republicans once the filibuster petered out and cloture could be invoked. At that time, a two-thirds majority was required to terminate all debate. Johnson also wanted to be assured that no crippling amendments would be added that would limit the effectiveness of the legislation. The Southern senators, led by Richard Russell of Georgia, a personal friend of Johnson, knew it was their last stand. For 57 days they tied up the Senate. No legislation could be brought to the floor as 18 Senators, divided into shifts, droned on and on. Johnson knew that eventually this exercise in futility would collapse. When the vote finally came, and the first civil rights act had been passed guaranteeing Blacks the same rights as any other Americans, Johnson's nomination for President in 1964 was assured. He had established his bona fide credentials as a liberal President.

There was one more item on his domestic agenda that he was determined to have passed as legislation before the actual presidential campaign got underway — his war on poverty. He called upon his liberal advisors to develop a program that he would be able to push through Congress; they proposed the Office of Economic Opportunity. He appointed Sargent Shriver, who had been so successful in creating the Peace Corps, to administer the program. Until the passage of the Civil Rights Act, Blacks had been excluded from most jobs. Labor unions in particular were loathe to add them to their workforce. Ethnic groups, determined to maintain their status, viewed them as a potential threat to their jobs. Finally, there were the Southern and border states, still licking their wounds from the passage of the Civil Rights Act, which would oppose the appropriation of any monies destined to ease the plight of their large Black population. But far more important to Johnson was that this legislation, if passed, would bear his imprimatur and not that of the late President Kennedy, as had been the case with the tax cut and the Civil Rights Act.

Johnson couldn't have selected a better candidate to run against than Barry Goldwater in the 1964 presidential election. The Senator from Arizona, later considered to be the progenitor of the conservative movement that would elevate the Republicans to the dominant political party, was above all honest to a fault. He was for dismantling Social Security by privatizing it, allowing people the opportunity to participate or reject it; campaigning in Tennessee, he told an audience he favored turning over the Tennessee Valley Authority to private interests. He did address one topic that later would resonate with a large segment of the American population, morality. He openly criticized Johnson for his association with Bobby Baker. He opposed the Civil Rights Act, viewing it as an infringement on states' rights. Goldwater was articulating, without knowing it, a return to the fundamental concept of the Founding Fathers, a republican form of government, with the federal power reduced to a bare minimum. Roosevelt's New Deal and Truman's Fair Deal were anathema to conservatives. To Goldwater and those conservatives who supported his views, the current trends were leading towards socialism, which they equated with communism. They did not comprehend that the Depression had altered the viewpoint of most Americans, who now expected the federal government to take care of their needs when the private sector could not. Moreover, they were insatiable. The more the government catered to their desires, the more they wanted.

In 1965 Johnson carried more than 61% of the popular vote in a landslide victory over Goldwater. On the strength of his margin of victory he had brought along huge liberal majorities in the House and Senate, which would enable him to have Congress pass the legislation that would bring to fruition his dream of the Great Society. The first item on his agenda was medical care for those 65 years old and over, now on Social Security. Some people saw this as the first step towards socialized medicine. The powerful and wealthy American Medical Association would spend a considerable amount of money lobbying against the bill, but to no avail. Then the AMA changed its strategy. Since the original bill only covered hospital care, the medical community proposed a bill that called for the inclusion of medical services on a voluntary basis. Labeled Elder Care or Better Care, it filled a gap that was missing in the original legislation. Most Democrats viewed the proposed legislation as an effort to kill Medicare. But Wilbur Mills, the chairman of the powerful House Ways and Means Committee, saw it as a golden opportunity for meaningful medical coverage. The bill devised by Mills would consist of three components. For the truly indigent, there would be free medical and hospital care provided by the government in conjunction with the states, which has come to be known as Medicaid. To this would be added the original Medicare bill, calling for 90 days of hospital care. The final component would be a voluntary option for medical treatment, which would be paid for partially by the patient and partially by the government. It was the best of all possible worlds for the elderly, and the overwhelming majority subscribed to the voluntary medical program. While the AMA originally threatened to boycott the program, which was enacted into law in July 1965, most doctors ultimately agreed to participate.

As it turned out, Medicare and Medicaid proved to be a bonanza for the medical profession. The number of patients using medical services increased dramatically, with people discovering aches and pains they previously ignored, thereby raising the income of most doctors. In addition, the increased demand created by Medicare and Medicaid necessitated the construction of new hospitals and clinics, which created the need for more nurses and technicians. But the major impact was to raise the general public's awareness of the necessity for health care. Liberals, naturally, sought to extend benefits to the entire population. Employers now were expected to provide some form of health insurance for their workforce. The number of Health Maintenance Organizations expanded enormously. Health was becoming a big business, not only for the private sector but for the federal and state governments as well. To handle the claims would require the addition of 9,000 permanent employees at the federal level alone. The influence of the legislation was far-reaching — from forcing the cigarette industry to include a warning label on every pack about the health risks of smoking, to increasing the focus on health education in the public schools. Johnson, with his theme of a Great Society, had set in motion the concept that the federal government was the arbiter of what was good or bad for society.

The next phase of the Great Society, actually the highest on the President's agenda, was education. It had proved to be his passport to success, and he viewed education as a necessary component of his war on poverty. Like educators and liberals today, he believed the major problems with the primary and secondary educational systems could be solved by allocating federal funds to the impoverished school districts in rural areas and in the inner cities. At least that is the picture of him drawn by his biographers.

The Elementary and Secondary School Education Act of 1965, a misnomer since the funds allocated for it where distributed to colleges and universities as well, was designed to expand educational opportunities for the poor and the disabled through expenditures of funds furnished by the federal government. Actually, the education bill as well as Medicare and the civil rights act were all concepts included in the platform that had been adopted at the 1960 Democratic Convention. Kennedy had attempted to put forth educational reform legislation for Congress to enact, but he ran into the same problem that Johnson would face and overcome: the question of the First Amendment, which calls for the separation of church and state. Catholic legislators in Congress, of which there were more in the eighty-ninth Congress than the usual majority of Methodists, insisted that parochial schools should share in any funds allotted to public schools. Congress would get around this Constitutional roadblock by allocating the funds to students rather than to the schools themselves, making use of a previous Supreme Court decision that allowed states to allocate funds for school busing to parochial as well as public schools. Unlike Medicare, where the original bill had been improved with amendments, Johnson insisted that this bill should pass as it was originally laid out. Despite the efforts of some Congressmen to make alterations or amendments, the bill was ratified overwhelmingly by both houses of Congress.

The aspirations of the education legislation were doomed to be unrealized from its very inception. The blame could be shared between Johnson, the pedagogues, and a dramatic change in society. Throughout his tenure in office, Johnson viewed domestic affairs through the eyes of a bona fide New Dealer. If there was a problem, the solution was to throw money at it. The TVA and the Rural Electrification programs were prime examples of how federal funds could make a fundamental difference in the lives of people. Johnson assumed, axiomatically, that federal monies would produce the same results for education. He did not understand the degree of change that had taken place in the theory of education. Thanks to Nicholas Murray Butler and Columbia Teachers College, instruction had evolved from the basic three R's to a more progressive attitude toward learning. The discipline of rote had been supplanted by a focus on creativity. Education no longer was to be a chore, as it had been for Johnson during his early years when he avoided attending class, but a pleasurable experience. Under those conditions, it should be far easier for a student to accumulate knowledge. At the same time, the role of the teacher should change. Instead of being that remote and authoritarian figure in the classroom, he or she should be more accommodating to the foibles of the students. When pedagogues were encouraged to apply this enlightened approach it destroyed the underlying foundation of education, discipline. Finally, Johnson's education act faced the obstacle of a society growing in affluence, where the accent was placed on instant gratification rather than the more laborious process of gradually developing the requisite tools for success. Add to that the fact that the parents of most of the children from poor families, to whom the program was directed, were either semi-literate or illiterate. Their children never were exposed to the idea that education is a necessity. In other words, the education bill was all form with no substance. It was the one piece of major legislation introduced as part of the Great Society that failed to live up to its expectations.

When the Voting Rights Act of 1965 was finally approved, after a long and intricate campaign highlighted by Martin Luther King Jr.'s successful efforts to get television coverage of the brutal tactics Southerners used to keep the Blacks subjugated, Johnson had attained his goal. He now could state that he was President of all the people in the United States. Only a Southern President could have accomplished what he did. With the two pieces of civil rights legislation, legally the Negro was on an equal plane with any other American. Johnson also knew, as Senator Richard Russell of Georgia had warned him, that the days of the solid Democratic South were numbered. The South would neither forgive nor forget that a white Southerner had betrayed them.

Politically, Russell was right. Economically and socially, the civil rights legislation finally united the South with the rest of the nation. The division of the nation into two distinct regions had commenced in Philadelphia with the ratification of the Constitution. In composing and adopting that revered document, the Founding Fathers reluctantly arrived at the conclusion that the only way the slave states in the South would accept the Constitution was to preserve the institution of slavery. At that time slavery existed in all 13 states to varying degrees. The difference, of course, was that in the South slaves were integral to the economy in more ways than one. Not only were they the field hands and the domestics, but the artisans and mechanics as well. They were the carpenters and brick layers who enabled Jefferson to continually rebuild Monticello. The absence of skilled, white craftsmen was the perpetual complaint of the Southern establishment. This almost total dependency on slave labor was the fundamental weakness in the Southern economy. The War Between the States was a continuation of what had taken place in 1787. The intensive production of cotton and tobacco had eroded the once fertile soil. From a strictly business point of view, the cost of feeding, housing and caring for its ever-growing Black population was not commensurate with the necessary return on investment. As the value of the South's slave population decreased, so too did the wealth of the large plantation owner. Secession was an act of desperation. Had the Southern establishment succeeded, it would have resolved nothing. The Negro would continue to procreate and his value to depreciate. Once the Negro was emancipated, the Southern establishment was bankrupt and remained in that condition for 100 years. As a result the Negro became the scapegoat for its poverty.

Now that the Negro had obtained political equality, with the right to vote, the white political establishment had to face reality. The Republican Party in the South viewed this dramatic change as its golden opportunity to drive a wedge in the political structure that had existed since the end of Reconstruction. The few liberal Democrats in the South believed the end of the political division in the electorate could be exploited to bring on a recrudescence of the Southern economy. The existing wealth of the South resided in cheap land, low taxes and non-unionized labor. Once northern manufacturers realized the advantages the South had to offer, they would move their operations there. Throughout the 1950s and early 1960s, there had been a mass exodus of the northern textile mills to the South. Falls River and New Bedford in Massachusetts had become ghost towns. Apparel manufacturers geared to volume production had set up plants in small cities where labor was cheap and unions were frowned upon. The local police cooperated in keeping union organizers out. As tensions between the two races continued to ease, more and more manufacturers began to take advantage of the South's advantages over the North. The Southern drawl still remained the dominant accent, but the hated Yankees now were seen as a blessing. Moreover, not only did Yankee capital come south, but Northerners migrated to the region as it became the fastest growing region of the national economy. The pace of growth in Florida no longer was led by retirees but by businesses taking advantage of its climatic and labor conditions. As the Southern and border states expanded their population, their representation in Congress grew accordingly. This was the greatest legacy of Lyndon Johnson. Through the civil rights legislation he had forced through Congress, he had united the country economically. The once solid Democratic South might now be referred to as the solid Republican south, but it had emerged finally from its economic isolation from the rest of the nation. Only a Southerner who understood the mind and the mindset of the Southern politician could have affected such a result.

The Great Society encompassed two other major programs, which did not appear to be as significant at the time. First was a radical change in the country's immigration laws, and the second was the first tentative steps towards facing the growing problem of the pollution of this nation's environment. The United States had long prided itself on its open-door policy toward new immigrants. The famous inscription on the Statue of Liberty — "Give me your tired, your poor..." — may have symbolized our humanistic intent, but a certain segment of the population found this intent anything but desirable. By the middle of the 1880s, the mix of immigrants would shift from mostly western and northern Europeans to eastern and southern Europeans, including southern Italians, Greeks, Poles, Hungarians, Ukrainians, Bulgarians, and a sizeable contingent of Jews. They were desperately poor and most of them were illiterate. Many were residents of the Russian empire who had fled to avoid forced military service in the tsar's army. These early immigrants were destined to be the vanguard of what would soon become the majority of immigrants entering this country. Most of these newcomers settled in large urban areas, in particular New York and Chicago, rather than spreading out across the country into rural areas, as previous immigrants had done. As a result, they were conspicuous.

The presence of these seemingly non-assimilative newcomers resulted in demands by some members of Congress to bring a halt to all immigration. The Depression of 1892, which was the most severe the country had ever experienced, forced the closing of thousands of businesses and more than a 100,000 workers were thrown out of their jobs. This spurred greater resentment towards the newcomers. The fact that anti-immigration legislation was an irrational response counted for little. Constituents called upon Congress to take some action to alleviate their economic plight, and this was the only answer the legislators could devise. Grover Cleveland, serving the second term of his split presidencies, vetoed the bill. It was only by one vote that Congress failed to override his veto. This was the first unsuccessful bill to limit immigration. The first nationality to be singled out for exclusion was the Chinese. Imported to this country by the developers of the western spur of the Union Pacific Railroad, they were seen as a threat to white labor once the line was completed. In 1882, Congress enacted the Chinese Exclusion Act, which not only forbade the Chinese to enter this country but also denied those already here the privilege of citizenship. A similar problem arose at the beginning of the twentieth century. This time, the group was the Japanese on the West Coast, who had acquired land and proved themselves to be more adept at farming it than their Caucasian counterparts. To meet the demands of the Californians without alienating the Japanese government, President Theodore Roosevelt negotiated an agreement whereby the United States officially would not discriminate against Japanese immigrants, but Japan would forbid any of its citizens to emigrate to this country. As a result, there would be a large influx of Japanese to the Hawaiian islands. From the beginning of the twentieth century and during all the years leading up to the First World War in 1914, more than a million immigrants would enter the United States annually. Placed in perspective, this mass immigration represented an addition of almost 20% to the existing US population. The ethnic makeup of the United States was undergoing a dramatic change. To cope with this, in 1907 Congress established a commission to study the subject. The results of the study, issued four years later, stressed the difficulty of the nation being able to assimilate the immigrants coming from southern and eastern Europe. It highlighted once again that the composition of the population was drawn largely from northwestern Europe and should retain that framework. The conclusion of the commission was that the national immigration policy of the government should be based on a quota system, taking into account the nationality of the immigrant. This time, in 1917, Congress was able to pass an immigration act despite President Woodrow Wilson's veto, invoking a literacy test as a method of restraining emigration from southern and eastern Europe. It also barred any emigration from Asia. But with the war in Europe still being played out, there was no necessity for concern over emigration.

Once the United States entered the war against the Germans in April 1917, the latent xenophobia first exhibited by the Know Nothing party against the Irish one hundred years before now was turned against the recent German immigrants, so that many of them changed their names. As far as some Americans were concerned, there was an enemy within the country. Congress responded by passing the Espionage Act. With US troops now in combat in France and sustaining casualties, Congress went on to pass the Sedition Act of 1918, effectively abridging free speech in this country.

It was the Bolshevik revolution in Russia in 1917, which precipitated the next attack on the policy of unlimited immigration. Americans had been exposed to anarchists for some time — notably, through the International Workers of the World and their tactics of using violence in order to attain their goals in strikes, and through the actions of Alexander Berkman who attempted to murder Henry Frick, the head of United

States Steel — but they were hardly prepared for the spate of bombings that began once the war was over. The Post Office confiscated 38 packages containing bombs, addressed to such high-profile Americans as Georgia Senator Thomas Hardwick, John D. Rockefeller, Chief Justice Oliver Wendell Holmes, and J.P. Morgan. Prior to these attempts by anarchists, Congress had enacted the Deportation Act of 1918. This piece of legislation authorized the deportation of any alien who was an anarchist; or who advocated the overthrow of the government by force or violence; or belonged to any organization whose avowed purpose met these criteria.

In June 1919, an Italian anarchist was killed by a bomb in front of the residence of Attorney General Alexander Mitchell Palmer. From his past record, Palmer appeared to be the last man to violate people's civil liberties. During his time in Congress, he had been an ardent supporter of women's suffrage and the right of labor to organize. But once violence touched his doorstep, he became determined to launch a crusade against radicals in the United States, by legal and illegal means. Palmer equated anarchists and Communists as being one and the same animal. In 1919, he hired as his assistant, a 24-year-old lawyer, J. Edgar Hoover. Hoover was named head of the Government Department of Investigations, a newly created division of the Justice Department. Hoover's basic function was to hire agents who would infiltrate subversive organizations and expose them before they could do any damage. Once Hoover had his assignment, he pursued it with diligence and speed. By December 1919, Hoover's agents had fingered 3,000 people who were either members of the fledgling Communist party or anarchists. Hoover then instructed agents of the Justice Department to conduct a series of raids and arrests on the evening of January 2, 1920. Known as Palmer's Raids, they resulted in the deportation of 246 radicals, among them Emma Goldman, the lover of Berkman, who convinced him to try to assassinate Henry Frick, and supposedly had convinced Leon Czolgosz to assassinate President William McKinley. She was one of the radicals deported to the Soviet Union.

Palmer's Red Scare convinced the newly elected Republican Congress that something had to be done to regulate immigration coming from eastern and southern Europe. The Immigration Act of 1921 limited entry to this country based on a formula of national origin reflected in the census of 1910. It was to remain in effect for three years, after which Congress would address the problem once again. That same year would see the last massive emigration of people from those sections of Europe. More than 805,000 would be admitted to this country.

Even though Big Business, the major supporter of the Republican party, was vehemently opposed to this legislation, Palmer's Red Scare was far more compelling to members of Congress. The world famous Sacco-Vanzetti case would add fuel to the fire. Nicolo Sacco and Bartolomeo Vanzetti, two Italian anarchists who had immigrated to this country, were accused of having killed the factory paymaster and a guard during a robbery in Braintree, Massachusetts on April 20, 1920. Both men were found guilty of murder despite the contention of the defendants' lawyers that the two men had been convicted not on evidence but by the fact that they were admitted anarchists. None of the cash from the robbery had been found in either of the defendant's homes; and while the appeals moved from one court to the next, a condemned criminal testified in 1925 that the robbery had been committed by a criminal group known as the Morelli gang. A committee of three looked into the evidence and decided that the trial had been fair. Thus the governor of Massachusetts refused to grant clemency. On April 23, 1927, the two men were executed.

It was thanks to the extreme amount of publicity generated by the Sacco-Vanzetti trial that when the temporary Immigration Act of 1921 expired in 1924, the National Origins Act was passed. With this legislation, all of Europe was placed under a system of quotas, with the total number of immigrants to be admitted fixed at 164,000. Furthermore, the quotas were not based on the census of 1910, when massive immigration from southern and eastern Europe had already taken place, but on census of 1890, when the initial emigration of southern and eastern Europeans had just begun. In 1929, the total number to be admitted underwent a further reduction. The restrictions against any Asians entering the country still remained in place. During the early years of the Depression, there was very little immigration. But with the rise to power of Adolph Hitler and his imposition of anti-Semitic laws, there was a massive effort by Jews to leave Germany. Despite the appeals of American Jewry to FDR to lift the quota and allow the 20,000 German-Jewish children sponsored by America Jews to enter this country, the President's response was that the quota had been filled. It was only at the end of the Second World War, when the horrors of the Holocaust had been exposed, that some exceptions were made. The much-despised McCarran-Walter Act, passed in 1952 despite the protests of liberals, did nothing to impede the post-war flow of immigrants to this country. Its focus was mainly on preventing the admission of Communists and Fascists. When 200,000 Hungarians fled to Austria, following the squelching of the Hungarian revolution by the Soviets, President Eisenhower made special exceptions for their admission to the United States. The same held true for Cubans under both Presidents Eisenhower and Kennedy.

Once Johnson had been elected President, he placed immigration reform high on the list of Great Society programs. After the usual debate and wrangling over unlimited versus a fixed number of immigrants to be admitted from Europe, Asia and Central/South America, the final number arrived at was set at 300,000 per year, with 120,000 from this hemisphere and 170,000 from Europe and Asia. Family members were given preference over those with occupational skills. The laws barring immigration from Asia and the Pacific were lifted. A quota of 10,000 was set aside for people fleeing communism and for immigrants from the Middle East. Any country automatically was allowed a minimum of 200 per year. However, there was a provision in the legislation that would permit far more than 300,000 to enter the country legally: citizens and legal aliens would be allowed to bring children, wives and husbands into the country, regardless of the allotted number. The new law would go into effect in three years. During the interim time, any unused quota from any nation would be placed in a general pool and could be drawn upon by any nation. The old formula, which had been in place for 40 years, limiting immigration to the country of origin, was dead and buried.

As would prove to be the case with the other programs of the Great Society, this immigration legislation had a far greater future impact than could be foreseen. Senator Robert Kennedy thought that perhaps 5,000 immigrants would arrive from India. By the mid-1990s, there were over half a million and still growing. The lifting of immigration restrictions turned out to be the salvation and the curse of the major metropolitan areas of this country. As Americans became more prosperous, they left the inner cities for the suburbs, creating a labor shortage. The new immigrants drove the taxis, waited on tables in the restaurants, or served as bus boys and dishwashers in hotels and restaurants. They would become the doormen and the janitors and handymen, as well as the maids and the nannies. They would perform all the menial jobs necessary to existence in a large city. And the better-educated and more motivated would elevate themselves as entrepreneurs or white collar workers. The Hispanic population is the fastest growing segment of US society, outstripping Blacks as the single largest minority in the nation. The second largest segment is from Asia and the Pacific islands. While the ideal of the melting pot has been achieved among most immigrants coming from Europe, it has yet to be attained in any substantial way by other nationalities or by Blacks.

Following the publication of a book by Rachel Carson, entitled *Silent Spring*, in the early 1960s, the growing problem of pollution became a priority issue. The book detailed how the industrial revolution had polluted the nation's waters and air. Carson, who had devoted her entire adult life to studying waterways and seas, had brought this problem to the attention of the US establishment through her book. But if any action was to be taken, it would be up to the Johnson administration and Congress. Here, government would have to fight industry interests and expand the reach of government still further into realms not envisioned by the framers of the Constitution.

Acts regulating clear air, clean water, endangered species, land and water conservation, and solid waste disposal eventually made their way through Congress and were signed into law by the President, but they fell far short of addressing the problems. This was the beginning of the ongoing clash that would take place between free-wheeling capitalism and a government ostensibly of the people, for the people and by the people. It was impossible to resolve then, and it is still a thorny issue today.

The legislation enacted during the Johnson administration was not limited to these major programs. To set in motion the wheels for a Great Society, there was far more legislation: an anti-poverty program for Appalachia; an excise tax reduction; a new administration within HEW to oversee the problems facing the elderly; expanded drug controls; rent supplements for low-income families; a program designed to encourage regional development; a new Cabinet post for Housing and Urban Development; a new National Endowment for the Arts and one for Humanities; and dozens of other programs were shepherded through Congress. In his first year as an elected President, Johnson had shown that there was no replacement for experience. The years he had spent in the House, and as majority leader of far more cantankerous Senate, had not been in vain. Some of the legislation passed was initiated by Kennedy and his liberal advisors, but the "poster boy" President did not possess the insider's knowledge that formed the basis of Johnson's success.

There was nothing tragic about Lyndon Johnson's presidency, as some of his biographers contend, going so far as to use that word in the title of their biographies. Had he stayed the course he would have been nominated by his party and would have defeated Nixon. Whether he would have had the foresight or the courage to recognize Communist China is questionable. Johnson arrived at the decision not to seek reelection because he was physically and mentally exhausted. Those who contend that his presidency was marred by his expansion of the war in Vietnam refuse to admit, for one reason or another, that he had inherited the war from Kennedy. Nor was it Kennedy's war. It was just another facet of the Cold War, which led to the prosperity that has enabled this nation to support Johnson's Great Society.

Chapter 9. The Renegade Republican: The Nixon Presidency

The man known as Tricky Dick to his detractors possessed all the talent and abilities to become one of America's greatest Presidents, except for one failing: he was incapable of trusting anyone other than his wife and children. Yet he was the first President in modern US history to capture 49 out of the 50 states when he ran for a second term. The best word to describe Richard Nixon is the French word *méfiance*. Difficult to translate, the word literally means mistrust of the motives of other people. But, in French, *méfiance* also connotes "get the other guy before he gets me." Nixon's *méfiance* about individuals would propel him to national fame and launch his political career when he alone was convinced that Alger Hiss — testifying before the House Un-American Activities Committee in 1948 — was lying when he said he had never met Whittaker Chambers. Hiss, with his credentials, appeared to be too perfect to ever be a Soviet spy, but in Nixon's mind, those credentials were the attributes that would make a perfect secret agent.

Nixon yearned to be a great President who would leave a legacy that would establish his presidency as one of the greatest in American history. At the same time, his political base was narrow minded and locked into economic and ideological principles that made no sense in the second half of the twentieth century.

Nixon's view of the Cold War was at odds with those of his supporters. Where they took literally his anti-Communist rhetoric, Nixon merely used it for his political purposes. He was well aware that any direct confrontation with the Soviet Union was out of the question as long as the USSR possessed equivalent atomic weaponry. He was also the second Cold War President to realize that the Soviet Union feared America's military power far more than most Americans realized. He had arrived at that understanding during the eight years he served as Dwight Eisenhower's Vice President. He used that knowledge in his negotiations with Russian leader Leonid Brezhnev and with Communist China's Mao Tse-tung. In all Nixon's dealings with the leaders of the two major Communist nations, he dealt from strength, not as an equal partner. He was neither boastful nor apologetic. As a successful poker player during his service with the Navy during the Second World War, he never attempted to bluff. He didn't have to. Once he had taken the unorthodox step of recognizing China, he knew that from then on the Soviet Union was on the defensive. He exploited that fact to bring an end to the war in Vietnam. Nixon was aware that an honorable peace with North Vietnam only could be attained when the source of its military and economic supplies could be cut off. He also knew that South Vietnam's President Nguyen Van Thieu never would agree to a peace treaty until he was assured that the Soviet Union and Communist China were part of the final settlement.

One of the curious aspects of the Nixon presidency was his close relationship with Henry Kissinger, first as his National Security Advisor, and after Nixon's first term, as both his Secretary of State and the head of NSC. From the taped conversations in the Oval Office, finally released after Nixon was forced to resign from the presidency in order to avoid impeachment, it appeared that Nixon was a virulent anti-Semite. His constant denigration of Jews and their influence in the media appeared to be proof positive that Nixon hated and feared Jews. Yet it was not only his close relationship with Kissinger that belied the accusation but the fact that his personal counsel, Leonard Garment, was Jewish as well, as was one of his major speech writers, William Safire, who had been with Nixon from the time he was Vice President. Moreover, the man who was originally responsible for elevating Nixon from a Congressman to a Senator was Murray Chotiner, a Jew from California. Nixon's attitude toward Jews was as complicated as his attitude towards the conservative elements of the Republican party. There is no doubt that Nixon's attitude towards Jews, especially those in the media, was colored by their attitude toward him. With his initial hard-line approach to Communists and fellow travelers, he alienated a notable percentage of influential Jews in New York City and Hollywood who had supported the general aims of communism, believing it would put an end to anti-Semitism. They contended that his persecution of Communists in government was a subtle form of anti-Semitism. Jews in the media were among Alger Hiss's prime defenders. This may sound strange to the non-Jewish readers who are unfamiliar with the insecurity of many Jewish intellectuals and of those German-born American Jews who had become financially successful in America and were vehemently opposed to the state of Israel, fearing it might create a backlash against American Jews. Among the leaders of that movement was the Ochs family, the owners of *The New York Times*. Even though a few hundred thousand Jews were desperate to find a homeland in Israel, *The New York Times*, in its slanted news and editorial columns, viewed the creation of a Zionist state as a threat to their status as patriotic Americans. Where Nixon had always been pro-Zionist, these fully assimilated Jews felt that a Jewish state might bring into question their loyalty to the United States.

Once Nixon achieved renown as a member of the House Un-American Activities Committee, among whose leading members there were some suspected of harboring anti-Semitic sentiments, axiomatically he was thrown in with the others. The committee's initial attack on Hollywood — when those who were called to testify and name Communists or fellow travelers in the industry instead took the Fifth Amendment — did not result in their prosecution by the government. The famous "Hollywood Ten" were cashiered by the Jewish executives who owned the movie studios, who feared an anti-Semitic backlash if the accused were allowed to remain in their jobs. Many of the "Hollywood Ten" weren't even Jewish. Yet many liberal Jews, especially in New York City, were convinced that Nixon harbored anti-Semitic sentiments. Even though they appeared to be accepted as Americans in this post-war world, they still harbored insecurity and were alert to any possible threat of anti-Semitism. To them, Nixon epitomized the narrow-minded Anglo-Saxon who, while not overtly anti-Semitic, accepted such sentiments. They blamed Nixon for the rise of McCarthyism. Nixon viewed their hostility towards him as unjustified. To a large extent, this was true. Israel had no better friend in the White House than Nixon. Jewish liberals dominated almost every aspect of New York City from the arts to the media to popular culture to its politics, and Nixon's attitude towards the state of

Israel did not necessarily coincide with their own. Many of them viewed Israel's arrogance as fostering anti-Semitism. A certain percentage of these Jewish liberals expected Israel to return the Arab territories gained in the Six Day War. In other words, no matter what Nixon did or didn't do, he was their number one enemy once Senator Joe McCarthy had died.

When Nixon finally realized his dream of the presidency, after defeating Hubert Humphrey in a close election, his focus was on how to bring the Vietnamese War to a successful end. Not only were the North Vietnamese unwilling to enter into negotiations other than on their terms of an unconditional surrender, but Thieu's South Vietnamese government was just as adamant in refusing to promote and enforce the reforms that would make his regime more palatable to the American public and justify the war itself. If South Vietnam was as much a dictatorship as North Vietnam, then what was the purpose of supporting Thieu's regime? Thieu was shrewd enough to understand that Nixon could not abandon South Vietnam without destroying his presidency and his chance for reelection. Nixon viewed his first job to be the reduction of the US forces in Vietnam. He mistakenly believed this move would take the immediate pressure off his presidency and allow him the time to arrive at some sort of negotiation with the North and South Vietnamese. But the general concept that a newly-elected President would receive a six-month honeymoon from his critics did not apply to Nixon when he took office. In fact, his election only served to intensify the animosity of his critics. Moreover, the leadership in the Kremlin had long subscribed to the view that Nixon epitomized the hard-line anti-Communist warrior who was determined to defeat the Soviet Union and its system of government. Meanwhile, US casualties continued to mount, despite the reduction of forces in Vietnam. It soon became more apparent that a drastic move was essential. Unless he could resolve the Vietnamese War, which was dividing American society, the blame for its continuation would rest on Nixon's shoulders.

It is difficult to pinpoint the moment when Nixon made the decision to enter into negotiations with the leadership of the Peoples Republic of China. Armed fighting was taking place along the border between China and the Soviet Union. Then there was the story of the members of the US ping-pong team visiting Tokyo, who were invited to China to participate in a ping-pong tournament with the Chinese, the first break in the hostility and enforced isolation between the two nations. Far more important were the hints from the leadership in Pakistan that Mao Tse-tung was not averse to establishing relations with the United States. Nixon, as *méfiant* as ever, still saw this potential opening for dialogue with the Chinese Communists as the necessary first step toward extricating the United States from the war in Vietnam, and at the same time, as a potential club to achieve a meaningful arms reduction treaty with the Soviet Union. He was aware that his reputation as the hard-line anti-Communist would serve him well if the Chinese leadership was sincere in ending the long-term animosity between the two nations.

He viewed Kissinger's belief in *realpolitik* as conforming to his own viewpoint. The only man Nixon trusted to bring this initial contact to a meaningful fruition was Kissinger. His secret mission to China is well known. Nixon's confidence in Kissinger was more than justified by the results. Nixon's triumphant visit to Peking in 1972, televised in color to the entire world, was the highlight of his presidency. Nixon had achieved what no other US politician had dared to attempt during the 18 years of estrangement between the US and China. While his conservative base was appalled, some of them rationalizing it by blaming it on the influence of Kissinger, the attitude of the majority of the American people was to view Nixon as a hero. Moreover, this initial step of Nixon alarmed the leadership of the Soviet Union. For the first time since the inception of the Cold War, the Soviet Union was threatened by a possible alliance between the United States and the largest Communist nation in the world. Later that year, Nixon and Brezhnev would sign the finalization of the first meaningful treaty on arms reduction, the SALT I agreement.

Nixon, despised by Democrats and liberals, had accomplished what no Democrat had dared to contemplate. By recognizing Communist China, he had forced the Soviet Union to enter serious negotiations with the United States. Far more important to Nixon was that he now had two allies that for their own reasons would enable him to bring to an end the Vietnam War. Both nations, for different reasons, were anxious to cement their relations with the US. It was their pressure that forced Hanoi to come to the bargaining table and enter into serious negotiations to end the conflict. When at the last minute the North Vietnamese balked at arriving at a final agreement, Nixon was not afraid to bomb the major harbor of Haiphong, knowing that the bombs might strike Soviet ships in the harbor. Although the Soviet Union protested vigorously, it did nothing more. By Christmas 1972, following Nixon's incredible reelection victory, Kissinger could report that the North Vietnamese were prepared to sign an agreement that would include the repatriation of US prisoners of war as well as the end of the conflict and the division of North and South Korea into two sovereign nations. Nixon believed he could maintain the stability of the South Vietnamese government once the last of the US forces were withdrawn, and he might have done so but for Watergate and his forced resignation from the presidency. Kissinger was far more doubtful and believed that the government of Thieu would collapse because of its corruption and its unwillingness to deal with the problems of the majority of the population, the landless peasant class.

In terms of domestic affairs, as a candidate Nixon had hewed to the conservative line of the Taft-led Republicans and it was expected that he would take the same approach once he was in office. That was a result of the media having pigeon-hold Nixon as another Republican reactionary. In the same way he would shock the conservative wing of the Republican party, as well as the liberals and the media, by his recognition of Communist China, he would dismay conservatives and astound liberals by his approach to domestic affairs. Nixon had no agenda other than to burnish his reputation as President. While he was in Congress, both as a two-term Representative and for two years as a Senator before becoming Vice President, he had adhered to the basic philosophy of the Republican party of achieving a balanced budget. Like Eisenhower, Nixon was an advocate of America assuming the responsibility of leading the effort to prevent Soviet aggression in the non-Communist world. Unlike Eisenhower, however, he understood the popularity of Johnson's programs with the American public. Thus, although the leaders of the Democrat-dominated Congress were certain he would make an effort to dismantle the programs of Johnson's Great Society, when Nixon took office in January 1969 he surprised not only his supporters but his political opponents as well — as had been the case throughout his political career.

Nixon's entrance into national politics was purely accidental. Upon his discharge from the Navy as a Lieutenant Commander, he returned to California to resume a law practice in a small firm. Seeking a candidate to run against a popular Democratic incumbent, that state's Republican leadership drafted Nixon haphazardly. With his exposure of Alger Hiss as a Soviet agent, this freshman Congressman was elevated into a national figure of such stature that when he ran for reelection, he faced no opposition. Yet Nixon campaigned as intensively as if he were running behind in the polls. Nixon had found his calling. This inner burning for success and fame, which had marked his academic career, now would be played out in the national political arena.

With the perjury conviction of Alger Hiss at his second trial, Nixon's initial judgment had been vindicated. The announcement by the popular Democratic Senator from California, Sheridan Downey, that he would not run for reelection left the Senate race wide open. Nixon was the obvious choice for the Republicans. His rival for the seat was Helen Gahagan Douglas, a protégé of Eleanor Roosevelt, and the wife of movie star Melvin Douglas. She had been elected to Congress from a district that encompassed Hollywood. Downey refused to endorse her. It was not Nixon who first brought up the charges that she was soft on communism, but rather her Democratic opponent in the primary, who went so far as to claim she was a Communist sympathizer. And it was a Los Angeles newspaper that first dubbed her the *Pink Lady*. Despite the savage attacks, she readily defeated her opponent in the primary. Now she faced her major trial, defeating Nixon. To the liberal wing of the Democratic party, still convinced that Hiss was innocent, Nixon had become its number one nemesis. Even when Senator McCarthy would replace Nixon as the principal *bete noire* of the Democratic party, Nixon continued to be viewed as the progenitor of the label that the Democrats had been soft on communism and Communists. What would have ordinarily been a race confined to the voters of California took on all the trappings of a crusade against Nixon. Liberals on both the east and west coasts raised huge sums of money to defeat him. Nixon won the election by a large margin. It was the last election he would win on his own until he ran for reelection as President in 1972.

Nixon's victory in the 1968 presidential campaign was largely a result of the third party candidacy of Governor George Wallace, whose segregationist views resonated not only in the South but among white unionist voters in the North who ordinarily supported the Democratic ticket. Nixon was not one who concerned himself with such petty details. Once he had been elected President, he now was his own man. He would pay lip service to the conservative wing of his party, but he intended to conduct his administration as he saw fit. In addition to being a pragmatist, he was an opportunist He understood that while Johnson's legacy had been tarnished by his expansion of Kennedy's war in Vietnam, he was still revered as the creator of the Great Society, which had transformed America through his social programs, and as the President who had liberated the American Negro from his second-class citizenship by pushing through the first meaningful civil rights legislation. Carrying Johnson's initiative a step further, Nixon appointed Arthur Fletcher as Assistant Secretary of Labor. Fletcher, a Negro and a life-long Republican, was determined to break down the labor-union-established barriers that prevented Negro employment in industry. He devised regulations whereby federal funds were withheld from contractors working on federal projects if they were not in compliance with fair employment practices and did not set specific goals for hiring minorities. Fletcher's so-called Revised Philadelphia Plan was the first time that affirmative action was adopted as a federal mandate.

This was only the first step Nixon would take in his effort to preempt the image established by the Democrats as being the only party that initiated progressive legislation for the majority of the American people. As a result of the growing threat of inflation on the incomes of older Americans living on Social Security, he proposed and Congress enacted the first legislation that indexed Social Security benefits to the Cost of Living Adjustments established by the Department of Commerce. Not only would these COLAs be applied to Social Security recipients but to members of the military and others collecting government pensions. Nixon even went one step further. He asked Congress to enact legislation that came to be known as SSI or Supplemental Security Income. The monies for this legislation would not be funded by the Social Security Trust Fund but would be drawn from the federal budget. The purpose of SSI was to provide funds for food, clothing and shelter to the aged and disabled who were unable to survive on the benefits provided by their Social Security monthly checks.

Nor did Nixon's social legislation stop there. His most ambitious measure was the creation of the Environmental Protection Agency. While the goals of this legislation were admirable, there were unforeseen consequences: they increased the cost of doing business in the US, which ran counter to the basic philosophy of the Republican party. Nixon, however, was more concerned with his own legacy than with Republican dogma. Strange as it might appear to some liberals, it was Nixon who advocated gun control and even proposed a minimum income for all Americans. He was also the first President to initiate a federal drug policy.

While Nixon was emulating Johnson by adding to the Great Society programs and was immersed in bringing the war in Vietnam to a successful conclusion, he and his advisors were less successful in managing the overall US economy. When Johnson was able to enact the Kennedy tax cut in 1964, the budget deficit in 1965 showed a sharp decline because of the ensuing increase in federal revenues. (See Appendix, Table 6.) But in 1966, when Johnson began the military buildup in Vietnam, despite a major increase in revenues of $14 billion, the budget deficit began to escalate again. By fiscal 1967, even with $18 billion more flowing into the Treasury, the budget deficit totaled almost $9 billion. But it was in 1968, when Johnson heeded General Westmoreland's demand for 534,000 troops that the budget deficit got out of hand, totaling more than $25 billion. Accustomed to almost no inflation, the steady increase in the inflation rate from 2.9% in 1966, to 3.1% the following year, and 4.2% in 1968, only served to convince those who were opposed to the war, the upper middle class, determined to avoid the draft, that the nation could not afford guns and butter. (See Appendix, Table 7.) In fact, it was the budget deficits that were putting butter on the table. In the last budget that Johnson submitted to Congress, that of 1969, he called for a temporary 10% across-the-board tax increase to reduce the deficit. Even with the tax increase, revenues coming into the Treasury soared by $34 billion, and for the first time since 1960, the budget showed a surplus (of $3.242 billion). Nixon's plan to reduce troop levels began once he took office in January 1969, and the following year revenues increased by $6 billion; even so, there was a deficit of $2.842 billion in 1970. On the other hand, the rate of inflation seemed to be getting out of control. From 4.2% in 1968, it increased to 5.5% in 1969, and 5.7% in 1970. Even though the troop withdrawals continued in fiscal 1971, and this was reflected in a decrease in defense spending of $3 billion, the budget deficit soared to $23 billion. Organized labor, in particular, with its three-year contracts that couldn't be renegotiated for another two years, descended upon the White House, demanding that Nixon institute wage and price controls since the war in Vietnam was still in progress. Nixon called in Arthur Burns, chairman of the Federal Reserve, and John Connelly, the lifelong Democrat who had switched to the Republican party and had been named Treasury Secretary by Nixon. Since Connelly knew next to nothing about finance, even though he had been Governor of Texas, and Nixon knew even less, it was Burns who suggested a temporary six-month imposition of wage and price controls in order to stem the inflation from getting further out of hand. Appearing on national television, Nixon announced Phase I of his program to rein in inflation. There never was a Phase II.

At the same time that Nixon was wrestling with how to control inflation, a far more significant event occurred that would alter the economic system of the United States and the rest of the non-Communist world forever. As previously noted, it was the decision forced upon the Nixon administration to abandon the artificial gold standard that had been in place since the Bretton Woods conference of 1944. The Nixon administration would have to bite the bullet and announce to the world that it would no longer redeem gold for dollars. The announcement to the world's financial market was like a seismic shock that registered 10 on the Richter scale. The world of gold as the last means of exchange, which nations had lived with since time immemorial, had been swallowed up in the financial earthquake and disappeared. Immediately, the central banks of other nations readjusted the value of their currency upward, in relation to the dollar. The value of the dollar now would float freely on the international market. But despite the despair of the Cassandras, the world did not come to an end. Free trade between nations continued much as before. The real aftershock, which had nothing to do with the dollar or gold, was still two years away. Although inflation had declined from 4.4% to 3.2% in 1972, the Nixon administration was still plagued by the ever growing deficits in the federal budget. Military expenditures were no longer responsible; by 1972, the US military presence in Vietnam had been drawn down to 69,000 troops. Rather, the increasing cost of Johnson's Great Society and the additions Nixon had added were the cause. Nor was there any indication that these expenditures could be reduced in future years because they were all mandated by Congressional legislation.

All of Nixon's domestic initiatives pale when compared with the fundamental change he initiated and saw enacted by Congress — the creation of a professional army to replace the draft. The rationale behind Nixon's original decision to end the draft was the work of Martin Anderson, an economics professor at Columbia University, and a free market economist who joined Nixon's administration. According to Gary North, who heard the details from Anderson, the idea for an all-volunteer army was first broached to Nixon during the 1968 presidential campaign.

On the campaign plane, Anderson was asked by Nixon if there was any policy recommendation that might make a difference in the campaign. Anderson's answer was "an all-volunteer army," and he followed up with a 17-page report on the subject. Later, when a *New York Times* reporter asked Nixon what he intended to do about the draft, Nixon replied: I think we should do away with the draft and go to an all-volunteer force. Following up on the media attention the interview received, Nixon outlined the details of this proposal in a radio address two weeks before the election.

After just three months in office, in March 1969, he appointed a 15-man commission to study the possibilities of ending the draft without endangering the security of the nation. The Gates Commission report was released less than a year later. The recommendation was unanimous; it was time to end the draft. As to be expected, the immediate reaction of the Joint Chiefs of Staff was negative, as were the opinions voiced by Melvin Laird, Nixon's Secretary of Defense, and Henry Kissinger, his National Security Advisor. But a young congressman from Illinois, Donald Rumsfeld, immediately introduced legislation supporting the proposal. Although hearings were held in the House and Senate, his proposal went nowhere. But in May 1973 when the draft came up for renewal, Congress enacted legislation officially ending the draft. Today it can be seen that the all-volunteer army led to the development of a high-tech military. In societal terms, the end of the draft signified something deeper: it deepened the national divide between the affluent and the less affluent, as those who choose the army for a career are predominantly lower-middle-class or poor.

In 1970, Egypt's Nasser, the idol of the Arab masses, died of natural causes. He was replaced as head of state by Anwar al-Sadat. Ever since the disaster of the Six Day War in 1967, the Soviet Union had been supplying Egypt with aircraft and tanks to replace those destroyed in that war. Moreover, Soviet military advisors were omnipresent in Egypt. Sadat, along with the Syrian leader Hafiz al-Assad, in conjunction with Soviet military advisors, had been planning a joint attack against Israel for a year. They chose the holiest day of the Jewish religion, Yom Kippur, the Day of Atonement, to launch their two-pronged attack, rightly assuming that the Israeli defensive forces would be lightly manned and caught off guard. Heat-seeking missiles, manned by Russians, were destroying the vaunted Israeli Air Force. Israeli leaders made a call to

Washington to replace their lost aircraft and tanks — Israel wanted to be assured that its equipment losses would be replaced. Whether Nixon was pressured by Kissinger, as some contend, or his judgment was clouded by the pressure of events from the Watergate investigation, the President ordered the Defense Department to make round-the-clock deliveries.

To the Arab nations belonging to OPEC, this US decision to rearm the Israelis turned the fortunes of war. In an emergency meeting, OPEC initiated a boycott of oil shipments to the United States. On the international market for oil futures, the reaction was immediate. The price of a barrel of oil escalated from $3 to $7 overnight. (See Appendix, Figure 1.) The oil crisis would send the world's economies as well as the economy of the United States into a period of inflation that lasted until 1983. By the end of 1973, inflation had increased from 3.2% to 6.2%. By 1974, after Nixon had resigned and Gerald Ford became President, it had soared to 11%, with the worst yet to come. Along with inflation came a rise in unemployment. (See Appendix, Table 7.)

At the time of Nixon's resignation, few recognized the implications of the abandonment of the gold standard and the existence of the oil crisis in changing the economy of the United States and the world. No longer tied to an arbitrary fixed value, the economy of the United States was able to weather the oil crisis. And, its continuing strength enabled President Ronald Reagan to force the Soviet Union to spend its wartime economy into bankruptcy. With US currency so widely diffused, it could not be replaced by any other; the dollar could remain supreme no matter how large the debt accumulated by the nation.

Watergate and the events leading up to Nixon's resignation have been more than amply covered in one book after another. The only thing his critics have overlooked is his rationale. The one characteristic of Nixon was his consistency. Even though every poll showed Nixon defeating any Democratic opponent in the 1972 presidential race, he remained the same Nixon who had campaigned for his second term in Congress as though he faced an opponent when in fact his name was the only one on the ballot. It was the same *méfiance* which had catapulted him to being a celebrity with his exposure of Hiss that would lead to Watergate. Nixon never trusted anyone, including his own pollsters.

CHAPTER 10. FRUSTRATION: THE PRESIDENCIES OF FORD AND CARTER

Every President in the twentieth century, beginning with Herbert Hoover, has left to his successor in the White House a legacy of an insoluble national problem. In the case of Hoover, it was the Great Depression; in that of Roosevelt, the Cold War with the Soviet Union; Truman's gift to Eisenhower was the Korean War; and Eisenhower, in turn, left the problem of Castro and Cuba to Kennedy, who left to Johnson the Vietnam War, which Johnson handed over to Nixon. Having successfully resolved that problem, Nixon handed over a new one, which plagued the presidencies of Ford and Carter — the oil crisis of the 1970s and the ensuing runaway inflation that threatened every facet of the economy.

On November 14, 1972, the Dow Jones average rose 6.09 points to pass the magic 1,000 mark, hitting 1003. At the end of that month, the US troop withdrawal from Vietnam was substantially complete, with only 16,000 Army advisors and administrators remaining there. The future looked rosy indeed: it was generally believed by the US business community that the previous budget deficits of the war years would begin to decline and by 1975 would fall into the low-single digits, delivering the "peace dividend." Ignoring the reality behind the economic boom of the wartime period — the ever growing federal deficits that were the force behind the prosperity — US business continued to act as though the boom would last forever. Corporate executives, their eyes focused on their stock options, threw all caution to the wind during the following year. The important thing was to show growth in sales and profits to Wall Street if the price of the corporation's stock was to advance. The large retailers, as concerned with the price of their stock as all businessmen were, increased their inventories above normal. In 1973, they planned for the biggest Christmas on record. But the day after Thanksgiving, normally the biggest retail day of the year, sales were disappointing. As Christmas sales failed to meet projections and worse yet fell behind the previous year's figures, the controllers at major department stores stepped in and called a halt to all purchases not already placed.

Retail sales are the most important barometer of the health of a nation's economy; at that time, they accounted for about two-thirds of the nation's GDP. As goes retail, so goes the nation's suppliers to retail and their suppliers as well. By spring 1974, while the eyes of the nation were focused on the impending impeachment of Nixon, the economy had entered a recession. As the year progressed, there were massive layoffs as firms tried to bring their inventories in line with market demands. Mills and factories were being shut down in order to reduce companies' overhead.

What had happened? In 1973, the deficit was $14.9 billion, which was about $8.5 billion less than the previous year, and in 1974, it dipped to $6.1 billion. (See Appendix, Table 6.) The deficit was plunging downward, and the economy with it. And, military spending had nothing to do with it. In 1973, defense expenditures were only $2.5 million less than the previous year, and in 1974, they increased to $79.3 million — reflecting the institution of the voluntary armed services in 1973. (See Appendix, Table 4.) Yet, throughout 1973, corporations were more focused on the price of their stock than on the inventories they were accumulating, which exacerbated the recession.

At the end of 1973, the elevation in the price of a barrel of crude oil, the result of the Yom Kippur War, began to affect the economy and fuel the recession. (See Appendix, Figure 1.) This was reflected in the index for inflation. From 3.2% in 1972, it had almost doubled, to 6.2%, the following year, and averaged 11% in 1974. (See Appendix, Table 7.) The inflation caused by the rise in oil prices took Wall Street completely by surprise, and the one thing Wall Street cannot tolerate is an economic event that has no precedent. The bear market began. Stock prices on the NYSE started to decline in 1973 and continued to fall throughout 1974. By

December 6, 1974, the Dow Jones average closed at a 12-year low of 577.60. It was the worst bear market since the 1930s. The purchasing power of the American public had gradually eroded as a result of the inflation, and the artificial bloom was off the roses. For 10 years Americans had been living in a world of economic fantasy, first fueled by the war in Vietnam and later by the programs of the Great Society. In 1974 and for the next seven years, they would experience a new kind of inflation over which no administration had any control — the growing cost of imported oil, which the economy required in order to survive.

Economists were bewildered. Alan Greenspan, then Chairman of President Ford's Council of Economic Advisors, was not alone in calling for a return to the gold standard. But despite classic economic theory, the world could not go home again. If the world's economy was to continue to expand, it could not rely on a limited supply of gold. The emergence of the dollar as the world's currency for commerce between nations would allow the world's economies to expand ad infinitum. Thanks to the dollar, the industrial nations would eventually be able to absorb the increases in the price of crude oil. As for the stock option, which had contributed to the initial onset of the recession, it was far from dead. It would return once the oil crisis was resolved and push the Dow Jones average into heights never before believed possible. It would lead to the consolidation of industries and the move towards off-shore production in order to gain the advantage of price and growth. It would abet the bull market of the 1980s and 1990s as well as that of the twenty-first century. It was the passport that opened the door to today's multi-millionaires and billionaires.

In 1973, Vice President Spiro Agnew had been forced to resign from office in order to avoid prosecution for taking bribes from contractors in Baltimore. Under the 25th Amendment to the Constitution, the President could appoint a successor to that office, provided the nomination was approved by both houses of Congress. If he didn't make an appointment, the next in line for the presidency was the Democratic Speaker of the House, Carl Albert. Nixon knew that one candidate, Gerald Ford, Republican minority leader of the House, stood the best chance of being ratified by Congress. Nixon — with his back against the wall, and knowing but not yet ready to admit that his days as President were numbered — called in Albert and Mike Mansfield, the Senate's Democratic Majority leader, who confirmed that Ford's nomination would be ratified. On August 9, 1974, to avoid certain impeachment, Nixon resigned his presidency and Gerald Ford was sworn in as the next President. For eight months while the country was mired in a recession, Nixon, immersed in his own troubles, had taken no steps to resolve the economic problem facing the nation. The country had been adrift without a chief executive.

Gerald Ford's basic qualifications for his new role as President were that he was accepted as an honest man, and after 25 years in Congress he was intimately familiar with the workings of that institution. Other than those two important and necessary traits, no one had the vaguest idea as to how he would perform in his new role. Since he possessed no experience in foreign affairs, it was assumed that he would maintain in office Nixon's Secretary of State and National Security Advisor, Henry Kissinger. He was one of the few intimate figures in the Nixon entourage who had been kept clear of the Watergate cover up. Because of Kissinger's extreme visibility, most Americans viewed him as the architect behind the country's recognition of Communist China and the Vietnam peace accords that were signed in Paris; thus, they assumed that the nation's foreign policy would be in firm hands. With his famous shuttle diplomacy he had negotiated the peaceful withdrawal of Israeli troops during the Yom Kippur War and prevented the conflict from developing into an armed confrontation with the Russians. The major question remained: how would Ford cope with the recession, the inflation now resulting from the sharp increase in the price of oil, and the growing unemployment.

Most men who aspire to the presidency possess an oversized ego and a firm belief that they are men of destiny. Ford, by contrast, had the office thrust upon him. Based on discussions with Nixon when Ford accepted the vice presidency, Ford assumed that Nixon was innocent. It is hard to believe that a man sitting in the office of the presidency would destroy his legacy over a petty burglary. Moreover, he admired Nixon and what he had accomplished while in office. A month after taking office, Ford almost destroyed his own presidency by extending a presidential pardon to Nixon. The only President ever called to testify before a congressional committee, Ford dissipated some of the anger directed against him and his action by his candor. Above all, Ford was honest to a fault. He explained to the committee that before he was asked to become Vice President, he had been approached by Nixon's then Chief of Staff, Alexander Haig, who asked whether, if he were offered the vice presidency, he would pardon Nixon. Ford admitted that it took him a few days before he answered in the negative. On the other hand, he was naïve enough to accede to Nixon's request, once he had pardoned him, to turn over the audio tapes that had led to the President's resignation. Fortunately, Nixon's request was blocked by the Special Prosecutor, Leon Jaworski, and the tapes remained the property of the federal government. Ford's explanation for his pardon of Nixon was logical and practical: if Ford was to function as President, Watergate had to be put behind him and the American public, and was better left to the history books than to the current political arena. His action did not cost him the presidential election of 1976, as some have contended. Most Americans were more concerned with inflation, the growing deficit, and the sluggish US economy.

At the time Ford took the presidential oath, Haig had become the *de facto* President of the United States. When Ford assumed the presidency, even though a group of friends and confidantes had been assembled to help him make the transition, he was still completely dependent upon Haig to familiarize him with the day-to-day operations of the White House. Haig, as a member of Kissinger's National Security Staff, had been drafted by Nixon to become Chief of Staff once he fired H. R. Haldemann and John Erlichman. While Haig served a purpose during the initial months of the Ford presidency, Ford's needs were different from Nixon's. The new President had no experience as an executive. Where Nixon's style was to run a tight, disciplined organization with limited access to the President, Ford preferred to delegate authority to the members of his Cabinet and his economic advisors. He finally dispatched Haig to NATO as Supreme Allied Commander. To replace him as Chief of Staff, Ford chose a young Republican ex-congressman, Donald Rumsfeld, who had worked for Nixon for a brief period before his impeachment. Rumsfeld possessed all the efficiency and discipline of Haig and Haldemann without projecting the air of a commanding officer. Rumsfeld, as the public would learn 30 years later, combined confidence in his own judgment with the ability to smile.

The basic problem facing Ford in fall 1974 was not his staff but the recession, which seemed to be growing worse. The price of oil, vital for industrial purposes and transportation, was climbing upward with a vengeance, a further blow to an economy already staggering from a recession. Even worse, Ford's key economic advisor, Alan Greenspan, seemed not to have the vaguest notion, nor did any of the others, as to why the economy had slipped into a recession, which was deepening rather than improving. Economic textbooks could not provide an answer because never before in recorded history had industrial economies become so dependent upon a single commodity for which there was no replacement. Without a sufficient and steady supply of oil, the economy of the US and every other industrialized economy would come to a screeching halt. It was as simple as that. Oil had become the oxygen that allowed every economy to breathe. No matter what the cost or the inflation that would result from its escalating price, the industrial world couldn't survive without it. Moreover, Ford was as blind as his economic advisors about the cause for the steady rise in inflation. He viewed inflation as an abstraction rather than the direct result of the price of imported oil more than doubling. His initial program was one of austerity as a means of defeating inflation. He wanted to put a cap on the federal budget; to impose a $5 billion surtax on corporations; and to increase personal income taxes. In his mind, and that of his economic advisors, taking those steps would soak up the excess money in circulation that was the driving force behind the inflation. In place of increasing the purchasing power of business and the public, he wanted to decrease it, thereby adding to the growing unemployment figures.

To rally the American public, Ford proposed a consumer campaign he called *Whip Inflation Now*, complete with a red, white and blue button printed with the letters WIN. It was a short-lived campaign. As a fiscally conservative Republican, Ford was appalled by the growing budget deficits that were adding to the national debt. The programs, mandated by Congress under the Johnson and Nixon presidencies, were the main culprit. Between 1974 and 1976, the cost of funding Human Resources increased from $135 billion to $256 billion. (A sizeable amount of that increase, $52 billion, was a result of Congress changing the date of the federal fiscal year from July 1, to October 1, extending the 1976 fiscal year by three months.) But the Human Resources budget was not alone in adding to the deficit. During that same period of time, Physical Resources jumped from $25 billion to $48 billion, with $9 billion a result of extending the fiscal year. Not all of these increases were the result of the expansion of the Johnson and Nixon social and medical programs. Inflation had to be factored in as well. Nevertheless, as the population continued to age and more advances were made in medicine and pharmacology, the demands for health care continued to grow. In 1974, the rate of inflation hit 11%; in 1975, with the economy gradually adjusting to the high cost of oil, inflation declined to 9.1% and by 1976 it had dropped to 5.8%. While inflation appeared to be coming under control, the unemployment rate had surfaced as a major problem. From a rate of 5.6% in 1974, it had climbed to 8.5% in 1975 and still remained a major problem in 1976 at 7.7%. (See Appendix, Table 7.)

It soon became obvious that Ford's nostrums were not the answer to the recession. Worker layoffs in every industry continued to accelerate. The unemployment rate remained a serious problem with no solution in sight. Greenspan conceded that he had no idea how deep the recession could advance or how long it would last. It was obvious that what the economy needed was an infusion of money to stimulate business and not Ford's notion that tightening the belt was the solution. Furthermore, in January 1975 Ford would be delivering his first State of the Union message to Congress. All of his economic advisors convened for a conference with the President, including Federal Reserve Chairman Arthur Burns. Once again the question of the growing deficit was raised, but absent an agreement among his economic advisors, it was decided to put off any decision until the New Year. Rumsfeld, on the other hand, a workaholic, was tying his future career to the President. (Later, in 1975, when Ford was prepared to make some changes in his Cabinet, Rumsfeld would convince Ford to name him Secretary of Defense, replacing Nixon's appointee, James Schlesinger.) Ford postponed any final decision on what approach to take to bring the economy out of its growing state of recession. He was a creature of habit. His two semi-annual vacations, skiing at Vail and playing golf at Palm Springs, were sacrosanct. They were the only times he had an opportunity to spend some relaxing moments with his wife and four children. To do what some of his economists now were suggesting — increasing the national deficit by pump-priming the economy through pork barrel projects — was against all the principles he had supported throughout his years in Congress. On the other side of the coin, he liked all the perqs that went with being President: the personal steward; a helicopter at his beck and call; a private retreat at Camp David; and the glory and honor of being the most important man in the non-Communist world. It was a potent cocktail, and he wanted four more years of it.

Once Ford returned to Washington, Rumsfeld became the driving force that would prod the President to take decisions that went against his economic concepts. Instead of Ford waiting for his State of Union message to announce his program designed to fight inflation, reduce unemployment and resolve the energy crisis, Rumsfeld believed it would be far more effective to preempt that address with a fireside chat from the White House; the President would be surrounded on three sides by floor-to-ceiling shelves of books, indicating that Ford was an intellectual who had pondered for some time before arriving at his decision on how to combat the grave problems facing the nation.

Ford's preamble to his proposed program was brief and to the point. He was going to put the nation's economic house in order by waging a three-pronged campaign against inflation, unemployment and energy dependence. The gist of his program contained several simple points. Raise taxes on imported and domestic oil and natural gas to encourage conservation. Return the revenues from these taxes to individuals, businesses and state and local governments. Speed the development of nuclear, geothermal and solar energy and increase incentives to produce more domestic coal and oil. Cut taxes by $16 billion in the form of rebates to individuals and incentives to companies that build more plants and hire more employees. Veto new government spending programs other than those devoted to energy projects, and limit increases in government and military pensions as well as Social Security benefits to five percent to combat the still persistent inflation.

Since many of these proposed cuts, such as Social Security and Veterans benefits, were impossible because they were mandated by Congressional legislation, the President's words apparently were meant to calm the public's fears more than to effect any real change. It was the conservative Nixon who had initiated the legislation that tied these programs to the cost-of-living index. Ford's proposals were a mélange of pieces of the New Deal combined with conservative Republican philosophy. His State of the Union message to Congress, which followed two days later, was a repetition of his fireside chat with a few details filled in to indicate that his programs had been well thought out and were not merely smoke and mirrors.

The Democrats, having increased their representation in both the House and Senate as a result of Nixon's forced resignation, were unwilling to impose a tax on gasoline and heating oil, which would hurt their constituents. The only part of Ford's program that appealed to them was his tax reduction. Moreover, instead of a $16 billion tax reduction, Congress upped the amount to $24.8 billion. The first reaction of Ford and his economic advisors was to veto the legislation since it would further increase the national deficit. As the unemployment figures continued to increase and the tax cut proposed by Congress was geared solely to lower income workers, the President felt that it would be prudent to accept the legislation as written. Even with the increased tax cut, the economy continued to stagnate throughout 1975 because unemployment still hovered between 7% and 9%. Even with inflation still a major problem, the Federal Reserve Board finally realized that the discount interest rate of 12% was impeding a recovery. Gradually the Fed began to reduce this rate in an effort to stimulate business. The President also came to the conclusion that what the economy needed was further pump-priming. He was also deeply concerned about his chances for reelection. Ford's basic dilemma, which he could never overcome, was his fundamental belief in fiscal conservatism. Nor was he alone in hewing to that credo. Thus, when he proposed a further tax reduction of $28 billion, he insisted that Congress reduce government expenditures by an equal amount. However, that reduction would cancel out the stimulating effect of his tax cut. Furthermore, except for the pork Congress required for its constituents, most of the federal programs in place required mandatory spending. Thus Congress quickly approved the $28 billion tax cut but refused to make any reductions in government spending. Ford vetoed the legislation and Congress responded by passing it a second time, offering vague promises to hold down spending. Frustrated by Congress's intransigence, the President reluctantly conceded defeat and signed the measure.

By May 1976, the continued efforts by the Federal Reserve to lower the discount rate as a means of stimulating the economy finally had taken hold. Interest rates, which had been 12% when Ford took office, now were about 6%, which allowed business to borrow money at an equitable rate. The $28 billion tax cut also had served its purpose. Shuttered automotive factories were reopened, as well as those of other industries. Consumer spending and confidence increased, but the unemployment rate still averaged 7.7%, a disturbing figure for a President seeking reelection. While lowering the discount rate had helped some segments of the population, the number of hard-core unemployed remained constant. In place of a continued resurgence, the economy appeared to have stalled. The $28 billion tax cut had jump-started the economy but was not enough for it to maintain its momentum. Neither Ford nor his successor in office, Jimmy Carter, understood that the economy required continuous injections of fresh funds in order to keep it rolling along. It was something new in economic thinking and contradicted all past economic theories. There was no way to prevent an increase in inflation as long as the price of a barrel of oil continued to escalate, and the economy had not grown sufficiently to absorb it. Even in retrospect, when the huge budget deficits under the Reagan presidency gradually reduced the unemployment rate and led to national prosperity, most of the nation's politicians and economists continued to believe that deficit spending and adding to the national debt eventually would lead to an economic disaster. In 1976, they were certain that the country was on the wrong track. Despite their complaints, no one in either party had a solution beyond the status quo. The US economy was drifting, and until a new approach could be invented, the only thing to do was to let it drift.

Ford, by inclination as well as necessity, focused on domestic issues. However, he was instrumental in pursuing several foreign affairs agendas. His first was his trip to Vladivostok in November 1974, where he met with Soviet General Secretary Leonid Brezhnev. The two leaders laid the foundation for the SALT II agreements. In 1975, Ford made two significant trips abroad. In August, he traveled to Helsinki to sign the Accords. Later, he explained: "The people who were critical in the United States didn't realize that the human rights provision would end up with the kind of freedom they wanted for the Baltic nations. And it took even more time to convince the skeptics that Helsinki was a great step forward and a time bomb for communism." And, in December, he made a five-day visit to the Peoples Republic of China. Although the conference was cordial, it produced no joint communiqué.

In October 1975, a little more than a year into the presidency, Ford decided to make the first serious changes in his administration. Prodded by Rumsfeld, in addition to removing Schlesinger to make room for Rumsfeld as Secretary of Defense, Ford promoted his assistant Dick Cheney to Chief of Staff. He promoted Kissinger's number-two man, Brent Scowcroft, to National Security Advisor, and Elliot Richardson, the Ambassador to Great Britain, was named to replace Secretary of Commerce Rogers Morton. Then, following the exposure of illegal CIA activities (which had been countenanced by every administration since its inception), Congress mandated reforms and its director, William Colby, was asked to resign. He was replaced by former one-term Congressman George H. W. Bush, whom Nixon had named as US representative to the Peoples Republic of China following Bush's unsuccessful campaign to move up to the Senate. But the biggest surprise was Ford's decision to drop Vice President Nelson Rockefeller from his 1976 presidential campaign. Ford knew that his major opponent in the Republican presidential primaries would be the extremely popular former governor of California, Ronald Reagan.

Reagan had become the idol of the conservative wing of the Republican party following his opening speech at the Republican national convention of 1964 that nominated Barry Goldwater. Faced with the possible conservative backlash from having the liberal former governor of New York on his ticket, Ford asked Rockefeller to step aside. Keeping him on the ticket might have cost Ford the nomination, even though Reagan chose a liberal Republican for his running mate. However, if Ford had won the nomination with Rockefeller on the ticket, they might have won the election by carrying the all-important electoral votes of New York.

Ford left the same legacy that he inherited — inflation, high unemployment, and the uncontrolled escalation of the price of crude oil. But those men whom he had appointed to high positions in his administration were rewarded in their future careers, not only politically but also in the field of business. The most successful of all was George H. W. Bush, whose political career eventually brought him to the vice presidency and the presidency. But the others did almost as well financially and politically. While the Ford presidency accomplished little in terms of tangible results, his unquestionable honesty enabled most of the public to put the political misdeeds of Nixon behind them.

The man who defeated Ford (in one of the closest presidential elections to date), James Earl Carter, Jr., soon to be known as Jimmy Carter, was a mass of contradictions. It is hard to account for his meteoric rise on the American political scene. None of the political pundits gave him any chance of winning the Democratic presidential nomination. He campaigned in every one of the 30 Democratic primaries as the people's candidate, in opposition to the political bosses who had previously been instrumental in choosing the candidate. This reform of the usual Democratic political process, initiated by the anti-Vietnam war protestors in

1972, had led to a fundamental change in the rules for nomination. While previously the winner of a primary received all the delegates, under the new rules there was proportional division between those who finished first and second. As a result, while not winning all the primaries, Carter amassed enough delegates to give him the nomination. Moreover, unlike the ill-fated George McGovern, whose campaign resulted in a landslide victory for Nixon, Carter possessed the advantage of being a Southerner, and once he was nominated his fellow Southerners rallied around one of their own. The civil rights legislation enacted under Johnson, which had resulted in many white Southerners abandoning their long-standing allegiance to the Democratic Party and casting their votes for Nixon, was set aside for the moment. Southern pride took precedence.

A major factor in Carter's phenomenal success story was his determination to win, sometimes by discarding his principles. After serving two terms in the Georgia Senate, where he showed himself to be a liberal Democrat in the highly polarized South, he decided to run for governor. To his shock and disbelief, running on the same liberal platform that he had championed as a senator, he came in third — running behind the arch conservative, Lester Maddox. It was then that Carter had his second spiritual awakening. In the next gubernatorial election he campaigned as an arch conservative, and was elected. Once in office, he would revert to his real views and attempt to establish harmony between the two races. Of course, this turn-about meant he had no chance at reelection, so he had nothing to lose by running for the presidency instead, as much as a long shot it might appear to be.

Carter's approach to the presidency differed dramatically from those of his predecessors. For one thing, he had been a successful businessman and understood the necessity for fiscal responsibility; on the other hand, he was a man of deep religious faith with a steadfast belief in what was morally right or wrong.

As a result, in his initial dealings with the Soviet Union, Carter ran into trouble because of his sharp criticism of the Soviet leadership for its record on human rights. Carter had hoped to reach an accord on SALT II, which had been a work in progress under Ford. Although Brezhnev was anxious to reach some accord after his meeting with Ford and Kissinger, he could accept only a proposal that would be favorable to the Soviet Union. When Secretary of State Cyrus Vance traveled to Moscow in March 1977, the proposal offered by the Americans was patently geared to US interests. Coupled with Carter's continued public criticism of the Soviet Union's record on human rights, the meeting ended without any proposals being discussed. He had a major triumph in foreign affairs in normalizing relations with the Peoples Republic of China. Although Nixon received the credit for recognition of China, the old leadership of Communist China, Mao Tse-tung and Chou En-lai, refused to formalize relations through an exchange of ambassadors because of the Taiwan question. Once these leaders had died, however, some of the original members of the Chinese Communist hierarchy, who had been dismissed by Mao, returned to power. With relations between China and the Soviet Union deteriorating, the new leadership, led by Deng Xiaoping, was open to normalizing relations between the United States and China. Although the future of Taiwan still remained a sticking point, Deng did make a visit to the United States as a sign of the new relationship between the two governments.

Carter also had promised during his campaign to remove the US troops stationed in Korea, in order to gain votes from the anti-Vietnam war contingent. The protests from Senators and some of the press were so strong that he was forced to back down. On the other hand, despite enormous pressure from Congress, he refused to give up on his plan to eliminate the B-1 bomber, already in the experimental stage and ready for production. Industry and military interests were solidly in favor of the bomber and tens of thousands of jobs would have been created if he had signed onto it. But Carter's economic policy tended to be conservative. When his domestic policy advisor, Stuart Eizenstadt, informed him early on that if the economy continued to grow at the 6% annual basis inherited from Ford, it would be possible to achieve a balanced budget by 1981, it became the goal that would determine Carter's economic policies. He became so fixated on attaining that end that in the process of attempting to realize it, he alienated various segments of the US economy. But such a goal can only be something to aim for; it is not fixed in stone. With the oil crisis still hovering and with the resulting inflation, there was no possible way to project the future of the economy. His first effort to eliminate pork-barrel spending by Congress resulted in a compromise. Carter had attempted to eliminate the waste associated with water and dam projects but he came up against a stone wall. Finally, a compromise was reached whereby the $147 million requested by Congress was cut back to $63 million. Unaware that Congress viewed the compromise as a sign of weakness on the part of the White House, he signed the revised legislation. This reduction, of course, was small potatoes in the greater scope of the economy. Carter had predicated his major reforms on three pieces of legislation — reform of the welfare system; reform of the tax code; and an energy plan to cope with the rising prices of oil and natural gas. In addition, in order to bring the budget in line, farm subsidies would have to be lowered. All of these legislative initiatives were designed to meet the goal of a balanced budget in 1981.

Carter soon learned that it was easier to propose legislation than to have it enacted. Within the Democratic Party there were too many pressure groups, each with its own conflicting agendas. He also learned to his dismay that Eizenstadt, who had been so optimistic in his economic projections for the second half of 1977 after experiencing a 6.5% economic growth in the first six months, now was revising his projections downward for the balance of the year and for 1978. It was deficit spending that had extricated the economy from the recession. And the farm lobby covered all the 50 states, so that each state's Representatives and Senators had to satisfy their farm constituents. Despite Carter's objections, Congress raised the price supports on such basic commodities as wheat, corn and cotton. Remembering that Ford's decision to veto similar legislation had resulted in his loss of the electoral votes in the farm states, Carter signed the legislation. Like Social Security, the farm bloc is a guaranteed stumbling block in American politics.

By fiscal 1977, the deficit — which had peaked in 1976 when the end of the fiscal year had been changed from July 1 to October 1 — was reduced to $54 billion. Carter's and Eizenstadt's original belief that the budget could be balanced by 1981 now appeared to be overly optimistic. The energy bill, one of the three legs of Carter's initial proposal that would lead to his goal of a balance the budget, immediately ran into trouble. Thanks to the powerful oil lobby in Congress, the bill was stripped of its principal feature, a tax on oil at the wellhead, which would provide the government with additional revenue. However, Congress finally approved Carter's proposal to deregulate natural gas. But the other two legs of the stool, tax and welfare reform, remained in limbo. While Carter and Eizenstadt focused their attention on alleviating the plight of the poor, Howard Jarvis, a wealthy Californian, was rousing from apathy his state's middle class, which represented the majority of the state's population. Convincing middle class residents that they were bearing the brunt of the tax load by ever increasing property taxes, Jarvis was successful in placing Proposition 13 on the ballot; it called for a cap on property tax rates. By an overwhelming majority of 2 to 1, the proposition was passed; with the rollback in taxes, the state of California had to scramble to make up the difference. Moreover, other states followed California with similar referendums. Congress heard the plaints of the middle class loud and clear.

While inflation showed no signs of moderating, increasing from 5.8% in 1976 to 6.5% in 1977 and 7.6% in 1978, the rate of unemployment was on the decline. From 7.7% in 1976, it had declined to 7.1% in 1977 and 6.1% in 1978. (See Appendix, Table 7.) The Carter administration would attempt to make the most of these small declines by declaring them an indication that the economy was finally on the right track (and in fact it was). At the same time, the administration was concerned about the growing negative balance of trade, which was decreasing the value of the dollar on the world's currency markets. However, there were two sides to that coin; while there was no way to prevent the exodus of dollars to the oil producing nations, cheap imports from other countries, especially Japan, were helping to keep inflation down, and Japan's far more fuel-efficient cars were reducing US oil consumption. In other words, as long as the price of oil imports remained relatively stable, thanks to the growing importance of imports of fuel-efficient Japanese cars, the economy appeared to be able to adjust itself to the slow but steady increases in the price of crude oil. While the liberal wing of the party wanted the administration to focus on the plight of the poor and the disadvantaged, Carter's main concern was to bring down the deficit.

There was also the problem of Senator Edward Kennedy and other liberals who were pressing for a national health insurance plan that would cover the 40 million taxpayers without any insurance. Kennedy was a potential contender for the 1980 presidential nomination and could hardly be ignored. By the end of 1978, polls showed that Kennedy was ahead of the President in electoral support for the nomination, despite Carter's success in managing the economy. Carter was beginning to learn a bitter lesson. No matter how successful his administration was in its overall approach to the economy, the US consumer and the media only saw the dark clouds.

Unfortunately for Carter, and undermining all of the economic projections of Eizenstadt, events taking place in Iran, the major oil-producing ally of the United States in the Middle East, soon would throw the administration into total disarray. America's close relations with Iran dated back to 1953, when a coup organized by the CIA overthrew the nationalist government and returned the Shah to his throne as an absolute ruler. For the first time in Iran's modern history there was neither an elected Assembly nor a Senate to act as a counterweight to the Shah's policies. The Shah owed a huge debt to the United States and over the intervening years, he had more than reciprocated. Not only was he America's principal ally among the members of OPEC, but he was one of its best customers for military equipment. American military advisors worked hand in hand with the generals of the Iranian armed forces. The Shah also was intent on modernizing and Westernizing his regime. The proscriptions against women exposing their heads in public were removed, alienating the religious fundamentalists in the country. In addition, Iran was the only Muslim country to recognize Israel. The efforts of Iran's Communist party to gain a foothold in the country were repressed by the Shah's secret police, SAVAK. Iran, like its Arab neighbors in the region, was a totalitarian regime. The basic support for the Shah was the military and the secret police. But in his efforts to westernize the nation he was alienating the Mullahs, the Shiite religious leaders, the only vocal opposition to his absolutist rule. Angered by their vocal opposition to his policies, he responded by reducing the government subsidies that supported their lifestyle. The result of his action was to create a powerful group of enemies determined to overthrow his regime.

The rebellion began with a fire in a movie theater in which 377 people died. Since the perpetrator was never uncovered, the Mullahs spread the rumor that the fire had been set by SAVAK, under the instructions of the Shah. Demonstrations against the Shah were provoked throughout the country, organized by the Mullahs and members of the Iranian Communist party In Tehran, close to 100,000 demonstrated against the Shah and his regime. The response of the Shah was to invoke martial law and ban any future demonstrations. The reaction of the Mullahs was to organize a large group that assembled in one of Tehran's principal squares to protest the imposition of martial law. The Shah called out the military. The demonstration was broken up by killing or wounding 700 civilian protestors. For the first time since 1953, signs appeared in the capital calling for the Shah's resignation or death. Moreover, the protests continued over the succeeding months of late fall and into the winter of 1979. No one in the US intelligence community was aware that the rebellion was being directed from Paris by the Ayatollah Khomeini until he issued a public call for a general strike throughout the country and the overthrow of the Shah. Responding to their leader's instructions the Mullahs called upon their supporters to shut down the oil fields and close one of the largest oil refineries in the world.

The Shah, incapable of coping with the situation, appointed one of the opponents to his policies in the National Assembly, Shamour Bakhtar, the head of the National Front party, to organize a new government and cope with it. He compounded this action further by announcing to the Iranian people that he was temporarily leaving the country and that upon his return he would establish a constitutional monarchy. In his defense, it must be added that the Shah was undergoing treatment for cancer and had gone to Egypt for more advanced treatment.

With the only vestige of temporal authority gone, the crowds led by the Mullahs took over the streets. Bakhtar was powerless. In February 1979, the 78-year-old Ayatollah Khomeini returned to Iran from Paris to take charge of the rebellion. The only serious opposition he faced would be the reaction of the military who owed their loyalty to the Shah for the favors he had bestowed upon them.

The Carter administration was paralyzed by these events. Its only source of information was Ambassador Walter Sullivan and his staff. Carter, along with his Secretary of State Cyrus Vance, was determined to maintain a neutral policy and watch events unfold. Khomeini now replaced Bakhtar with his own Prime Minister, Mehdi Barzagan. Shortly after, Iranian students seized the US Embassy and held its occupants hostage for two hours. This event was followed by a personal apology delivered to the US by the Ayatollah. Early in November 1979, another group of supposed students seized the US Embassy and refused to vacate it unless the Shah, who was being treated for cancer in New York, was returned to Iran to stand trial for his misdeeds. The only counterforce to the Ayatollah was the Iranian military, with whom the US military had an extremely close relationship thanks to the continued arms shipments under the Shah. The commanding generals were waiting to act on America's behalf. Instead of Carter attempting to enlist their support for the release of the hostages he made the decision to undertake negotiations through third parties to gain their release. It was only six months later, after the Ayatollah's rule over Iran was entrenched, that Carter sent an a US general to confer with them. It was too late. It was then that in desperation Carter initiated the aborted American attempt to rescue the hostages.

Until 1979, despite the rising price of oil on the international market, the US was able to lessen the inflationary pressure on its economy because the United States produced 52% of its oil needs domestically — unlike Western Europe and Japan. Helping to keep oil prices down was the Energy Policy and Conservation Act passed by Congress in 1975, during the Ford administration. Under the EPCA, a three-tiered system of pricing was created. Old oil, from wells already in existence before the oil crisis, was priced at $5.50 a barrel; new domestic oil discovered after 1975 was priced at$12.50; and imported oil, which accounted for 48% of America's needs, was currently selling at $15.20. However with the temporary shut down of Iran's oil fields, a result of the revolution that brought Khomeini to power, the price of imported oil increased 17%, adding to the inflationary pressure on the economy. President Ford's original response to the world's energy crisis had been to impose a wellhead tax on US oil producers and use the funds collected by the government to aid those people suffering from the rise in prices. But the increase in the price of oil had an impact not only on transportation and home heating but on industry and agriculture as well. Plastics and manmade fibers were totally dependent on oil to produce finished products, pushing prices up in a multitude of industries as well as textiles. Farmers were faced with the rising costs of pesticides and oil to operate their farm machinery, driving up the cost of food. Food prices were up 18% over the year before, and the Consumer Price Index (better known as inflation), which had been at 7.6%, moved up to 11.3% in 1979. Since Social Security benefits and other government pension plans were tied to the CPI by law, this placed a further strain on the economy. As if the economic news wasn't bad enough, the head of the Social Security Trust Fund announced that the fund was in the red, and unless Congress raised the payroll tax, the fund would not be able to meet its obligatory payments to retirees.

Inflation creates a vicious cycle. To complicate the economic situation further, Carter in his 1980 budget insisted on bringing the federal budget deficit down from $40 billion to $30 billion. Thus far, he had succeeded in reducing the 1978 budget deficit from $59 billion to its 1979 level of a little more than $41 billion. At a three-day conference attended by the Democratic leadership, an open revolt by the liberals of the party ensued, led by Senator Kennedy. Each of the party's basic constituencies — labor, Blacks, the cities and the environmentalists — were opposed to the President's conservative economic philosophy. Rumors picked up by the press spread the word that Kennedy intended to challenge Carter for the presidential nomination. While the Senator denied it, the press wouldn't let go. Polls commissioned by the media showed that Kennedy was far ahead of Carter among potential Democratic voters and could easily defeat such Republican contenders as Ronald Reagan and George H. W. Bush.

But in spring 1979, the only constituency interested in polls was the media. The public was far more concerned with the increasing inflation. Moreover, Carter's voluntary wage and price controls were beginning to fray as the edges. The wage increases sought by both the Teamsters and the United Auto Workers exceeded the guidelines established by the administration. Corporate profits were at an all-time high, having increased 25% over the previous year. Meanwhile, thanks to the ever increasing price of foreign oil, inflation which had been at 8.3% in early spring was at 11.3% by summer. Because Congress refused to decontrol the price of oil as it had that of natural gas, certain sections of the country were experiencing shortages. In the Northeast, Midwest and California, gas stations were resorting to rationing. It was at this moment that the President undertook to make major changes in his Cabinet. He appointed William Miller, head of the Federal Reserve Board, as Treasury Secretary; to fill Miller's role as chairman of the FRB, he named Paul Volcker, head of the New York branch of the FRB.

With OPEC continuing to raise oil prices, Congress finally agreed to adopt the President's emergency oil program. In exchange for deregulating the price of oil, Congress passed a 60% windfall tax that was supposed to generate $227 billion in revenue. Of course it never did. Carter's rationale was that the increased revenues would enable his administration to balance the budget, his primary goal. In addition, Congress enacted a standby gas rationing bill along with an Energy Mobilization Board, whose function was to facilitate the construction of energy-related facilities. As a final approach to the energy shortage, another agency, the Energy Security Corporation, was to be created to facilitate the development of alternative energy sources. Carter also was able to persuade Congress to enact a $5.7 billion dollar welfare reform bill. Finally, in order to prevent the Chrysler Corporation from going out of business, Congress provided the ailing automotive giant with a guaranteed loan of more than $1 billion.

While Carter had managed to have most of his programs enacted, including the new Cabinet position of Secretary of Education, he was still unable to tame the ever increasing inflation. The decision to deregulate domestic oil only exacerbated the inflation while making the oil companies more profitable. What it did accomplish was to promote an effort to revive old oil wells where drilling for oil previously had been too expensive. Throughout Texas, there was a mad rush to get in on the oil bonanza. While domestic oil production increased slightly, this did not affect the rate of inflation because domestic oil was now priced at the same level as OPEC's — i.e., higher than $20 a barrel.

About the only good news the President had was that a final agreement had been reached with the Soviet Union on the SALT II agreement to limit production of atomic missiles. The treaty was never ratified by the Senate because shortly thereafter the Soviet Union invaded Afghanistan. Nonetheless, both sides honored its terms. Despite this success in reducing the threat of nuclear-weapon proliferation, Carter's approval ratings continued to decline. Given this, Kennedy decided to challenge Carter for the Democratic nomination.

Problems other than those on the domestic front also surfaced. The Castro-supported Sandinistas in Nicaragua defeated Somoza's forces, forcing him to flee the country, and installed a Marxist regime. Furthermore, once in power, they began to export arms to other leftist rebel groups in neighboring El Salvador, Guatemala and Honduras. This was soon followed by the decision of the Soviet Union to gain a stronger hand in Afghanistan and send in 85,000 troops to fight the insurgency that had forced one prime minister after another to leave office. America's inaction (and then the failed attempt to rescue the hostages) had left Moscow and others with a sense that they were free to act with impunity.

Carter's response to the Soviet invasion of Afghanistan was to feel as though he had been personally betrayed. He held up final ratification of the SALT II agreement. He cancelled grain shipments to the Soviet Union and asked his European allies to do the same. He threatened to cancel US participation in the Summer Olympics to be held in Moscow. He called for $400 million in aid to Pakistan. To prevent the loss of the farm vote in the 1980 elections, he promised to reimburse farmers for the losses they incurred from the ban on shipments of grain to the Soviet Union. He granted China most favorable nation trade status, something that had never been accorded the Soviet Union. He also agreed to sell China certain high-tech military equipment. He increased military spending for the fiscal year from 3% to 5%, and he proposed that all men between the ages of 18 and 26 register for the draft, even though America had abandoned the draft in favor of a professional army. Now Carter was obliged to set aside his goal of bringing the budget deficit down to $30 billion for fiscal 1980.

With the threat of an invasion of Iran by the United States, and the actual invasion of Iran by Iraq, the price of oil on the international market soared into the stratosphere. Day by day, nations were outbidding each other in order to ensure a sufficient supply of oil to maintain their economies. Until it became apparent that the Iran-Iraq war would not interfere with the supply of the world's oil, its price on the international market increased from $20 a barrel to the unheard of price of $38 a barrel. The majority of economic prognosticators were speaking in terms of a barrel of oil increasing to as high as $80.

While in 1978 the inflation rate had increased to 7.6% from 6.5% the previous year, it was still manageable. In 1979, the rate continued its upward march, hitting 11.3%; in 1980, it peaked at 13.5%. Unemployment, which had decreased to 5.8% in 1979, shot up to 7.1% in 1980 when inflation hit its historical pinnacle. The newly appointed chairman of the Federal Reserve Board Paul Volcker decided it was time to take drastic action to curb the return of inflation. Volcker's remedy almost killed the patient. He couldn't fix the oil price, but he could reduce the perceived excess of money in circulation; he curbed the use of money for investment by raising the discount rate to 13%, which forced business to retract on expansion plans. His plan had the desired effect as far as inflation was concerned. By 1981, it had come down from its high of 13.5% to 10.3%, and by 1982, to 6.2%. But as an unexpected result of the high interest rates, the economy went into a recession. With more people entering the workforce every year and with business forced to eliminate any plans for expansion, the unemployment rate began to climb from an annual rate of 5.8% in 1979 to 7.1% by 1980; 7.6% by 1981; and 9.7% by 1982. It was not Volcker's policy that brought inflation down, but rather the collapse of the OPEC cartel as US imports decreased as a result of the mileage standards that had been imposed by Congress. The attempted rescue of the savings and loan institutions and the necessity to increase payroll deductions to save Social Security are discussed in the next chapter. But the FRB had been taught a lesson. While the control of the nation's money supply was important, it was not the only factor influencing the direction of the economy.

At least Carter beat back the presidential challenge of Senator Kennedy in 1980. Kennedy had taken the gamble that the scandal surrounding Chappaquiddick, which had occurred in 1969, could be overcome. But a scandal of that magnitude is easy to revive.

The defeat of Kennedy was the only satisfaction Carter enjoyed during the campaign against Ronald Reagan. Whatever attitude the US public had about Reagan and his bellicose attitude towards the Soviet Union was altered by one devastating question Reagan asked during a campaign debate. Were Americans better off than four years before? No, they were not. Election Day they responded by giving Reagan a landslide victory. On his coattails the Republicans took control of the Senate for the first time in 28 years. In addition, the Republicans added 34 seats to the House and took control of additional governorships.

If historians have not been fair to Carter, it is in part because his self righteousness grated on people. It also led to his tendency to blame everyone except himself. Had he reacted immediately to the taking of the hostages, he might have been viewed in a better light. His aborted attempt to rescue them only compounded his original failure. The twice born-again Christian viewed himself as a man of destiny. He was — but his presidential legacy is one that he did not envision.

Chapter 11. America on the Attack: The Reagan Presidency

What was Reaganism, and what was it supposed to mean? Ostensibly, Ronald Reagan's philosophy centered on less government interference in the private sector of business; reducing taxes; balancing the budget; and where possible, eliminating government regulations. In other words: allow the free market economy to do its job. Yet none of these basic principles that supposedly define Reaganism, with the exception of the tax cut, occurred during his eight years in office. Every government regulation that had been in place before he took office remained in place. If anything, the bureaucracy in Washington continued to grow. Instead of the budget being balanced, under his administration the national debt soared and when he left office, the gross federal debt was almost triple the one he inherited, which included the deficits of all previous administrations combined. At the end of his presidency, all that remained of Reaganism was his 25% across-the-board tax cut on individual margin rates, and even that was negated somewhat by the need to raise the payroll tax for Social Security. Was Reaganism a myth that has been perpetrated by loyal adherents? Even the philosophy of Supply Side economics, which was supposed to reduce the national debt while growing the economy, instead increased the government debt. Yet under his presidency, the economy flourished as it never had before; the standard of living for the majority of Americans reached heights previously thought unattainable; the rate of inflation was low enough that increases in wages and prices produced real economic growth; profits were at an all-time high; and the Dow Jones average passed the 2,500 mark for the first time. Although his initial goals never were realized, the legacy of his administration, prosperity at home, would be passed on to future presidencies

Of far greater significance were his accomplishments in foreign affairs. A hard-line anti-Communist by his rhetoric, he not only was a fervent supporter of the Vietnamese War but accused Richard Nixon of having betrayed his country when he recognized Communist China. During the presidential campaign, Carter, the Democrats and the liberals sought to portray Reagan as a loose cannon who would alienate the Soviet leadership and possibly bring about an atomic war with Russia. Once in office, he continued his inflammatory rhetoric, publicly denouncing the Soviet Union as an "evil empire." Yet he brought the Russians to the bargaining table and negotiated the first meaningful treaty for arms reduction. Arguably, it was his adamant promotion of new military technologies and the concomitant obligation of the Soviets to follow suit that provided the impetus for the eventual collapse of the Soviet Union. Reagan's inflexible attitude toward an adopted concept, whether it was Supply Side economics or the Strategic Defense Initiative (SDI), was what would come to define Reagan's strength and his weakness; the incredible success of his two administrations remains truly remarkable and difficult to understand.

Who was Ronald Reagan, and did he actually espouse a new philosophy for the federal government? Or was he playing the lead role in the movie, *Mr. Smith Goes to Washington*, in which a newly elected congressman attempts to reform government? Even Edmund Morris, the Pulitzer-Prize-winning biographer whom Reagan personally selected to describe his life and career, was incapable of getting a bead on the man and ended up writing a fictional/non-fictional biography. Even his two wives and his children were unable to pierce that inner core. Yet this was the man who came to be known as the Great Communicator. Throughout his life and career, his actions were a series of endless contradictions.

In many instances, his critics thought he was stubborn to a fault. Once he believed that the action he had taken was right, he would not budge. When a deep recession struck the country following his 1981 across-the-board tax cut, and it appeared to most that he would be a one-term president, he refused to compromise with Congress on a reduction in the tax cut or on its elimination. He maintained that he was certain it was the right step for the country to take. As it turned out, the tax cut stayed in effect and the country entered a period of prosperity that has continued until the present day. Not that Reagan was prescient. Outside factors, mainly the huge deficits that were amassed during his tenure in office, played a far more important role. All of the positions he espoused, whether in domestic or foreign affairs, which his political opponents contended would be disastrous, instead proved to be the right medicine for this country's domestic and foreign policies. Could it be that his success could be attributed to nothing more than dumb luck?

The economic prosperity that began in his presidency and has continued until the present day was his legacy to the nation. But it was not his fundamental belief in free trade that altered the US economy and witnessed it gradually move from one based on industrial production to one where the service sector came to dominate. As was the case with so many events that seemed to begin during his administration and to which he was assigned the credit or the blame, Reagan had nothing to do with it. The consolidation of America's corporations fostered by the stock options for key executives had begun in the late 1950s and had continued throughout the intervening years. Likewise, the decisions to source more and more merchandise overseas in order to gain a competitive advantage had followed along the same track. At the same time, the programs of the Great Society were creating job opportunities in the service sector. It was the advent of the personal computer, with its multitude of applications that served to accelerate what had been a growing trend in the US economy.

The same could be said about his emergence as a major factor on the American political scene. In the 1964 presidential campaign, the Republicans suffered their worst defeat since Franklin Roosevelt carried every state with the exception of Maine and New Hampshire. In that same year, when Lyndon Johnson carried California by a million votes, Reagan's fellow actor and friend, George Murphy, was elected to the Senate as a Republican. The Republican political leadership in California realized the value of name recognition and the glamour associated with a movie celebrity in winning an election. Following Goldwater's crushing defeat, a committee from the California Republican party approached Reagan as a potential candidate in the 1966 race for governor. Republican millionaires would fund it. Reagan positioned himself as the average public-minded citizen determined to root out the political corruption in the state capital. When the votes were counted, Reagan had defeated incumbent Governor Pat Brown by a margin of almost one-million votes. The new political star was rising, and he now was determined to seek the presidency.

The odyssey of Reagan's thoughts from a New Deal Democrat to a conservative Republican took place over a number of years. It began even before he left Hollywood and became the master of ceremonies for the General Electric Theater and the company's spokesman. When Reagan was president of the Screen Actors Guild (SAG), there was a hard core group within the organization — a few, members of the Communist party and other sympathizers with the Soviet Union — who sought to radicalize the programs of the Guild and become more confrontational with the studios. With his Midwestern upbringing, he was a patriotic American who believed that America was the greatest country in the world and felt that its fundamental values were superior to those of any other system of government. The idea that any American would support the philosophy expounded by the Soviet Union was anathema to him. It was at that moment in his life that his strong stance against communism emerged. In 1947, Reagan, and former SAG presidents Robert Montgomery and George Murphy were subpoenaed by HUAC to testify about Communist subversion within the Screen Actors Guild. When queried, he did not mention any names, but he did admit that there existed a hard core within the organization determined to take control of the Guild. Reagan was very circumspect, contending that 90 percent of its members were good Americans and anti-Communist. He also was very much aware that if he named names, that would be the end of his acting career; as the country later learned, with the Hollywood 10, a large percentage of the directors in Hollywood were either card-carrying members of the Communist party or fellow travelers. And directors played a major role in selecting the cast. Reagan also knew that while only 10 percent were active members of the party or fellow travelers, the percentage of those who sympathized with their philosophy was far greater.

However, Reagan still remained an ardent believer in the philosophy of Roosevelt's New Deal programs. Growing up during the Depression, he had witnessed the long lines of the unemployed and the people foraging through garbage cans for food. His father's employment had been sporadic. His first exposure to a viewpoint other than the one he had adopted was a result of his marriage to the actress, Nancy Davis in 1952, when he met her stepfather, a successful physician. For the first time in his life he was exposed to an economic philosophy different than his own. Nancy's stepfather was vehemently opposed to the programs of the New Deal and Truman's Fair Deal, and he tried to convince his new son-in-law how this legislation had impeded initiative taken by the individual. Reagan remained unconvinced. As he would demonstrate throughout his political career, he had a stubborn streak, so his own thoughts on the subject would be difficult to change. It was when he joined GE as its spokesman that he was forced to examine the alternative to his previous belief. His role was to travel the country delivering speeches to the wholesalers and retailers of the company's products. Known already from his career in movies, and as the master of ceremonies for General Electric's Theater, everywhere he traveled he was greeted as a celebrity. With his extensive repertoire of anecdotes and jokes and the inside dope on Hollywood celebrities, he drew a wide audience wherever he spoke. For the first time in his life, he was exposed to the problems of small businessmen, who informed him that the growth of their businesses was impeded by the excessive taxation of the federal government. It was an eye-opener for the former actor, and he began to reconsider the views he had held up to that point in his life. It was while he traveled the country that he developed his habit of writing down his thoughts on what made the economy tick. These random reflections, uncovered when the Reagan Library was opened, proved that Reagan was not the lightweight thinker that he had been portrayed to be by the media and the intellectuals. A great deal of thought and consideration had preceded the formulation of his theory of government. Bureaucrats and politicians had no accountability for their actions; they had no bottom line to worry about, nor did they fear going out of business. It wasn't their money that they were investing in government programs, but the funds of the taxpayer. Once he had adopted his new-found theory of the role for government, the same stubborn streak that had dominated his previous thinking took over.

As governor, Reagan was determined to show a surplus in the state's budget. He managed to reform welfare and was successful in replacing the huge hospitals where the mentally ill were warehoused with community centers throughout the state. He reduced taxes by 5%, and he imposed tuition in the state's higher education system for the first time in the state's history. In his second term, he presented a balanced budget of

$258 billion, which produced a surplus of $1.1 billion. In the past, because the state's Constitution mandated a balanced budget, governors and the legislature had resorted to the issuance of state bonds, a practice common to many states. When the students at the University of California at Berkley closed down the school in protest against the war in Vietnam, with some faculty members joining the students, Reagan called out 2,000 members of the state's National Guard, armed with tear gas, to break up the demonstrations and restore order on the campus. While roundly criticized by the Democrats in the legislature, the public in general applauded his action. His record established him as the leading conservative in the Republican party. At the end of his second term as governor, Reagan had become a national figure and a symbol of law and order. With Nixon's overwhelming victory in 1972, Reagan set in motion his plan to capture the Republican nomination for the presidency.

The unexpected resignation of Nixon and the elevation of Gerald Ford to the presidency delayed his ascension. Although Reagan came close to winning the nomination in 1976, the power of Ford's incumbency proved too difficult to overcome. In 1980, Reagan defeated Jimmy Carter and at 69 years of age became the oldest man in history ever elected to the presidency.

When Reagan took office in 1981 the economy was in a shambles; inflation was still the major problem, along with massive and growing unemployment. With the Iran-Iraq war still going on, the price of crude oil was up to $38 a barrel, with most pundits speaking of it mounting to as much as $80. There was good reason for this pessimistic view. Iraq and Iran were the second and third largest suppliers of oil in the Middle East. If they destroyed each others' oil fields, it would be a disaster for every major industrial nation in the world and especially for the United States. Paul Volcker, appointed as Chairman of the Federal Reserve Board by Carter, sought to stem the inflation by raising the discount rate to 13% while at the same time reducing the supply of money used by the Fed to stimulate the economy, thereby placing a further strain on an already weakened economy. Inflation continued to grow, and the tight money policy contributed to the inflation as businesses were forced to increase prices in order to pay for the higher interest rates on the money they borrowed. Unless Reagan took some action, his presidency faced an economic disaster.

Forces that were set in motion in 1975 when the Energy Policy & Conservation Act was passed would rescue the economy. The CAFE standards issued under that legislation mandated increased gas mileage for new autos and light trucks beginning in 1978 and increasing each year until 1985. They dramatically decreased the amount of oil consumed in the US and created a glut of oil on the international market. The United States used one-fourth of the world's total oil supply, and about one third of that amount was used by cars and trucks. The OPEC monopoly was broken as the individual members of the organization reduced oil prices in order to maintain their share of market. As already noted, the American automotive industry was too slow to respond to the sharp increase in the price of gasoline at the pump, thus allowing the Japanese (who had always been totally dependent upon imported oil and had traditionally engineered their cars and trucks to produce the maximum mileage per gallon) to capture 20% of the US auto market.

Reagan arrived at the presidency with certain entrenched ideas, some better than others. He, as well as most economists, failed to recognize the ultimate effect of the steep rise in the cost of oil. It was not only responsible for the inflation that was debilitating the economy; it was not only flooding the world with dollars, which was reducing the value of America's currency; but by doing this, it was insuring the supremacy of the dollar as the sole means of exchange in commerce. Furthermore he, as well as his economic advisors and Congress, failed to realize that the huge budget deficits would continue to grow, even after the OPEC monopoly had fallen apart and the price of a barrel of oil had decreased to the low $20s. It was the cheapened dollar that was adding to the deficits. It was this basic fact that every economist had overlooked and continues to ignore. From 1971 onward, the programs of the Great Society would be the major contributor to the budget deficits, even though Reagan did increase the expenditures of the Defense Department. In other words, despite his belief that the budget could be balanced by growing the economy through tax cuts, the continual increase in non-defense expenditures made this impossible. Government figures show the futility of his effort. In 1981, when he inherited Carter's budget, federal outlays at the end of the fiscal year totaled about $678 billion. Of that amount, Defense accounted for $158 billion; Human Resource, $362 billion; Physical Resources $71 billion; Net Interest on the debt, $69 billion; Other Government Functions, $47 billion. In fiscal 1989, the last budget submitted by Reagan, total expenditures were $1.144 trillion. Of that amount, Defense accounted for $304 billion; Human Resources, $569 billion; Physical Resources, $82 billion; Net Interest on the debt, $169 billion, Other Government Functions, $58 billion. When broken down into categories between the two budgets of 1981 and 1989, Human Resource expenditures on Health had almost doubled, increasing from $27 billion to $48 billion. The increase in Medicare costs was even more dramatic — rising from $39 billion to $85 billion. The federal debt had grown from $995 billion to $2.867 trillion, and the gross domestic product had increased from $3 trillion to $5 trillion. (See Appendix, Tables 5, 6 & 7.) All of these increases, to a major extent, were a result of the decreased value of the dollar.

Reagan's belief that a balanced budget was the *sine qua non* for a successful economy, a view that was held by his predecessors and successors, was an anachronism no longer feasible or desirable, once the gold standard had been destroyed. His decision in early 1981 to pass an across-the-board tax cut as a means of stimulating the economy, which had been paralyzed by eight years of ever-growing inflation, paid off. The fact that it would take two years before effect of the tax cut took hold was a result of the decision by the Federal Reserve Board to maintain its tight money policy throughout 1982, even though the decrease in the price of oil had lowered the inflation rate to 6.2%. Disregarding the lower inflation rate, the Fed continued to maintain a discount rate of 13.5%. With money now available only at usurious rates, there was no desire on the part of the business community to expand operations. Instead, a contraction took place, increasing the unemployment rate to 9.7%, which meant that more than 10 million people were out of work. It wouldn't be until early 1983 that the Fed would change its policy of tight money; once it did, the recession would end and business was prepared to expand. Only Reagan's decision to hold firm against the counsel of most of his economic advisors and the Republican members of Congress, who feared that the recession of 1982 would result in a major defeat for the party in the mid-term elections, kept Congress from eliminating the tax cut or modifying it. His only support came from his Treasury Secretary Donald Regan. Later, Reagan would modify his tax cut by making small increases on the vague promise from Congress that it would match these increases with comparable reductions in federal spending. While Reagan's tax cut would provide the necessary jolt to spur economic growth, his assumption that the Supply Side economic theory espoused by Arthur Laffer — i.e., that tax reductions by themselves would lead to a balanced budget — was nothing less than Voodoo Economics, as his critics ridiculed. As previously explained, the continual increases in government expenditures, largely a result of the Great Society programs, outstripped the additional tax revenues that the tax cut generated, but were also responsible for the country's economic growth. Although the deficit increased, as did the interest expenditure necessary to service the debt, the overall effect was to increase employment and, in turn, tax receipts.

Economists underestimated the dramatic change in the world's economy as a result of establishing the dollar as the official currency for international exchange of currencies. The inflation produced by the OPEC price increases flooded the international money markets with inflated dollars. In turn, the OPEC nations circulated these inflated dollars throughout the economies of other nations as well as our own. It resulted in entrenchment of the dollar as the world's official currency. The value of every commodity continued to be measured in terms of dollars. Moreover, as the US negative trade balance continued to increase, the circulation of inflated dollars continued to mushroom as well. The world's economies were on a treadmill from which there was no escape. If they didn't support the bonds issued by the United States Treasury to pay for the increased deficits, a result of deficit-spending on the part of every US administration, their own economies would collapse since a major part of their financial assets were tied up in inflated dollars. This was the basic reason why the US economy could continue to grow. It was not, as some economists tended to believe, that deficit spending hurt the economy but rather that deficit spending had allowed the US economy to enjoy a continual growth, and in turn, the highest standard of living in the world.

Reagan also was a firm believer in free trade between nations. He believed that competition was the essence of capitalism. The one and only time he compromised that belief was when he threatened to raise the duty on Japanese automobile imports unless Japan voluntarily agreed to limit its car exports to the US to a fixed figure, equaling about a 20% share of the American automotive market. (This limit involved a slight rollback in Japanese exports.) Reagan's reasoning was as follows: lowering the tariff barriers imposed by countries would increase trade between nations and lower prices in the marketplace, thereby leading to increased consumer spending and an increase in the gross domestic product. But the wage and cost differential between foreign countries and our own would decimate America's basic heavy industries and result in the creation of what has been termed the Rust Belt, those Central Eastern and Midwestern states whose economies had been based on such heavy industries as steel, automotives and coal. As a result, US Steel, at the turn of the twentieth century the largest corporation in the world, would shrink to a pale ghost of its former self. But it was not solely the differential in labor costs that accounted for the loss of heavy industry's domestic market. Far more significant was the unwillingness of management to invest in new equipment to update their facilities. The motive for this attitude was the growth in the value of securities traded on the stock exchanges, and the emergence of the stock option as a form of remuneration for top executives. Designed to maximize compensation for those executives in the higher income tax brackets, the stock options could be cashed in as capital gains, which were taxed at a considerably lower rate than straight income or bonuses. As a result, the focus of top management was on the bottom line, which would lead to a rise in the price of their stock holdings, rather than on expending capital on purchases of more productive machinery to streamline their operations. The Japanese were the ones who took the lead in the development of robots to replace manual labor. In defense of management, it is also a fact that any attempt to improve productivity was opposed by the unions. But there was another factor that has been overlooked that also explains the disappearance of the steel industry in this country. In its effort to prevent Western Europe from succumbing to communism the US had instituted the Marshall Plan to reconstruct their basic industries. Whereas America's steel plants had seen no reason to invest in new equipment during the Depression, those countries receiving aid under the Marshall Plan were provided with the latest in technology. The same would apply to Japan and later South Korea. This combination of lowering trade barriers and failing to invest in more efficient would lead to the loss of jobs and to America's dependence upon foreign imports for a commodity like steel. The resulting domino effect caused a decline in the production of coal and coke for the steel furnaces. Pittsburgh has lost its place as steel capital of the world. A similar scenario would take place in the cities that surround Detroit when the Japanese automotive manufacturers began to construct their own plants in this country and seize an additional market share from Detroit's Big Three. In an effort to entice the Japanese to invest in this country, the government agreed that only 50 percent of the finished product would have to be manufactured domestically to avoid paying custom duties. In order to have a level playing field for US auto producers, they were accorded the same privileges of sourcing some of their parts overseas, where it was less expensive to produce these components. In a one world market, unionized US manufacturers that had previously supplied parts for Detroit no longer were able to compete, and their communities in Michigan and Ohio soon became ghost cities. While the Japanese facilities in the US were non-unionized, their wages, pensions and benefits were the same as those of unionized shops. The advantage these Japanese auto producers possessed was enjoying far more freedom in assigning workers to various jobs within the plant. While competition lowered prices, it also created unemployment. Reagan's contention that competition reduced the cost of merchandise and expanded the market for consumer goods was accurate. He didn't forecast the negative effect it would produce on America's unionized labor force.

Prime examples of this effect were the labor-intensive apparel and footwear industries. As more and more apparel and footwear manufacturers moved their production facilities to off-shore locations in the Far East, in order to gain a price advantage over their competitors, other manufacturers in the same industries were forced to follow suit or go out of business. What began as a trickle developed into a groundswell that appeared to have no end. Old respected brand names in men's tailored clothing, unable to pry themselves loose from union contracts, disappeared from the retail landscape. The final blow to these domestic industries was the decision of the Chinese leadership of the Communist party to open up China's economy to private enterprise. Today, China is the number one creditor nation to the United States, supplanting Japan. Not only is China the largest supplier of apparel and footwear for the United States but that country has made notable inroads in the toy, luggage, and electronics markets as well. The annual negative balance of payments between the two nations was more than $200 billion in 2005 and promises to grow annually. Today China (along with Japan, South Korea and others) supports our growing national debt by purchasing US Treasury bonds that cover the interest on our debt. Reagan, of course, was not directly responsible for the dramatic changes that would alter the US economy from one geared to manufacturing to one centered on service industries, other than by his continued advocacy of free trade as a means of expanding the growth of the world's economy. At the economic summit meetings of the seven largest industrialized economies, he harped on that point. His only major ally at those conferences was Britain's *Iron Lady*, Prime Minister Margaret Thatcher, who after breaking the back of England's powerful labor unions, had charted a new and successful course for Britain's economy.

Reagan faced a major a challenge in attaining the Republican nomination. His main opponent was George H.W. Bush, the one-term congressman who was appointed by Nixon to be Ambassador to the Peoples Republic of China after losing his race for the senate in Texas and who was appointed by Ford to head up the Central Intelligence Agency. During the campaign, Bush positioned himself as a moderate Republican with experience in foreign affairs, which Reagan lacked. He also ridiculed Reagan's theory of Supply Side economics, referring to it as Voodoo economics. To Reagan's shock, Bush carried the majority of delegates at the Iowa caucus. With the New Hampshire primary next, and with Bush considered to be a New Englander and likely to carry the first primary in the nation, the Reagan camp panicked. John Sears, who had managed Reagan's unsuccessful bid in 1976, was cashiered. Should Bush win in New Hampshire with a large majority of the delegates, it would appear that Reagan's hard line against the Soviet Union and his theory of Supply Side economics were making him unelectable in the forthcoming presidential race. The "California Mafia" that had surrounded Reagan when he was governor in Sacramento had never liked Sears, and his wife Nancy convinced him to change horses in mid-stream. Nixon suggested he replace Sears with Bill Casey, another outsider.

Casey, a native New Yorker and like Reagan a self-made man, hardly possessed the expected background for a campaign manager. A successful lawyer and one-time Chairman of the Securities and Exchange Commission, he had become a millionaire on Wall Street representing various financial interests. During the Second World War he had served under Bill Donovan at the Office of Strategic Services (OSS), from which would emerge the CIA. It was not Casey who turned the tide in New Hampshire but an unknown non-political figure, Max Hugel. Enlisted by William Loeb, the publisher of the Manchester Union-Leader, one of the most conservative newspapers in the country, Hugel was a successful businessman. He employed the unorthodox approach of dividing the New Hampshire electorate into its various ethnic groups, and then selecting a leading personality from each ethnic group as a co-chairman of the Committee to Nominate Reagan. It was this unorthodox method of vote gathering that enabled Reagan to capture New Hampshire and provided the momentum for his nomination. Following Reagan's sweeping victory, Casey sought the key post in the new administration, Secretary of State. Reagan, claiming that Casey's rapid-fire New York speech pattern made him hard to understand even in Washington, much less in foreign capitals, offered him the post of Director of the CIA instead. Given Casey's wartime background with the OSS, Reagan assumed it would be a reasonable fit. He also elevated the post to that of Cabinet status.

While Reagan, by dint of his perseverance and his unwillingness to compromise, eventually forced a reluctant Congress to enact his 25 percent across-the-board tax cut, he was soon faced with two major problems he inherited from Carter. The inflation caused by the OPEC oil crisis continued. Both the Social Security Trust Fund and the savings and loan institutions were affected by the soaring interest rates that followed. In the case of Social Security, the threat to its solvency was tied to the Cost of Living Allowances (COLAs), which in turn were linked to the Consumer Price Index. In the case of the S&Ls, the high interest rates threatened their solvency because their business was restricted by law solely to the issuance of mortgages for private home buyers.

During the Carter administration, the president and Congress faced the initial threat to the solvency of the Social Security system. Despite the end of the war in Vietnam, defense expenditures did continue to increase. But the major factors that forced the Carter administration to increase the payroll deduction from workers' paychecks and from business, was the slow but steady increase in inflation, a result of the increasing cost of a barrel of crude oil, and the rising costs of the Great Society programs. Even though Carter had managed to reduce the budget deficit from $54 billion to $41 billion in his 1979 budget, it was not reflected in the COLAs that automatically kicked in once the Consumer Price Index had risen. Now, three years later, in 1982, in order to maintain the system for current and future generations, the payroll tax would have to be substantially increased beyond Carter's small increase. As previously noted, the man responsible in large measure was Volcker, who increased the discount rate to 13% in an attempt to squeeze inflation out of the economy by reducing business expansion, which he believed to be the root cause for the runaway inflation. Instead, the high interest rates resulted in an economic recession and until the OPEC monopoly was broken, inflation continued to ravage the economy. By January 1981, when Reagan took office, the increases in the COLAs threatened the solvency of the Social Security Trust Fund. By the middle of 1982, even though the OPEC monopoly had ended and the inflation rate was reduced to 6.2%, the fund was teetering on bankruptcy. (See Appendix, Table 7.)

New York Senator Daniel Patrick Moynihan, a Democrat who had once worked in the Nixon administration, was at the forefront of placing the system on a sound economic basis that would insure its viability for the next half a century or perhaps longer. Reagan, who was opposed to any tax increase, especially one that sharply increased the payroll deductions from both individuals and business, proposed instead the privatization of the Social Security system. The number of senior citizens dependent upon it for their income had increased dramatically as advances in medicine and pharmacology extended the average lifespan of Americans. Despite the protests of organized labor and business as well as Reagan, Congress passed the legislation that would ensure the safety of the Trust Fund for the proposed half a century. Despite Reagan's threat to veto the legislation, he grudgingly signed the measure. While the Social Security Trust Fund had been salvaged, the COLAs also applied to government employee pensions, as well as to military and veteran benefits. All of these increased expenses would have to be funded by government revenues, further increasing the federal budget deficits.

No segment of the economy had suffered more from rising inflation than the savings and loan institutions. As early as the late 1960s, as a result of the initial inflation induced by the Vietnam War, they had felt the pinch of the high cost of borrowing money to issue mortgages. But by the late 1970s, with inflation continuing to grow, their financial situation became precarious. The final blow was Volcker's decision to increase the discount rate to 13%. With the majority of their 30-year mortgages issued at lower interest rates and the cost of borrowing money prohibitive, an entire industry faced bankruptcy. The S&Ls sought the removal of the restrictions that confined them to the issuance of mortgages, so they could enter the same markets as commercial banks. This would enable them to extend loans to commercial businesses, sell securities, issue credit cards, and enter into risky adventures. Given the number of these institutions and the fact that they were located in all 50 states, Congress was sensitive to their plight.

Deregulation was in the air, and it meshed perfectly with Reagan's concept of a free market economy, which was envisioned as lowering the cost of goods and services and stimulating the economy. In 1978, Congress had deregulated the natural gas and airlines industries, which proved a boon to consumers. Two years later, it deregulated the trucking and savings and loan industries. The Depository Institutions Deregulation and Monetary Control Act began the process, which continued to evolve through the Reagan years. The limitations placed on where saving banks could locate new branches and in what proximity, which hindered the growth of these institutions, were lifted, allowing for further competition among the S&Ls. Federal guarantees on depositors' accounts were raised from $40,000 to $100,000, and the S&Ls became free to set their own interest rates on Certificates of Deposit. This would result in a bidding war for deposits as consumers sought the highest rates for their money. Commercial banks, which had previously ignored the individual-depositor market, now that these accounts were guarantee by the FDIC, entered the bidding war for consumer deposits. The competition between S&Ls vying for the consumer dollar and the commercial banks drove the interest rate paid to depositors up. On the surface, the deregulation of the S&Ls made sense. Where it failed was in not having a sufficient number of regulators overseeing these banks and making sure that the commercial loans they extended were backed by the necessary amount of the reserves they held in the event of defaults on the loans they granted. Furthermore, these banks had no previous experience in commercial banking. The combination of inexperience and a lack of regulators overseeing their business practices was deadly. In the commercial housing boom that followed the deregulation of the S&Ls, many went overboard in extending commercial loans. Since commercial buildings could be depreciated on an annual basis, pools of investors were created to invest in commercial real estate with the knowledge that their deposits were guaranteed by the government for up to $100,000. The investors were allowed to write off the annual depreciation on their personal income taxes. Finally, the savings and loan institutions were prime customers for the issuance of junk bonds, which paid an interest rate of between 12% and 14%. As a result of these forces coming together, the commercial housing market was overbuilt, and when the S&Ls called in their loans they were stuck with empty buildings; no tenants to occupy them; and insufficient reserves to weather the defaults. Finally, Congress enacted legislation to plug this loophole in the tax code, resulting in investors withdrawing their loans before the buildings had finished construction. The sudden decline of the stock market in 1987 resulted in a spate of bankruptcies among public companies that had only been able to survive by the junk bonds that they had issued. This left many of the savings and loan institutions holding worthless junk bonds. The bankruptcies of the S&Ls that followed left the FDIC, and eventually the federal government, having to absorb those funds that had to be paid out to depositors. The S&L crisis resulted in the closing of hundreds of savings institutions across the country. In order to salvage some of the assets of those banks — i.e., the ones that were only seriously crippled — Congress enacted legislation that removed the restrictions forbidding commercial banks to cross state lines. Naturally, those commercial banks that agreed to take over crippled S&Ls retained only those assets that were valuable and dumped those that weren't into the lap of the government. The cost of the S&L scandal eventually resulted in the government having to pick up a tab of about $250 billion. As for the S&Ls that managed to survive, now they function like any other bank. The original concept of the savings and loan institutions as the backbone for home ownership disappeared. The scandal's most important legacy was the consolidation of the commercial banking industry. With commercial banks now allowed to cross state lines, a spate of mergers took place, a trend that continues to the present day.

In his second term Reagan faced the first major crisis of his political career -- the Iran-Contra scandal, which almost led to his impeachment. It was the Boland Amendment, attached to the 1983 Defense Appropriations Act, which triggered all the events leading up to and ushering in the Iran-Contra imbroglio. The Boland amendment was a reaction to actions taken by the death squads of the Contras against those civilians who supported the Sandinistas. As a result, the annual appropriation for military and economic aid used by the CIA to support Contra activities was capped at $30 million for FY'83 and $50 million for FY'84. In fact many in Congress feared that supporting the Contras might lead to another Vietnam.

It was at this moment that Casey made the decision to continue the struggle against the Sandinista regime, by any means, legitimate or not. Casey, accustomed to the free-wheeling activities of the OSS in France, decided to take matters into his own hands. While Congress had enacted legislation limiting the covert activities of the CIA, it had never seen any reason to enact similar legislation that would cover the National Security Council (NSC), later renamed the National Security Agency (NSA). Originally designed for the sole purpose of advising the President on foreign affairs, this agency had gradually expanded its activities, as most bureaucracies in Washington tend to do, becoming an additional source of intelligence. (Nixon was the first president to alter its original function, when he chose his NSC chief Henry Kissinger to handle secret negotiations that led to the recognition of Communist China.)

Aside from being a devout Catholic and a virulent anti-communist, Casey, as head of the CIA, felt a deep obligation to protect the members of his organization. Hezbollah, the terrorist organization in Lebanon, which was supported financially by the Iranian government, had captured (among others in that country) the head of the CIA station in Lebanon. Casey was determined to save his life at all costs.

Robert McFarlane, who had been assistant Secretary of State under Haig and was later appointed NSC Advisor, played a major role in the arms-for-hostage deal. Casey now enlisted him in his cause. Through an intermediary it was suggested that the Iranian government would be open to exchanging the hostages held in Lebanon in return for replacement of the tow missiles needed to carry on the war against Iraq. Since all the military equipment used by the Iranian army had been supplied by the US prior to the fall of the Shah, the Iranian government had no place else to turn. Ostensibly, it was moderates in the Iranian government who had suggested the deal. McFarlane accompanied the first shipment of missiles from Israel to Iran, and when the Iranian moderates did not meet the original terms agreed upon, by releasing all the hostages, he refused to accompany the second shipment. When a Lebanese newspaper first disclosed the secret mission, and the article was confirmed by the Iranian authorities, he was forced to resign. Without Israel's complicity in arranging the arms for hostage agreement, it never would have been possible.

The government of Israel, which had taken the initiative in proposing the arrangement, had two motives for its involvement. First, it hoped to gain the release of Iranian Jews in Iran, and second, to ingratiate itself with the Reagan administration. Had it been a straight arms-for-hostages deal, there would have been a scandal but not of the proportion that ensued. Part of the funds paid by the Iranian government for the missiles was used to support the Contras fighting in Nicaragua. Throughout the controversy, Reagan insisted that his only motive in the shipment of arms to Iran was to normalize relations between the two governments and not to exchange prisoners in return for the arms shipments. For the press and Congress, this assertion was difficult to believe since Reagan had solicited money from some of the Gulf States to arm the Contras. When the scheme finally was brought to his attention, he professed to be shocked. Casey, now dead, had betrayed him. It remains a question how much Reagan knew, and if he did not know, then how could he have avoided being informed about the scheme. Only one thing is certain. Since the money used to support the Contra was funneled through a Swiss bank account, only Casey, among all the conspirators involved was knowledgeable enough to understand the use of such banking facilities.

In the end, Casey's determination to defeat the Sandinistas was successful. The tens of millions of dollars raised to fight them enabled the Contras to expand their original military force of several hundred men to a disciplined force numbering in the tens of thousands. Trained and directed by the CIA, they were able to establish bases in Nicaragua and hold them against attacks from the Sandinista army. As a result of the civil war that ensued, other Central American nations proposed free elections to decide upon the future government of Nicaragua. In the supervised elections the Sandinistas were defeated and a popularly elected government took over the country. The threat that regimes supported by the Soviet Union might come to power elsewhere in Central America was eliminated. This was Reagan's first success in blocking the further spread of Soviet influence in the American hemisphere. However, he had far bigger fish to fry.

Those who lived through that period of time referred to as the Cold War, whether citizens of the Soviet Union or the US, understood neither its rationale nor its end goal. The population in both nations had been so overdosed with constant propaganda about the aims of the other side that the ability to make a rational judgment was lost. Was it an effort to contain the expansion of Communist doctrine throughout the world, either by the use of naked force or propaganda? Or was it, as Americans were told, a contest between good and evil, freedom and totalitarianism, where the rights of the individual were subordinated to a few bureaucrats who had risen to the top of the power structure? For the Soviet citizen, it was a war against US imperialism and the last dying efforts of a capitalist system besieged by its own internal contradictions as it sought to destroy its inevitable successor, communism. It was also a conflict between an ideal of economic justice for everyone and the exploitation of the majority for the benefit of the few.

Neither the leadership of the Soviet Union nor the various US administrations throughout the half a century that the Cold War lasted saw any possible compromise. The only thing that prevented either side from abandoning the shaky status quo was the threat of mutual destruction from an atomic war. It was a prospect real enough to serve as a deterrent. Yet ironically both countries continued to increase the number of atomic weapons in their stockpiles as a form of insurance against a surprise attack from the other side. Because of all his rhetoric both before and after he assumed the presidency, Reagan was viewed as the epitome of the intransigent Cold War warrior, one who by might lead the United States into a hot war with the Soviet Union, resulting in the end of American civilization. His counterpart was the puzzling figure of Mikhail Gorbachev.

In a certain sense Gorbachev was the most tragic figure produced under the concept of state socialism. A devout believer in economic justice, he was unable to come to terms with the internal contradictions within the system. The economy of the Soviet Union had been constructed as a pyramid. Unless the pyramid was leveled and replaced by a new structure, nothing could be changed. For almost 60 years, ever since Stalin had converted an agricultural society into a modern industrial one, the objective sought had been reached. Social conditions had been improved tremendously, but once everything was in place — free education; free medical and dental care; pensions for the aged and disabled; housing and electricity; full employment — there was no incentive to move the system further along and risk upsetting what was already in existence. State socialism had gone as far as it could go.

When Gorbachev was finally elected to the leadership of the Soviet Union, he was the youngest man to lead the Soviet government since Lenin and Stalin. As was the case with these predecessors, whose economic policies shaped the original economy of the Soviet Union, Gorbachev also had a new formula intended to redirect and reform the economy in such a fashion that it would become more productive and raise the standard of living for the average Russian. But the system was incapable of being reformed without destroying it. In defense and space, they were in competition with the United States, but there was no internal competition within the system. The term *perestroika* might mean restructuring, but Gorbachev was prepared only to put his toe in the water before diving in. Gorbachev's first effort at privatization — allowing for the formation of private cooperatives in the service, manufacturing and foreign trade sectors, and introducing the concept of individual profits — was doomed to failure before it was initiated. First-time entrepreneurs faced excessively high taxes on any profits. The major roadblock, however, was the inability of the employer to fire workers in order to increase productivity. By the time the law was altered two years later, it was too late to convince would-be capitalists to trust the government. Gorbachev was hindered by his core belief in the fundamentals of the Communist doctrine, which prescribed that under state socialism every man and woman was guaranteed a job. As a result, there was no possibility of increasing productivity by utilizing efficient machinery to replace manual labor. This was one of the principal weaknesses of the system. The one dogma of communism that never could be amended was the guarantee of full employment.

The Reagan administration and its intelligence arm, the CIA, seem not to have recognized at that time that all of Gorbachev's actions were designed to prop up the Soviet economy. His repudiation of the Stalin doctrine — insisting on complete control over the destinies of all the East European nations that the Soviet army had liberated from Nazi Germany, a doctrine that had been reaffirmed by all of his successors — is just one of the steps he initiated to solve that basic problem. He did not heed Reagan's famous words: "Mr. Gorbachev, tear down this wall," without first talking Germany's Chancellor Helmut Kohl out of $4 billion. His decision to withdraw all Russian troops from Afghanistan stopped that financial hemorrhage. His decision to allow Western European nations to construct a pipeline from Siberia to Western Europe to supply those countries with of natural gas was predicated on the need to find a new source for additional government revenues. The motivation to initiate all of these radical steps is attributed in part to Reagan's refusal to abandon his Strategic Defense Initiative. As is the case with any leader of a nation,

Gorbachev believed his first and most important role was to defend his country from an attack.

Reagan meanwhile had continued with his inflammatory rhetoric denouncing the foreign policies of the leadership of the Soviet Union. Given the military advantage that the United States possessed, his rhetoric could only be perceived in Moscow as a threat to the safety and security of the Soviet Union. When Edward Teller, the father of the hydrogen bomb and a hard-line anti-Communist, suggested to Reagan the development of a nuclear X-ray laser curtain that would prevent Soviet missiles from striking the United States, he bit. Hans Bethe, the world-renowned physicist who had worked on the original atom bomb and the hydrogen bomb, was highly skeptical about its feasibility. But after visiting with Peter Hagelstein, the theory's developer, at the Livermore National Laboratory, Bethe pronounced it "a splendid idea." Unlike the Manhattan Project, which developed the atomic bomb during the Second World War and was kept top secret, the commencement of work on SDI was announced to the world in an address to the nation by on March 23, 1983.

To the Soviet defense ministry and the members of the Politburo, this announcement came as a seismic shock. If in fact the United States was in the process of developing such a shield against Soviet ICBMs, it meant that Soviet strategy against a preemptive attack from the United States now had been rendered obsolete. If the project was still on the drawing board, then perhaps a preemptive attack could prevent the system from becoming operational. In the lead-up to the 1984 election, experts from MIT were called by Congress to testify against its feasibility. These open hearings convinced the Soviet leadership that they still had time to develop their own system. Meanwhile, the theory developed by Hagelstein ran into difficulties when an attempt was made to test it in practice. Undeterred, the scientists at Livermore developed a second system known as Brilliant Pebbles. In this system, satellite-based mini-missiles would track down incoming ICBMs and destroy them in the air. Numerous tests were made using the system, and while some were successful, others were not. Since this system was less than perfect and still was in violation of the SALT II treaty, ground-based interceptor missiles were developed — the Patriot used in the first Gulf War being an example. But when Gorbachev came to power in 1985, he could not be sure whether the Brilliant Pebbles would be implemented and would be effective.

Since Soviet scientists were unable to develop anything comparable to either SDI or Brilliant Pebbles, Gorbachev decided to take a new tack. First, he would increase Russia's offensive ability; next, he would set in place Soviet intermediate missiles designed to destroy all of Western Europe in the event of a preemptive strike by the United States. He hoped to use the implantation of those missiles as a deterrent to any first strike by the United States. Reagan's response was to place the same number of intermediate missiles in Germany. When Gorbachev held his initial meeting with Reagan in Reykjavik, Iceland, considered neutral territory, he spoke of his plan for massive disarmament by both superpowers so that by the year 2000 all offensive weapons held by both sides would be made inoperative and eventually destroyed. In exchange, all work on the SDI would be confined to the laboratory. Reagan would not give an inch; he cut off all discussions after three days and returned to Washington. Other meetings followed in Geneva and Moscow between Reagan and Secretary of State George Shultz and Gorbachev and Russian Foreign Minister Eduard Shevardnadze. Agreement was reached to destroy all intermediate ballistic missiles on both sides. It was the first meaningful agreement between the United States and the Soviet Union, and in the US, credit is given to Reagan's philosophy, "trust but verify." This was expected to become the first stage in what would lead to mutual disarmament.

Reagan's revolution is comparable to FDR's revolution, which made the Democrats the majority party for 40 years. The combination of the Southern and border states, loyal to the Democratic Party for more than a century, was broken by the Reagan phenomenon. These Southern and border states, combined with a number of Western and Midwestern states like Ohio, eventually led to Republican majorities in both the House and the Senate and Republican domination of the presidency. (The election of Clinton in 1992, to be covered in the next chapter, was only an aberration and mainly the result of the bizarre independent candidacy of Ross Perot.)

Furthermore, following the disaster of the Iranian hostage taking, Reagan restored American confidence that indeed the US was a superpower and that such humiliation would never occur again. While the national debt almost tripled while Reagan was in office, at the same time, the GDP increased from $3 trillion to $5 trillion. After a temporary crisis in 1987, the New York Stock Exchange recovered and once again exceeded the 2000 level before the one-day sell-off. Best of all, his exuberant confidence in the future of this country washed over the American public. Once again, the United States was the leader of the free world.

Chapter 12. The End of the Cold War: The George H. W. Bush Presidency

George H. W. Bush, who was President when the Soviet Union imploded and who had been instrumental in putting together the coalition that defeated Iraq's Saddam Hussein and expelled him from Kuwait, should have been a shoo-in to be reelected to a second term in 1992. With a ninety-one approval rating after the Desert Storm victory, he enjoyed a public popularity that dissuaded the more high-profile Democratic candidates from entering the race. This vacuum led to the nomination of the relatively unknown governor of Arkansas, William Jefferson Clinton, who despite a dubious personal record pulled off an upset in the general election. Historians and political pundits blamed Bush's defeat on two ostensible causes. One was the economic recession of 1991, from which the nation only began to emerge in the third quarter of 1992, too late to help his campaign; this issue was highlighted by the Clinton mantra: "it's the economy, stupid." The other was Bush's reneging on his 1988 pledge: "read my lips: no new taxes," which was deemed to alienate the conservative base of the Republican party. There is no question that both the economic downturn and the tax increase resonated with the supporters of Ross Perot.

The effect of the independent candidacy of Perot upon the election results was dismissed because he failed to acquire any votes in the Electoral College. Yet, if the results of the popular vote are analyzed, Perot was more than likely the determining factor in the President's defeat.

Perot captured almost 20 million votes compared to Bush's 39 million and Clinton's 45 million; if he had stayed out of the race (he dropped out in June on a dubious pretext, then reentered the campaign two months before the election) Bush might well have won. Perot was an anomaly among third party candidates. A self-made billionaire, he postured himself as the only man who could save the country from its impending financial disaster. His program called for fiscal austerity and term limits for members of Congress. Two years later, in 1994, Newt Gingrich, an outspoken voice among the Republicans in Congress, would adopt Perot's program under the rubric of a Contract with America and the Republicans would capture both houses of Congress for the first time in 40 years. Moreover, once the Republicans had implanted themselves as the majority party, they continued to remain in power. Perot's proposals would have reduced government expenditures in programs that had been the backbone of the philosophy of the Democratic party. Bush lost to Perot the moderate Republican and independent voters who, now that the Cold War was over, were naïve enough to believe that the so-called peace dividend would result in lower taxes for them. This segment of the population was the base for Perot's 20 million votes, and Gingrich was foresighted enough to understand its implications and reap the benefits. In other words, it was Perot who inadvertently completed the Reagan Revolution that had propelled the Republicans into being the majority political party.

But another dynamic was taking place within the Beltway. The end of the Cold War had also seemed to annihilate any modicum of civility between the Republicans and Democrats. While the ideologies of Ronald Reagan and House Speaker "Tip" O'Neill were diametrically opposed, at the end of the day they were capable of polite banter. One cannot imagine such a scenario involving Bush and any of the post-O'Neill Democratic leaders. Although Bush had been a very successful businessman, in the dog-eat-dog world of Texas oil exploration, he was a lost soul in the milieu of Washington politics, and his effectiveness was hampered by his inability to be an impressive public speaker. He owed his rise to prominence in the Republican party to political appointments by both Richard Nixon and Gerald Ford. He had been elected to the presidency not on his own merit but as the successor to Ronald Reagan.

The denigration of the first Bush presidency by liberals in general and by the media in particular had its roots back in the early days of the Cold

War, when the Democrats were assigned the blame for the loss of China to the Communists and were plastered with the label of being soft on communism. The efforts by Presidents John Kennedy and Lyndon Johnson to erase this image by involving the US in the Vietnam War not only backfired but led to the election of the liberals' number one nemesis, Nixon, who brought the war to a successful conclusion by recognizing Communist China. It was the Vietnam War that led to the great schism within the Democratic Party, which continues to the present day.

George H. W. Bush's presidency was marked by his success in foreign affairs. Although some contend that it was the "Iron Lady," Margaret Thatcher, who pushed him into making the decision to expel Saddam Hussein from Kuwait, in the final analysis it was the President who marshaled the members of the UN, and in particular Mikhail Gorbachev, to support the invasion. It is ironic that almost every nation in the coalition Bush assembled, including the United States, had supported Saddam's regime during the eight-year-long Iran-Iraq War either through military or financial aid. But it was the United States more than any other country that had played a major role in the Iran-Iraq War. America's initial support for Iraq in the conflict was no doubt based on the decision of the Iranian government to hold US embassy personnel hostage for more than a year. Now, just three years after the unsuccessful conclusion of the Iran-Iraq War, the US was spearheading the coalition force intent upon removing Iraq from Kuwait.

From as far back as 1972, long before Saddam had come to power, Iraq had been a client state of the Soviet Union. Russia not only had sold armaments but had sent along military advisors as well. Furthermore, Iraq owed the Soviet Union tens of billions of dollars as a result of Iraq's conflict with Iran. Should the Iraqi armed forces be defeated by the coalition forces, as the Soviet military leaders expected, there would be no possibility of collecting those debts. Saddam mistakenly assumed that the Soviet Union, as a permanent member of the Security Council, would step in at the last moment and prevent the imposition of the UN's January 15, 1991 deadline for Iraq to remove its armed forces from Kuwait. Even Hosni Mubarak, the president of Egypt, who had called for a meeting of the Arab League to intercede before the invasion took place, found his efforts brushed aside by the Iraqi dictator. Mubarak then sent Egyptian forces to join the coalition army in expelling Iraq from Kuwait. Even stranger was the decision of the Syrian dictator Hafez Assad, also a client of the Soviet Union and no friend of the United States, to send Syrian troops to fight alongside the Egyptians. In a last-minute desperate effort to convince the Soviet Union to intercede, Tariq Aziz, Iraq's foreign minister, made a trip to Moscow, which proved to be of no avail.

The steps that led to the US decision to expel Saddam from Kuwait spanned a period of six months. From Saddam's initial invasion of Kuwait, at the beginning of August until the deadline set by the United Nations of January 15, 1991, a series of negotiations took place between the Bush administration and the other players in the drama. Bush's first priority was to get the support of Saudi Arabia's King Fahd, without whom a land invasion would have been impossible. The President had to convince the King of the seriousness of the problem that faced his kingdom. With Saddam's army now on the border of Saudi Arabia, it would require no great effort on the part of the Iraqi army to defeat the Saudi army, overrun the kingdom and bring to an end the Saudi dynasty — given the disparity in the strength of Iraq's armed forces and those of the Saudi kingdom. It was this real threat that convinced Fahd to permit the stationing on Saudi soil of the first 100,000 US troops. For the United States, its European allies and Japan, protecting Saudi's oil supplies was an economic necessity. If Saddam was to seize the Saudi oil fields, he would control 40% of the world's oil supplies. Already with his conquest of Kuwait, he controlled 20% of the world's oil reserves. The first item on the Bush agenda was to have the United Nations impose an embargo on all oil shipments from Iraq and Kuwait. By taking this step and getting Gorbachev to support that decision, Bush was able to cut off the flow of funds necessary to purchase the supplies needed to feed the Iraqi people. Since Iraq imported 75% of its food supplies, Bush believed this action might force Saddam to evacuate Kuwait peacefully. Prior to that embargo, the United States and its western allies had frozen all of Iraq's assets, leaving the regime bereft of any financial means with which to purchase food.

Even before Saddam had consolidated his power in Iraq, he played the dominant role in moving Iraqi society from its primitive state to that of a modern Western-oriented regime. In 1972, he prodded the Iraqi government to nationalize the country's oil fields by expropriating the monopoly held by Western oil companies. His decision couldn't have been taken at a more propitious time. A year later, the Yom Kippur War would break out, and to punish the United States for its support of Israel the OPEC nations instituted a temporary embargo on oil shipments to the United States. Traders in oil futures immediately jacked the price of oil up from $3 a barrel to $7. By 1982, the price of a barrel of oil had settled in the high $20s, after peaking at $38 following the Iranian revolution and Saddam's invasion of Iran in 1980, which at the onset threatened the oil supply to West should the oil fields of either or both sides be put out of commission. (See Appendix, Figure 1.) During this nine-year period, the OPEC nations found themselves enriched beyond their wildest dreams. Iraq, as the second largest producer of oil in the Middle East, found itself blessed with an enormous influx of dollars for the first time since it had been carved out of the old Ottoman Empire.

Saddam used most of his nation's newly found wealth not only to upgrade Iraq's infrastructure but also to revolutionize the country's social structure and move it on the road to becoming a secular society. In taking this approach, he had two objectives: to consolidate the position of the ruling Ba'ath party through improving the living standards of the population; and, to diminish the power of the Shiite clerics, who held sway over the 60 percent of the population that embraced that faith. He was convinced that only by transforming the society through secularization could Iraq emerge as the leading power in the Arab world. He would succeed where his idol, Nasser, had failed.

Throughout the 1970s, Saddam set in motion a series of programs designed to move Iraqi society from its primitive past into the modern world. He focused his initial efforts on education and the elimination of illiteracy among the Iraqi population. The government picked up the tab not only for primary and secondary education but for the university level as well. He also established the best public health system in the Arab world, including free hospitalization for everyone. In his desire to alter Iraq's medieval society, where two-thirds of the population remained peasants tilling the land, he decided to diversify the economy by using the revenues from the increases in oil prices during the 1970s to create an industrial base. Within a brief period of time, every city in Iraq was electrified and even some of the more remote areas of the country had been serviced. He broke up the large estates and divided the land among the peasants, and he personally supervised the importation of modern agricultural machinery to increase productivity. Pursuing the Ba'ath party's socialistic agenda, he established farm cooperatives in which the profits were divided according to each man's contribution to the final product.

He also established schools to train unskilled workers. By these measures, he upgraded the standard of living of Iraq's peasant class and earned their loyalty. All of these major reforms took place while Saddam was still vice president of the Ba'athist regime and had yet to assume total power over the nation. He had proven himself to be a tough and able administrator of the Iraqi economy.

In 1979, the sickly president of Iraq, Ahmed Hassan al-Bakr, negotiated an initial treaty with the Ba'athist president of Syria, Hafez al-Assad, which called for the eventual unification of the two nations. Under the terms of the agreement, Assad would become deputy leader of the two nations, which in effect would relegate Saddam to a far lesser role. Moreover, in the event that the merger of the two nations took place, it would be Assad and not Saddam who would assume the leadership of the two nations. However, for reasons that are unclear, al-Bakr resigned before the agreement went into effect and Saddam became president of Iraq. Immediately, negotiations between the two countries were broken off. Saddam had no need for a Syrian ally.

Five days after he took the oath of office, he made a wholesale cleansing of those members of the Ba'ath party who might challenge his authority. Saddam lifted whatever restrictions still remained on the dress code for women and appointed some of them to key positions in government and industry. If this offended the religious community, they were totally alienated when he changed the legal system from that based on Islamic law to one modeled after Western democracies.

Melding all of Iraq's different groups into a solid, unified nation was Saddam's major challenge. In addition to religious and ethnic complications, Iraq was to a great extent a tribal society, in which the tribal leader had far more influence over his people than the centralized government. To combat these tendencies within the Iraqi society, Saddam resorted to what became known as the cult of personality, which could be viewed as a form of self-deification. Not only were statues of his likeness erected in every city throughout the country, but his face was painted on the walls of office buildings, schools, airports and shops as well as printed on Iraqi currency. The only places that remained sacrosanct were the mosques. Throughout the 24 years of his absolutist rule over the country, Saddam's two greatest fears were a coup directed against his regime or an assassination. To prevent new cliques from forming, the key figures in his administration were either close family members or men who had grown up around the city where he had been raised, Tikrit. To make certain that a coup was not engineered from within the army, as so often happened in Iraq, in 1974 he appointed a close associate as commander of the People's Army, whose principal function was internal security against possible rebellions amongst the officers of the regular army. But he placed greatest dependency on his notorious secret police, commanded by his youngest stepbrother.

The ostensible reason for the Iran-Iraq war was the dispute over rights to the Shatt al-Arab waterway, which divides the two nations. Saddam's actual reason for initiating hostilities was to bring about the downfall of the theocratic regime of Ayatollah Khomeini and to annex the only province in Iran, Khazestan, where the overwhelming majority of the population was Sunni, and which possessed vast oil fields. Saddam committed two errors. First, he hoped the Iranian armed forces had been so weakened by Khomeini's elimination of the generals that the Iraqi army would meet no real opposition once it invaded Iran; he also overestimated the quality of his own armed forces. In order to prevent the possibility of a military coup, a longstanding tradition in Iraq, he deliberately weeded out those officers with any talent or following among the junior officers. As a result, instead of obtaining quick victory and the acquisition of Khazestan, he found himself mired in an interminable war that soon was being fought on Iraqi territory. His early efforts to establish a truce failed even when he resorted to the use of chemical weapons against the Iranians.

After eight years of continuous warfare, both nations were bankrupt and a truce finally was agreed upon. With Saddam's army in a weakened state, the quasi-independent Kurdish population in Iraq openly revolted against his regime in a bid for independence. Iraqi troops sent to crush the revolt attacked the Kurdish city of Halabja with chemical weapons. About 5,000 civilians are reported to have died. At the time of the massacre, the international community remained silent. Most countries, including the United States, as well as the United Nations, viewed the Kurdish rebellion as an internal Iraqi problem.

In 1990, two years after the truce had finally brought the Iran-Iraq war to an end, Saddam's government was in a precarious position. Even with the financial aid he had received from the neighboring Gulf States, the nation was in debt for $75 billion. Nor were the Iranians in a much better financial position. The number of deaths on both sides was in the neighborhood of 1.7 million, not to mention the number of soldiers and civilians permanently maimed. The vaunted Iraqi army had not performed as well as expected, and the US military equipment provided to the Shah was proven superior to that of the Soviet Union. It was the high-tech military equipment which the US had sold to the Shah during the 1970s, and not the waves of human cannon fodder, that had turned back the initial invasion of the Iraqis. The Iran-Contra scandal that tarnished the last two years of the Reagan's presidency was an effort by the conservatives in the Iranian government to replenish their stores of US military equipment. The Tomahawk missiles, sent as bargaining chips for the release of the Americans held hostage in Lebanon, played a major role in the war against Iraq.

Saddam's decision to invade Kuwait was a result of many factors, but the most important was his desperate need for money. He convinced himself that in fighting Iran, he was protecting the other countries in the Persian Gulf region from the religious threat coming from Iran. As a result, they had backed Iraq with massive loans during the war. Kuwait had loaned him $30 billion. He expected Kuwait to write off the debt. In addition, there was the long-standing belief — not only held by Saddam — that Kuwait was actually part of Iraq. The British, under their protectorate, had created this artificial country and thereby had cut off Iraq from an outlet to the sea. In reconstructing the former provinces of the Ottoman Empire, British imperialists viewed Kuwait as a buffer state between Iraq and Saudi Arabia. Because it was small in land mass and population, with only one Muslim faith (Sunni), and could be easily controlled, it suited British imperial interests. Desperate for funds, Saddam had asked the emir of Kuwait to reduce its oil production in order to increase the price of oil on the world market. Instead, Kuwait played a major role within the OPEC cartel to sustain prices at their current level.

Actually, it was Saudi Arabia, the leading oil producer among the OPEC nations that was responsible for maintaining the price of oil. Saudi Arabia also had provided the bulk of the funds that enabled Iraq to continue the war with Iran. These contradictory policies among the Arab oil-producing states were a reflection of their need and distrust of each other's government. On the one hand, they were all Arabs and followers of the same religious Sunni faith; on the other hand, the secular and socialist policies pursued by Saddam frightened the rulers of Kuwait and especially Saudi Arabia. Given their oppressive regimes their greatest fear was an internal uprising against the ruling elite.

By the summer of 1990, Saddam was experiencing trouble on several fronts. Not only were the Kurds in open revolt but the Shiite majority in the country also sought a greater voice in the country. Saddam also had been misled as to the position of the United States and the Soviet Union on the border dispute between Iraq and Kuwait. From conversations with US Ambassador April Glaspie and later with Secretary of State James Baker, Saddam convinced himself that while the United States was opposed to the use of force, it would take no action once an invasion was a *fait accompli*. Saddam also misread the events that had taken place in Russia. His ambassador to the Soviet Union had failed to keep Saddam apprised of the dire state of the Soviet economy and of Gorbachev's need for friendly relations with the United States. Instead of the usual stance of the Soviet government, which previously would have vetoed the United States resolution condemning the Iraq invasion of Kuwait, the Soviet Union added its voice to the condemnation. After moving the Iraqi army to its border with Kuwait, Saddam sent his negotiators to meet with the Emir of Kuwait. Either the Emir would submit to an unconditional surrender, or Saddam's army would move in. A few days later, on August 2, 1990, Saddam's army crossed the border and soon was in total control of Kuwait. Iraq now controlled 20% of the oil produced by the members of the OPEC cartel.

With an overwhelming international military force assembled against Iraq. Saddam offered to remove his troops from Kuwait if Israel vacated all the territory it had occupied during the Six Day War. It was Saddam's last effort to rally the other Arab nations to his cause in the hope that their anti-Zionist policies would focus their attention on their common enemy, Israel. On the other hand, the greatest fear that Bush faced was that Israel, if attacked, would retaliate. Iraq possessed Scud missiles capable of reaching Israel. Although the hard-line conservative Likud government was in power, Bush was able to convince Prime Minister Yitzhak Shamir to restrain Israel. To compensate for Israel's lack of defensive weapons against the incoming Scud missiles, the United States sent a huge airborne shipment of its Patriot missiles, designed to shoot down incoming Scuds. The Patriot missiles were the latest version of Reagan's Strategic Defense Initiative. While the Patriots enjoyed some success in demobilizing incoming Scuds, some got through, killing 31

Israelis and injuring 400. Israel's greatest fear was that Saddam would use poison gas. Although every Israeli was equipped with a gas mask, the principal deterrent came from Bush. Before the attack on the Iraqi forces began, Bush had warned Saddam that if he used chemical weapons he could expect the US to use its own weapons of mass destruction. The US possessed an arsenal of smart atomic weapons and that was enough to dissuade Saddam from the use of poison gas.

The war was over before it began. The initial bombardments in the middle of January 1991 destroyed most of the Iraqi air force on the ground. The land offensive finally began on February 24. The ground war was as lopsided as the war from the air; 300 Iraqi tanks were destroyed without the Americans suffering any hits on their tanks. Reagan's decision to double the defense budget over the eight years of his presidency had paid off.

General Norman Schwarzkopf planned to use part of the US-forces to drive the Iraqi forces out of Kuwait while the US-led coalition forces crossed into Iraq and surrounded the rest of Iraqi army. Everything went according to plan and had the coalition forces continued their advance one day longer, the entire Iraqi army would have been trapped. Instead, Bush called for a halt to all military operations and agreed to negotiate with Saddam, rather than insisting on an unconditional surrender.

In making that decision Bush was backed by Colin Powell, head of the Joint Chiefs, and Secretary of Defense Richard Cheney as well as Schwarzkopf. Two reasons were offered. First, going further would have exceeded the United Nations resolution, which called solely for the removal of Iraqi troops from Kuwait. Second, if US-led forces had marched onto Baghdad in order to remove Saddam from power, this action would have entailed street fighting and a huge increase in the number of US casualties. But there was a far more important reason why Bush ended the war when he did. In order to get King Fahd's permission to allow a half-million troops to be stationed in Saudi Arabia, Bush had to promise the King that Saddam would continue to remain in power. If Saddam's regime had been toppled, in the anarchy that would certainly follow the Shiite majority in Iraq might well have invited Iran to intervene and establish a second theocratic government, making it the most powerful force in the Persian Gulf region. Fahd, whose own regime rested on less popular support than that of Saddam, needed to maintain Saddam in power. With the exception of Iran and the Shiite population in Iraq, the majority of Muslims in the region followed the Sunni faith. Now that the US had decimated Saddam's army and air force, he no longer posed a military threat to the other nations in the region. For the Saudis, now America's major ally among the oil producing states, a weakened Saddam was far preferable to an alliance between the Shiites of Iraq and Iran.

For Bush, it was his moment of triumph. His ratings as President soared. The defeatist Vietnam syndrome had been broken. The United States had reestablished itself as the leader of the free world. The war was also good for the Republican Party, as many of those Democratic Senators who had vehemently opposed the decision to go to war were defeated for reelection.

A president receives credit or blame even though the events taking place are totally out of his control. Up until the last moment, when Gorbachev resigned the presidency of the Soviet Union, Bush must have assumed that Gorbachev was in control of the events taking place in Moscow. Bush was misled by the faulty information from the Central Intelligence Agency, upon which every president during the Cold War depended for accurate information about the Soviet Union and its intentions. Unfortunately, the agency had little understanding of events that were taking place in Russia. It possessed the latest and most sophisticate satellites to monitor Soviet military activities but its analysts were incapable of reading or interpreting events on the ground that were leading to the collapse of the Soviet economy. While one might now assess Glasnost and Perestroika as signs that the Soviet economy was in trouble, they interpreted it as signs of a thaw in Soviet-US relations. There were signals to indicate that Gorbachev's reforms were a last-minute effort to prevent the ship of state from sinking. The decision to withdraw Russian troops from Afghanistan; the construction of the pipeline to sell natural gas to Western Europe; the sale of East Germany to the West German Republic for $4 billion; the decision to grant the Baltic states their independence; the shakeup in the Politburo — every publicly reported event indicated that the Soviet system of state socialism was retreating. But the CIA, intended to be a source of reliable data, had instead developed into a secret and inept bureaucracy.

State socialism had been organized as a great hierarchy with layer upon layer of specialists with specific responsibilities. The result was a rigid structure that made change in any given sector dependent on change in others. Removing those at the top of the structure, either for inefficiency or corruption, did nothing to change the basic structure. Gorbachev and Yuri Andropov removed twenty percent of the governors and top administrators and replaced them with new bureaucrats, but nothing changed because the base remained intact. Gorbachev persisted in looking for solutions through modifying, rather than replacing, the structure. Bush supported him until the end.

The peace dividend that was supposed to follow the end of the Cold War never emerged. US outlays for defense were able to decline slightly but the increased costs stemming from social programs far outstripped any reductions in defense. The darkest moment in the presidency of Bush was when he reneged on his promise not to raise taxes, which had been the keynote to his 1988 campaign. The effort to control spending and achieve a balanced budget had been a priority for every post-war administration, beginning with Truman, and exists to the present day. As the Cold War continued to expand, it became more difficult for each succeeding administration to meet that goal. First, the excuse was the cost of the Vietnam War; this was followed by the oil crisis and the escalation in the price of a barrel of crude. Once the legislation of the Great Society was enacted, Congress paid no attention to the effect it would have in preventing a balanced budget. Nor did Congress understand that the driving force behind the nation's growing prosperity was the continuing and increasing budget deficits. Thus, when Reagan instituted his tax cut, followed by his increases in defense spending, a coalition of fiscally conservative Republican and Democratic senators, lead by Phil Gramm and Warren Rudman on the Republican side and Ernest Hollings from the Democrats, enacted in 1985 the Balanced Budget and Emergency Deficit Control Act. It was designed to bring the federal budget into balance by across-the-board reductions in federal spending once the federal budget exceeded the prescribed goal. Declared unconstitutional by the Supreme Court, the law was rewritten several times. In 1990, a revision was enacted that merely called for voluntary reductions in federal spending. Richard Darman, Bush's budget director, and John Sununu, his chief of staff, were strong advocates for bringing the nation's budget into balance as was the Democratic majority in the House and Senate. Since there was no possibility of reducing the mandatory spending programs or even attempting to cut into Social Security benefits, the only alternative was to raise taxes, promise or no promise. Bush was disappointed in his belief that Congress was capable of restraining government spending. Thanks to the Supreme Court decisions, the limits were merely goals and no longer mandatory.

The first indication that Bush was about to change his original stance was a meeting that took place at the White House between the Congressional leadership of both parties and Bush, Darman, Sununu, and Treasury Secretary Nicholas Brady. It was at that meeting that Democratic Senate Majority Leader George Mitchell forced Bush to admit that there were no preconditions to the discussion for the federal budget in fiscal year 1991. From that point on, it was no longer a question of whether there would be a tax increase but how much it would amount to and what form the tax increase would take. The reaction from the conservative wing of the Republican party was as expected. Bush was about to pronounce the death of Reaganism, which had produced seven years of continuous prosperity. Worse yet, with the midterm Congressional elections coming up in 1990, when the party in power generally loses seats in Congress, a tax increase would result in a loss of seats that would turn into a political disaster. With the October 1 deadline looming, when a budget had to be ratified by Congress or the country would shut down, Bush announced that he would veto any budget that called for a tax increase. It was pure bluster.

The following day, members of the administration and the leaders from Congress met in the Rose Garden of the White House to announce the compromise agreed upon. The proposed budget agreement called for cuts of $119 billion from entitlement and mandatory programs; $182 billion from discretionary programs, and a reduction of $67 billion in defense appropriations over a three-year period. It called for a cap on all discretionary spending and pay-as-you-go on all new programs initiated by Congress. On the negative side, it also sought a $134 billion tax increase to be raised by a gradual increase in gasoline taxes, starting the first year with a five-cent a gallon increase at the pump. Not only was it a regressive tax, disproportionately affecting the poor and lower middle class, but Bush's justification that it would decrease dependence on foreign oil imports was absurd. On September 30, Bush signed a continuing resolution that allowed the country to keep functioning until Congress ratified the proposed budget agreement. Led by House Republican minority whip Newt Gingrich, Republicans joined the House Democrats in rejecting the budget.

Bush, furious, vetoed the second continuing resolution in the hope that it would bring Congress to accept his budget proposal. Instead it resulted in a shutdown of the nation's non-essential facilities such the national parks and other recreational facilities. The public, more concerned with its own immediate needs than with what is taking place in Washington, often blames or praises the president for actions of others. With his administration under fire, Bush relented; on October 9, he signed the second continuing resolution. Over the next two weeks, the Democratic Congress passed the Omnibus Reconciliation Budget Act of 1990. The revenue that the regressive gasoline tax would have generated was replaced by raising the income tax for the upper brackets. Bush rationalized his defeat by stating that it would accomplish his goal of reducing government expenditures by a half-trillion dollars over the next five years. Of that $500 billion, $350 billion were in spending cuts, the largest amount ever proposed by Congress. Even though most Republicans, led by Gingrich, had voted against the legislation, the Republicans lost one seat in the Senate, eight seats in the House and two governorships.

While the Congressional Democrats were patting themselves on their backs for their fiscal austerity, the actual facts and figures belied their assertions. Begin with the promise to reduce defense expenditures by $67 billion over the next three years. In fiscal year 1991, the year the budget was enacted, Defense expenditures were $273 billion; in fiscal 1993, they had increased to $291 billon. Some might blame the increase on the cost of Desert Storm, but the war was over in 1991. The peace dividend from the collapse of the Soviet Union had yet to surface. Or take Human Resources, the single largest item in the federal budget. In 1991, the cost was $690 billon; by fiscal 1993, it had increased to $828 billion. (See Appendix, Table 4.) Every single category of government expenditures grew accordingly, including the revenues from the Social Security Trust Fund, which since the presidency of Johnson in 1967, had been used by succeeding administrations to disguise the amount of the government debt. In 1990, before Congress enacted its plan to reduce government expenditures, the federal debt amounted to $3.3 trillion; in fiscal 1993, it had increased to $4.4 trillion. (See Appendix, Table 5.)

Bush had risen to prominence in the party solely as a result of being Reagan's vice president. Reagan added him to the ticket because Bush was supposed to represent the moderate wing. But the group of people who constituted the moderate wing of the Republicans and their goals did not reflect the party's platform. Bush was neither a liberal nor a conservative; neither a Texan nor a Connecticut Yankee; neither a wimp nor a tiger. Most pertinent was the fact that he had virtually no experience holding elective office — only his one term as a Congressman. This was his fundamental handicap as president. Bush viewed himself as a statesman rather than a politician, when only a politician could have understood the intense rivalry that had emerged between the two political parties now that the Cold War had ended. Nor was Bush alone in not understanding this dramatic change. Its relevance had escaped the media as well. For 45 years the two political parties had set aside fundamental differences in philosophy to unite against the threat of the Soviet Union. Once that threat had disappeared, it was replaced by open warfare between the Democrats and the Republicans.

Epilogue: The Vanished Track

Strike me dead, the track has vanished,
Well, what now? We've lost the way,
Demons have bewitched our horses,
Led us in the wilds astray.

What a number? Whither drift they?
What's the mournful dirge they sing?
Do they hail a witches marriage?
Or a goblin's burying?

—Alexander Pushkin

Those lines of verse from Russia's greatest poet, used by Fyodor Dostoyevsky as the introduction to his most prescient novel, *The Possessed*, evokes not only the standard view of why the Soviet Union broke up, but the perplexity of America's leaders and economists as they try to fathom the new world without a Cold War.

The reforms instituted by Mikhail Gorbachev to revamp an outdated economic system not only led to its collapse but were destined to arrive at that outcome from their very inception. State socialism, or Soviet communism, was a well defined, rigid system that brooked no compromise with its basic thesis — i.e., the state controlled every aspect of the economic lives of its citizens. Since capitalism can take on some of the trappings of socialism when it deems it necessary, he assumed that Soviet communism could indulge in a similar approach. Instead it backfired. In place of reform there was confusion because Gorbachev was still wedded to the basic tenets of state socialism and Leninism-Stalinism. He was not prepared for the Soviet Union to espouse a free market economy since that violated one of the basic tenets of communism — guaranteed full employment. Nor was he about to abdicate the state's overall control and regulation of the economy. Gorbachev believed he could maintain the fundamentals of the Soviet economy while at the same time allowing for a certain degree of economic freedom. Both Glasnost and Perestroika were designed to allow a little fresh air into a system that until then had deliberately isolated itself from the capitalist world in order to avoid becoming infected by its ideas. He was an optimist. He had no idea how deeply the arteriosclerosis had affected the mindset of the Soviet leaders and the population. Nothing illustrates this better than the failure of the attempted coup by the very conspirators he had elevated to the Politburo. Having placed him and his wife, Raisa, under house arrest in a dacha for three days, none of the instigators knew what next to do. Under the old system, before Gorbachev had been elected president, there had been no problem. Khrushchev was eased out of his position as primus inter pares and retired to his dacha where he lived out the rest of his life. Now there had been an election, something entirely foreign to the system formerly in place. Unable to find an answer, they released him.

It was too late. Boris Yeltsin, whom Gorbachev had dismissed from the Politburo, stepped into the breach. While the world watched in utter amazement he climbed onto a tank, had the soldiers inside of it point the gun muzzle at the building housing the Central Committee of the Communist Party, and when its members refused to vacate it, had a shot from fired into the building. It produced the desired effect. With the leadership of the Central Committee dispersed, Yeltsin, who had previously headed the Moscow Soviet, the largest and most powerful of all the party organizations in the nation, had no problem taking advantage of the vacuum created by the house arrest of Gorbachev. Enormously popular with Muscovites, and with the country in confusion, Yeltsin exploited this opportunity by declaring himself president of the Russian republic, thereby challenging the very concept of the Soviet Union. At the beginning of December, the Ukraine voted for its independence. This was followed a week later by a meeting attended by Yeltsin, Ukrainian President Leonid Kravchuk and Stanislav Shushkevich, the leader of Belarus. All three agreed to dissolve the Union of Soviet Socialist Republics, and in its place, to establish a voluntary Commonwealth of Independent States. Not only had Gorbachev been sidelined; he had been end played. With the three largest and wealthiest republics of the former Soviet

Union having declared their independence, Gorbachev's title of president of the USSR was meaningless. On December 25, he tendered his resignation. The Soviet Union had lasted 70 years and the Cold War had lasted almost 50 years, and when both of them ended simultaneously, it was neither with a bang nor a whimper. The fantasy of Karl Marx, the dream of Vladimir Lenin and all the efforts by Joseph Stalin to create the first viable Socialist state evaporated. To President George H. W. Bush and the leadership in Congress, once it became clear that Yeltsin was determined to put an end to the Cold War through a mutual agreement to eliminate the threat posed by atomic missiles pointed at each nation, peace was finally at hand.

Once the threat of mutual destruction had been eliminated, it was time for the new Russian republic to undertake the next order of business: to convert the state socialist system to a free market economy and to establish the mechanisms of a democracy. The US rushed in with economists and lawyers from Harvard and other US institutions of higher learning to "advise" on reforms to the economic and legislative system. Anarchy set in. Managers of prosperous industries and other assets of the former Soviet Union attempted to privatize them, usually to the benefit of their own families. While efforts were made to privatize some of the businesses in the large metropolitan cities of Moscow and Leningrad, the rest of the Russian people living outside these major cities were confused and frightened by this sudden turn of events. Accustomed to the security of the Soviet system, even with all its limitations, they were ill prepared to face an unknown. Under the new democratic form of government not only was the Communist party alive and unwilling to give up its former perks, but a nationalistic party emerged, with strong tinges of anti-Semitism. Unlike in Western democracies, there was no presidential party. Instead, Yeltsin contended that he was president of all the people. With his choice of Vladimir Putin to replace him, a result of the Chechnya crisis, and Putin's seeming ability to stabilize if not control the situation in that part of Russia, Yeltsin turned over the reins of governing Russia to him. Putin has continued to follow the example set by Yeltsin and govern without heading a formal party.

Russia today reflects the ideals of pure democracy no better than does America, and is more transparent in its transgressions. Putin has used the office of the presidency to strengthen his grip on the nation by exercising control over the national media and appointing the formerly elected governors of the provinces. On the other hand, Putin is a realist. When he announced that the economy of Russia was equivalent to that of a Third World nation, he not only was stating a fact but was signaling what would be his first priority. Moving Russia from a controlled economy to a free market economy cannot be accomplished overnight or even in ten years. A new generation will have to emerge not only in Moscow and Leningrad but in the vast expanse of land that covers seven time zones and stretches from Russia's border with Poland to the Pacific Ocean. He is unwilling to follow blindly the United States in its foreign policies, nor does he wish Russia to become subservient to the European Union as it continues its expansion eastward; he views its efforts as an attempt to isolate Russia economically. With oil now liquid gold and Russia blessed with huge oil reserves, the country now has the income to make whatever transitions it wishes. The track that Russia followed for 70 years under the Communist system has vanished. What will replace it eventually is anyone's guess. Only one thing appears certain. It can't go back.

With the collapse of the Soviet Union, politicians led the American public to believe that a peace dividend soon would be forthcoming in the form of lower taxes and a balanced budget. Yet in the fifteen years that elapsed after the collapse of the Soviet Union, the national debt grew from $3.6 trillion to more than $8 trillion, and it shows no sign of declining either in the near or long term, especially with US military forces in Afghanistan and Iraq. Furthermore the growing debt, instead of becoming an albatross around the neck of the US economy, remains the root of our continuous prosperity. How this country has managed to eat its cake and still have it on its plate is the subject of this epilogue.

Ostensibly, Bill Clinton rode to the White House by focusing on the mantra, "It's the economy, stupid." To many Americans, this theme had a significance other than the one Clinton was emphasizing. Ross Perot, the independent candidate who amassed 19 percent of the vote, was only one of a number of successful US entrepreneurs who believed that the fundamental problem with the nation's economy was not the temporary economic slump but the continually growing national debt. They believed that if the deficit were allowed to continue unchecked, it would result either in the collapse of the capitalist system, at worst, or in leaving the unpaid bill to be shouldered by our children and grandchildren, at best. All of these successful entrepreneurs had built their fortunes on sound business practices. They assumed that, since a business could not continue to function year after year without balancing its books, neither could a nation

Nor is this concern limited to the national debt. The nation's trade deficit has resulted in a continuous decline in the value of the dollar on the international currency markets. While Clinton and the Democratic majority in both Houses of Congress possessed no solutions for the trade deficits, they did have an answer for reducing the nation's debt and bringing the federal budget into balance. With the Cold War over and the professional army capable of handling minor international problems, they reasoned, it was time to dismantle the defense programs instituted during the Reagan administration. His Strategic Defense Initiative could be put on the back burner; other areas of the defense budget could be trimmed as well. Most important of all, with the economy having emerged from the temporary recession, it was time for an across-the-board tax increase that would lead eventually to a balanced budget. Clinton's tax increase was passed despite vociferous Republican opposition. Two years later, in the Congressional mid-term elections of 1994, the American voters expressed their gratitude to the Democrats by installing the Republicans as the majority party in both houses of Congress. It was the first time the Republicans held that enviable role in 40 years. Even more galling to the Democrats was that it was not a temporary aberration but a lasting phenomenon. Over the next decade, the Republicans not only would hold onto both Houses of Congress, but in 2004 would increase their majorities. Furthermore, once the Republican Party had regained the White House in the 2000 election, the Clinton tax increases would be repealed and even larger tax cuts than those instituted by Reagan would be passed. Clinton had rationalized his tax increases by stating that the nation no longer was in a recession; President George W. Bush rationalized his tax cuts as a means to lift the country out of recession.

A recession in 2001? How was that possible? Over the last three years of Clinton's second term, the budget had shown an increasing surplus. Even in Bush's first year in office, despite the recession, the budget still showed a considerable surplus. (See Appendix, Table 6.) Most Americans believed that the economy finally was on the right track. The blame for the recession would be placed on the collapse of stock prices on the New York Stock Exchange and NASDAQ, the smaller stock exchange that serviced most of the start-up high-tech companies. Stocks on the NYSE lost 30% of their value and on the NASDAQ, as much as 80%. The consensus that emerged to explain the collapse of the value of securities on both exchanges was the unforeseen failure of so many of the Dotcoms, whose prospects were oversold and in turn whose stocks were overbought by the investing public. Not only is this explanation superficial but it defies all logic. The rise in stock prices that began in 1984, referred to as the beginning of the bull market, was a result of professional investors coming to realize the significance of the personal computer for the future growth of business worldwide. Whether these stocks were traded on the Big Board or the NASDAQ was immaterial.

To some on Wall Street this was a replica of the bull market that had begun in the early 1960s and lasted until the early 1970s when the US abandoned the gold standard and the oil crisis began. In that instance the boom followed the inventions of the transistor and the integrated circuit, which revolutionized the electronics industry, and was accelerated further by the emergence of the stock option and the spate of consolidations and mergers that followed. The institution of the conglomerate and the agglomerate was designed to increase the price of stocks because acquisitions add notable increases in volume and profit. But the aforementioned boom was peanuts when compared to the future of those companies in the forefront of the revolutionary Age of Information. The personal computer and all of its potential applications would affect every industry and business throughout the world. Many expected its future effects to be as far-ranging as those of the Industrial Revolution.

Fueled by the publicity surrounding those stocks that were leading the world into the Age of Information, the Dow Jones average had advanced passed the 3,000 mark by 1991. Over the next four years, the Dow continued to rise as the occasional investor reentered the market. In February 1995, the Dow passed 4,000. With the hundreds of mutual funds and brokerage houses realizing that a strong bull market was in the offing, they began to beat the bushes to ensnare the amateur who had never invested in securities. By November 1995, the Dow had crossed the 5,000 mark; less than a year later, 6,000; five months after that, 7,000; and five months later, in July 1997, 8,000. As the price of stocks on the NYSE and NASDAQ continued to grow at a dizzying pace, with more and more amateur investors now entering the market for the first time, the revenues coming into the Treasury from income tax returns increased proportionally. This was a direct result of the rising income of those selling the securities. It was neither the Clinton tax increase nor the efforts of the Republican Congress to hold down spending that resulted in the budget surplus in 1998, the first since 1969, but rather these new revenues. Beginning in 1995, the receipts from tax revenues was adding $100-billion-plus annually to the Treasury. By 1998, when the first surplus of $69 billion had been attained, the increase in yearly government receipts had increased to $142 billion. By fiscal year 2000, when the stock market craze hit its peak, with the Dow having passed 11,000 and approaching 12,000, and the NASDAQ having passed 5,000, the federal budget showed a surplus of more than $236 billion as treasury receipts advanced to $175 billion. The non-partisan Congressional Budget Office was projecting budget surpluses over the next 10 years.

Lost in the exuberance that followed this projection was a close analysis of the underlying reason for the surplus. Although the increased revenues coming into the Treasury as a result of the runaway bull market played a major role, far more important was the use of the surplus from the Social Security Trust Fund to balance the budget or reduce the deficit. (See Appendix, Table 6.)

Lyndon Johnson was the first president to use the surplus in the Social Security Trust Fund to bring down the deficit by sleight of hand. In his 1969 proposed budget, his administration added the receipts from the payroll tax, earmarked for Social Security, to general receipts. Every succeeding administration has done the same. Thus, the budget surplus shown in 1998, $69 billion, included the $99 billion surplus drawn from the Social Security Trust Fund. Likewise, the $125 billion surplus of 1999 was made possible by the addition of $124 billion from the Trust Fund. In 2000, when the surplus reached its peak of $236 billion, about $150 billion of that number came from the Fund. In 2,001, when the surplus declined to $127 billion, the contribution from the Fund was $160 billion.

The artificial nature of the Clinton years' surpluses is even more clear when we examine the GDP. While the GDP increased by $3 trillion under the eight years of the Clinton presidency as compared to its gain of $2 trillion under Reagan's two terms in office, the increased value of stocks on both exchanges during the Clinton years were beyond any reflection of the increase in the GDP. During the Reagan years, the Dow had doubled, moving from about 1,000 to 2,000. During the Clinton presidency, the Dow almost quadrupled, advancing from about 3,000 to almost 12,000, while the GDP had advanced only 50% more than under Reagan. In other words, the increased revenues coming into the Treasury were not the result of a massive growth in the economy but of the frenetic buying and selling on the two stock exchanges, as well the annual increased revenues from the Social Security Trust Fund. The bull market that began under Reagan continued under Bush and was out of control under Clinton, generating the revenue figures that led to the balanced budgets. It was not the economy, stupid, but the taxes paid by investment professionals and an expanding populace of investors, anxious to become instant millionaires, that generated the flow of income into the Treasury. Moreover, when the market showed signs that it had reached its peak in spring 2000, when it experienced its first serious decline, with investors continuing to buy and sell, the federal budget for fiscal 2001 still showed a surplus of $127 billion even though the receipts coming in to the Treasury were $37 billion less than in 2000. In this instance, it was the Trust Fund that made up the difference. On Wall Street, salesmen make money whether the investor is buying or selling. Going hand in hand with the explosion of stock prices were the growing number of mergers and acquisitions among corporations listed on the stock exchanges. This trend, which had begun in the late 1950s, and continued to accelerate with each succeeding administration, was a treasure trove for the investment banking firms and their legal consulting firms. The entire financial community and its support system were flying to the moon, and the public was being taken along for the ride. Had not the publicity surrounding those firms leading the world into the Age of Information drowned out any effort to view this revolution in context, the professional investors might not have lost all sense of reality. Once the amateur investor entered the markets, convinced that the purchase of securities could lead to his personal fortune, whatever logic existed in the system went out the window.

Behind the surge of unbridled optimism was the belief that Internet-related innovations would revolutionize retailing. On-line retail sales companies entail no investment in retail space or sales help. Furthermore, thanks to the credit card, retail transactions were simplified. Lost in projections for success was the cost of carrying inventory and of promotion. In the case of Amazon.com, which focused on books, there was no problem because books were sold on consignment. If they didn't sell, they were returned to the publisher. In most other industries, what you buy, you own. This simple fact led to the collapse of the majority of these start-up businesses. Where e-business was effective was among those retailers who possessed a large inventory for their retail establishments and could draw upon this supply to meet orders placed via the Internet.

It is only when viewed in the perspective of the 1990s that one can understand the rationale for this artificial boom. The most significant event that led to this madness was the collapse of the Soviet Union in 1991. This event signaled the dawn of a new era. The media was quick to announce that a peace dividend was in the offing. Their false assumption rested on the belief that with the threat of the Soviet military gone, defense expenditures would decline, leading to a balanced budget. But the budget deficits were not being created by defense expenditures; rather, the programs of the Great Society had ballooned, as described earlier. Furthermore, Americans sought a professional army so they wouldn't have to be subject to the draft; and maintaining a professional army is expensive.

However, neither the collapse of the Soviet Union nor the successful use of a professional military answered the question of how the US government could achieve a permanent balanced budget. The temporary increase in the value of stocks had not provided an answer. Instead, when the bubble finally broke, it led to the recession of 2001, a large increase in unemployment, and even greater deficits than under Reagan and the first President Bush. If not the stock market, then which elements of the US economy could provide the country with full employment, little or no inflation, and a balanced budget? Or does the US economy require consistent federal budget deficits to support simultaneously an aging public, with a continually increasing life span, and a growing number of young people entering the employment market annually? Finally, and even more important, what would happen to the American economy in the event other nations decide it is no longer in their economic interest to purchase US Treasury bonds, which pay the interest on our growing federal debt?

This brings up the second problem raised by Perot and the other self-made multi-millionaires — namely, America's continuing trade deficit with other major industrial nations, the result of a steady decrease in our domestic manufacturing facilities, and in turn, the loss of good-paying skilled labor jobs. Perot, as already noted, had served on General Motors' board of directors and understood the business philosophy of its key executives. When Clinton and the Republican Congress passed the

North American Free Trade Agreement (NAFTA), Perot predicted that there would be a mass exodus of good US jobs to Mexico, where labor rates are far less than those in the United States. Not only was his prognostication accurate, but while prior to NAFTA, the United States enjoyed a positive trade balance with Mexico, after NAFTA the trade balance was in the negative range.

The expansion of free trade to include Mexico and Canada was a continuation of a long tradition whose origins could be traced back to the Cold War, and was a major feature of the Bretton Woods agreement ratified by 42 nations in 1944. Free trade between nations enables their economies to grow as the number of markets available to their industries expands. Free trade is the very essence of capitalism since it permits competition to be the determining factor in the success or failure of a business. It can be cruel in the sense that it often results in the loss of jobs among those companies unable to compete, but it can be beneficial for the overall economy of a nation. It provides competitive companies with a larger market for their products, which in turn results in lower prices for the consumer, and increases employment to handle the expanding volume of the business.

There is no better example of how free trade can lead to the prosperity of many nations than the creation and development of the European Union. In 1967, Jean-Jacques Servan-Schreiber, the founder and publisher of *L'Express*, the first French newsweekly magazine, published a book entitled *Le Defi Americain*. A bestseller in France, it was translated into English and German and also enjoyed a large readership in translation. The title of the book translates as *The American Challenge*. The author's theme, heavily influenced by the ideas of French President Charles De Gaulle, was that unless Western European nations broke down their artificial trade barriers, especially those between France and Germany, they would be unable to compete with the economy of the United States. To Europeans, and especially to the French with their long-standing anti-German sentiment, Servan-Schreiber's thesis appeared unrealistic. On the other hand, the success of the European Coal and Steel Community, a joint venture with France, Germany and Belgium as participants, had been extremely successful. From that initial effort, over the next 30 years customs duties and other trade barriers gradually would be lifted, and a union of all Western European nations, including Great Britain, would evolve, with its own Parliament, its own justice system, and its own currency, the euro, introduced January 1, 1999. According to plan, within three years, the national currency of those member nations of the European Union that had opted for the euro would be phased out. The euro now was the official currency for almost all of Western Europe. What seemed impossible 30 years earlier had become a reality.

Following the demise of Soviet domination over the Eastern European nations, the economies of those countries evolved, some to the point where they have been admitted as members of the European Union. In 2005, the total population EU countries was larger than that of the United States; their gross domestic product exceeded that of the US; and the purchasing power of their currency was almost 20% greater than that of the US dollar. However, the standard of living of their citizens does not come close to matching that of Americans. There is a fundamental reason why their larger economy and its stronger currency do not translate into a better standard of living. Europe, where socialism was conceived and grew, in many ways remains loyal to its tradition of providing economic security for all of its citizens. In the same way that every person in this country who has contributed to the Social Security Trust Fund is eligible for its benefits, either because he or she is disabled or reaches the age of 62 or older, Western European nations, including Great Britain, also provide benefits for their citizens, but the benefits are far more generous. Not only do they include free medical and dental care, and pharmaceutical drugs, but also an elaborate pension system has been established for those permanently unemployed. To pay for this largesse from their governments, Europeans are heavily taxed, both on their personal incomes and on what they purchase. With the exception of food and beverages, a value-added tax is placed on all merchandise. Unlike US federal, state and city sales taxes, the value-added tax begins with the primary raw-material supplier and is added onto every stage of a product's development, until it is passed onto the consumer through the retailer. As a result, comparable merchandise in Europe is far more expensive than in the United States, inhibiting Europe's economic growth, reducing the purchasing power of its citizens, and effectively lowering their standard of living. Furthermore, because Europe is completely dependent upon imports of crude oil and natural gas, both of these products are heavily taxed by the government, especially gasoline at the pump

Despite the enormous growth in its overall economies and the prosperity that has followed, the EU has still not developed into an economic counter-force to the American challenge. The US economy with all of its weaknesses still remains the machine that drives the economies of the rest of the world. Believe it or not, the major factor in the US economy's continuing success is the massive trade deficit it accumulates with its trading partners. Despite the weakness of the dollar with respect to the euro or the British pound sterling, the United States still continues to have a negative balance of payments with Germany, France and Great Britain. These negative trade balances pale by comparison to those the United States has with China and Japan. This negative trade balance, which continues to grow every year (See Appendix, Table 3), has played a major role in the expansion of the US economy. Sourcing merchandise in low-wage countries not only has kept inflation down but also has increased the purchasing power of the American consumer.

The key to the success of the US economy is its consumer sector. Despite the growth and expansion of the EU, China and Japan, the United States still remains the single largest consumer market in the world. Moreover, the retail sector continues to grow as a percentage of the GDP while at the same time consolidating into fewer and more efficient operations. This vibrant retail economy, which enables Americans to possess the highest standard of living in the world, is fueled by several factors, in addition to imports. The expansion of consumer credit through the ubiquitous credit cards has played a major role. More important is the use of debt to sustain growth by both manufacturers and retailers. Finally, there is the growing indebtedness, not only of the federal government, but in many cases, of state and municipal governments.

This situation is made possible by the Almighty Dollar. Ever since it was determined at Bretton Woods that the dollar would be the official means of exchange for every other currency, the stage had been set for its dominant role in the development of the economies of the rest of the world. Although the actual value of the dollar was predicated on a certain weight of gold, the eventuality of the Cold War and the ensuing deficit spending needed to wage that war, had not been factored into that original decision. As a result, the number of dollars in circulation soon exceeded the supply of gold housed in Fort Knox, Kentucky. When the US Treasury no longer could redeem dollars for gold, by default the US dollar became the official currency of the world. As the number of dollars in circulation continued to increase over the next 35 years, there was no other currency that could replace it.

Should our leading creditor nations, China and Japan, abandon their support of our debt, and no other nations with a surplus of dollars take their place, the United States government would be forced into bankruptcy; the current value of the dollar would disappear, and along with it, the dollar reserves held by every other nation. But without an international currency capable of replacing the dollar, commercial transactions between nations would come to an abrupt halt, and the world would enter a depression that would make that of the 1930s seem like a picnic. In other words, because of the dollar's overwhelming presence in the economy of almost every other nation, the dollar has become the cement that binds the world's economies to each other. To paraphrase the words of Dr. Pangloss in Voltaire's famous satiric novel, *Candide*: for Americans, this is the best of all possible worlds. As long as nothing comes along to replace the dollar, Americans can eat their cake and still have it on their plate.

At the same time that America enjoys this unprecedented prosperity, it also has produced an unexpected backlash against what is viewed by many nations, even in Western Europe, as the arrogance of the world's only superpower. During the 50 years of the Cold War, the United States was seen by the non-Communist nations of the world as their protector. In their eyes it was only America's military prowess that contained the Soviet Union from expanding. With Russia no longer posing a military threat, the role of the United States as the leader of the free world no longer resonates to its former degree. The enormous outburst of anti-American feeling, partly generated by the US invasion of Iraq and other international interventions, is also a symptom of something far more profound. For better or for worse, most of the world's population no longer entertains the idea of a superpower that exerts its authority by virtue of its military power. Regardless of whether the war in Iraq was justified or not, we must recognize the end of an era. Whether we acknowledge it or not, the United States no longer leads the world. That track also has vanished.

Appendix

Table 1. Bretton Woods Agreements: Contributions to World Bank (in millions of dollars)

Country	Amount	Country	Amount
Australia	200	Iran	24
Belgium	225	Iraq	6
Bolivia	7	Liberia	.5
Brazil	105	Luxembourg	10
Canada	325	Mexico	65
Chile	35	Netherlands	275
China	600	New Zealand	50
Colombia	35	Nicaragua	.8
Costa Rica	2	Norway	50
Cuba	35	Panama	.2
Czechoslovakia	125	Paraguay	.8
Denmark	*	Peru	17.5
Dominican Repub.	2	Philippines	15
Ecuador	3.2	Poland	125
Egypt	40	South Africa	100
El Salvador	1	USSR	1,200
Ethiopia	3	United Kingdom	1,300
France	450	United States	3,175
Greece	25	Uruguay	10.5
Guatemala	2	Venezuela	10.5
Haiti	2	Yugoslavia	40
Honduras	1		
Iceland	1		
India	400	Total	9,100

**The quota of Denmark shall be determined by the Bank after Denmark accepts membership in accordance with the Articles of Agreement.*

Note: *Deposits were to be made 25% in gold (at the established rate of one ounce of gold equivalent to $35) or in dollars. The balance was to be made in each country's local currency at a specified rate to the dollar.*

Source: *The Avalon Project at Yale Law School*

Table 2. Bretton Woods Agreements: Contributions to International Monetary Fund (in millions of dollars)

Country	Amount	Country	Amount
Australia	200	Iran	25
Belgium	225	Iraq	8
Bolivia	10	Liberia	.5
Brazil	150	Luxembourg	10
Canada	300	Mexico	90
Chile	50	Netherlands	275
China	550	New Zealand	50
Colombia	50	Nicaragua	2

Costa Rica	5	Norway	50
Cuba	50	Panama	.5
Czechoslovakia	125	Paraguay	2
Denmark	*	Peru	25
Dominican Repub.	5	Philippines	15
Ecuador	5	Poland	125
Egypt	45	South Africa	100
El Salvador	2.5	USSR	1,200
Ethiopia	6	United Kingdom	1,300
France	450	United States	2,750
Greece	40	Uruguay	15
Guatemala	5	Venezuela	15
Haiti	5	Yugoslavia	60
Honduras	2.5		
Iceland	1		
India	400	Total	8,800

**The quota of Denmark shall be determined by the Bank after Denmark accepts membership in accordance with the Articles of Agreement.*

Note: Deposits were to be made 25% in gold (at the established rate of one ounce of gold equivalent to $35) or in dollars. The balance was to be made in each country's local currency at a specified rate to the dollar.

Source: The Avalon Project at Yale Law School

Table 3. U.S. Trade in Goods: Balance of Payment (BOP) Basis (in millions of dollars)

Year	Trade Balance	Percent Change	Exports	Imports
1960	4,892		19,650	14,758
1961	5,571	13.9	20,108	14,537
1962	4,521	-18.8	20,781	16,260
1963	5,224	15.5	22,272	17,048
1964	6,801	30.2	25,501	18,700
1965	4,951	-27.2	26,461	21,510
1966	3,817	-22.9	29,310	25,493
1967	3,800	-0.4	30,666	26,866
1968	635	-83.3	33,626	32,991
1969	607	-4.4	36,414	35,807
1970	2,603	328.8	42,469	39,866
1971	-2,260	-186.8	43,319	45,579
1972	-6,416	183.9	49,381	55,797
1973	911	-114.2	71,410	70,499
1974	-5,505	-704.3	98,306	103,811
1975	8,903	-261.7	107,088	98,185
1976	-9,483	-206.5	114,745	124,228
1977	-31,991	227.9	120,816	151,907
1978	-33,927	9.1	142,075	176,002
1979	-27,568	-18.7	184,439	212,007
1980	-25,500	-7.5	224,250	249,750
1981	-28,023	9.9	237,044	265,067

1982	-36,485	30.2	211,157	247,642
1983	-67,102	83.9	201,799	268,901
1984	-112,492	67.6	219,926	332,418
1985	-122,173	8.6	215,935	338,088
1986	-145,081	18.8	223,344	368,425
1987	-159,557	10.0	250,208	409,765
1988	-126,959	-20.4	320,230	447,189
1989	-117,749	-7.3	359,916	477,665
1990	-111,037	-5.7	387,401	498,438
1991	-76,937	-30.7	414,083	491,020
1992	-96,897	25.9	439,631	536,528
1993	-132,451	36.7	456,943	589,394
1994	-165,831	25.2	502,859	668,690
1995	-174,170	5.0	575,204	749,374
1996	-191,000	9.7	612,113	803,113
1997	-198,104	3.7	678,366	876,470
1998	-246,687	24.5	670,416	917,103
1999	-346,015	40.3	683,965	1,029,980
2000	-452,414	30.7	771,994	1,224,408
2001	-427,188	-5.6	718,712	1,145,900
2002	-482,297	12.9	682,422	1,164,720
2003	-547,296	13.5	713,421	1,260,717
2004	-665,390	21.6	807,536	1,472,926

Source: U.S. Census Bureau, Foreign Trade Division

Table 4. Human Resources vs. Defense Expenditures (in millions of dollars)

Year	Human Resources*	Defense**	Year	Human Resources*	Defense**
1960	26,184	48,130	1983	426,003	209,903
1961	29,838	49,601	1984	432,042	227,413
1962	31,630	52,345	1985	471,822	252,748
1963	33,522	53,400	1986	481,594	273,375
1964	35,294	54,757	1987	502,200	281,999
1965	36,576	50,620	1988	533,402	290,361
1966	43,257	58,111	1989	568,684	303,559
1967	51,272	71,417	1990	619,329	299,301
1968	59,375	81,926	1991	689,667	273,292
1969	66,410	82,497	1992	772,440	298,350
1970	75,349	81,692	1993	827,533	291,086
1971	91,901	78,872	1994	869,410	281,642
1972	107,211	79,174	1995	923,765	272,066
1973	119,522	76,681	1996	958,232	265,753
1974	135,783	79,347	1997	1,002,336	270,505
1975	173,245	86,509	1998	1,033,426	268,456
1976***	255,659	111,888	1999	1,057,717	274,873

1977	221,895	97,421	2000	1,115,481	294,495
1978	242,329	104,495	2001	1,194,409	305,500
1979	267,574	116,342	2002	1,317,437	348,555
1980	313,574	133,995	2003	1,417,707	404,920
1981	362,022	157,513	2004****	1,497,286	453,684
1982	388,681	185,309	2005****	1,566,477	450,586

* Human Resources include education, training, employment and social services; health includes Medicare and Medicaid; income security, Social Security; veterans' benefits and services.

** Defense includes the salaries and benefits paid to personnel in order to maintain a professional army as well as research and development and intelligence.

*** Reflects the decision by Congress to change the fiscal year from July1 to October 1, 1976.

**** Figures are estimates.

Source: Office of Management and Budget – Historical Tables for Fiscal Year 2005

Figure 1. World Nominal Oil Price Chronology: 1970-2005

This chronology was originally published by the US Department of Energy's Office of the Strategic Petroleum Reserve, Analysis Division. Updates for 1995-2005 are from the Energy Information Administration.

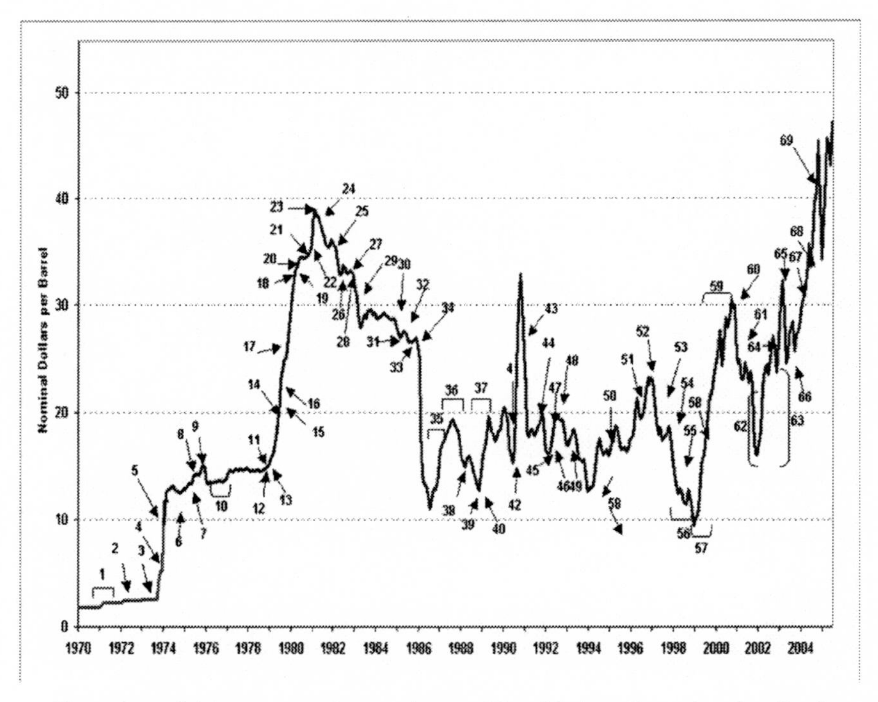

The price data graphed above are in nominal terms, i.e., they are in "dollars-of-the-day" and have not been adjusted for inflation.

Table 5. Gross Domestic Product vs. Gross Federal Debt (in billions of dollars)

Year	GDP	Debt	Year	GDP	Debt
1940	96.8	50.696	1973	1,311.0	466.291
1941	114.1	57.531	1974	1,438.9	483.893
1942	144.3	79.200	1975	1,560.8	541.925
1943	180.3	142.648	1976*	2,198.4	643.561
1944	209.2	204.079	1977	1,974.4	706.398
1945	221.4	260.123	1978	2,218.3	776.602
1946	222.7	270.991	1979	2,502.4	829.467
1947	233.2	257.149	1980	2,725.4	909.041
1948	256.7	252.031	1981	3,058.6	994.828
1949	271.3	252.610	1982	3,225.5	1,137.315
1950	273.2	256.853	1983	3,442.7	1,371.660
1951	320.3	255.288	1984	3,846.7	1,564.586
1952	348.7	259.097	1985	4,148.9	1,817.423
1953	372.6	265.963	1986	4,406.7	2,120.501
1954	377.1	270.812	1987	4,654.4	2,345.956
1955	395.9	274.366	1988	5,011.9	2,601.104
1956	427.0	272.693	1989	5,401.7	2,867.800
1957	450.9	272.252	1990	5,737.0	3,206.290
1958	460.0	279.666	1991	5,934.2	3,598.178
1959	490.2	287.465	1992	6,240.6	4,001.787
1960	518.9	290.525	1993	6,578.4	4,351.044
1961	529.9	292.648	1994	6,964.2	4,643.307
1962	567.8	302.928	1995	7,325.1	4,920.586
1963	599.2	310.324	1996	7,697.4	5,181.465
1964	641.4	316.059	1997	8,186.6	5,369.206
1965	687.5	322.318	1998	8,626.3	5,478.189
1966	755.8	328.498	1999	9,127.0	5,605.523
1967	810.2	340.445	2000	9,708.4	5,628.700
1968	868.5	368.685	2001	10,040.7	5,769.881
1969	948.3	365.769	2002	10,373.4	6,198.401
1970	1,012.9	380.921	2003**	10,828.3	6,760.014
1971	1,080.3	408.176	2004**	11,466.0	7,486.447
1972	1,176.9	435.936	2005**	12,042.4	8,132.945

** GDP includes additional revenues from July 1 to October1, 1976 when Congress changed the beginning of the fiscal year.*
*** GDP for fiscal years 2003-2005 are estimates. Federal debt for 2004-2005 are estimates.*
Source: Office of Management and Budget – Historical Tables for Fiscal Year 2005

Table 6. Budget Surplus/Deficit and Gross Domestic Product (in billions of dollars)

YEAR	TOTAL			OFF-BUDGET*			GDP
	Receipts	Outlays	Surplus or Deficit (-)	Receipts**	Outlays	Surplus or Deficit (-)	
1930	4.058	3.320	0.738				97.4
1931	3.116	3.577	-0.462				83.8
1932	1.924	4.659	-2.735				67.6
1933	1.997	4.598	-2.602				57.6
1934	2.995	6.541	-3.586				61.2
1935	3.609	6.412	-2.803				69.6
1936	3.923	8.228	-4.304				78.5
1937	5.387	7.580	-2.193	0.265	-0.2	0.267	87.8
1938	6.751	6.840	-0.089	0.387	-0.10	0.397	89.0
1939	6.295	9.141	-2.846	0.503	-0.13	0.516	89.1
1940	6.548	9.468	-2.920	0.550	-0.14	0.564	96.8
1941	8.712	13.653	-4.941	0.688	0.35	0.653	114.1
1942	14.634	35.137	-20.503	0.896	0.66	0.830	144.3
1943	24.001	78.555	-54.554	1.130	0.89	1.041	180.3
1944	43.747	91.304	-47.557	1.292	0.114	1.178	209.2
1945	45.159	92.172	-47.553	1.310	0.143	1.167	221.4
1946	39.296	55.232	-15.936	1.238	0.210	1.028	222.7
1947	38.514	34.496	4.018	1.459	0.303	1.157	233.2
1948	41.560	29.764	11.796	1.616	0.368	1.248	256.7
1949	39.415	38.835	0.580	1.690	0.427	1.263	271.3
1950	39.443	42.562	-3.119	2.106	0.524	1.583	273.2
1951	51.616	45.514	6.102	3.120	1.277	1.843	320.3
1952	66.167	67.686	-1.519	3.594	1.730	1.864	348.7
1953	69.608	76.101	-6.493	4.097	2.330	1.766	372.6
1954	69.701	70.855	-1.154	4.589	2.912	1.677	377.1
1955	65.451	68.444	-2.993	5.081	3.983	1.098	395.9
1956	74.587	70.640	3.947	6.425	4.972	1.452	427.0
1957	79.990	76.578	3.412	6.789	6.016	0.773	450.9
1958	79.636	82.405	-2.769	8.049	7.503	0.546	460.0
1959	79.249	92.098	-12.849	8.296	8.996	-0.700	490.2
1960	92.492	92.191	0.301	10.641	10.850	-0.209	518.9
1961	94.388	97.723	-3.335	12.109	11.677	0.431	529.9
1962	99.676	106.821	-7.146	12.271	13.535	-1.265	567.8
1963	106.560	111.316	-4.756	14.175	14.964	-0.789	599.2
1964	112.613	118.228	-5.915	16.366	15.734	0.632	641.4
1965	116.817	118.228	-1.411	16.723	16.529	0.194	687.5
1966	130.835	134.532	-3.698	19.085	19.715	-0.630	755.8
1967	148.822	157.464	-8.643	24.401	20.424	3.975	810.2
1968	152.973	178.134	-25.161	24.917	22.336	2.581	868.5
1969	186.882	183.640	3.242	28.953	25.204	3.749	948.3

1970	192.807	195.649	-2.842	33.459	27.607	5.852	1,012.1
1971	187.139	210.172	-23.033	35.845	32.826	3.019	1,080.3
1972	207.309	230.681	-23.373	39.907	36.857	3.050	1,178.9
1973	230.799	245.707	-14.908	46.084	45.589	0.495	1,311.0
1974	263.224	269.359	-6.135	53.925	52.089	1.836	1,438.9
1975	279.090	332.332	-53.242	62.458	60.440	2.018	1,560.8
1976***	379.292	467.767	-88.476	84.405	89.030	-4.625	2,198.4
1977	355.559	409.218	-53.659	76.817	80.716	-3.899	1,974.4
1978	399.561	458.746	-59.185	85.391	89.657	-4.266	2,218.3
1979	463.202	504.028	-40.726	97.994	99.978	-1.984	2,502.4
1980	517.112	590.941	-73.830	113.209	114.329	-1.120	2,725.4
1981	599.272	678.241	-78.698	130.176	135.196	-5.020	3,058.6
1982	617.766	745.743	-127.977	143.467	151.404	-7.937	3,225.5
1983	600.562	808.634	-207.802	147.320	147.108	0.212	3,442.7
1984	666.486	851.853	-185.367	166.075	165.813	0.262	3,846.7
1985	734.088	946.396	-212.308	186.171	176.807	9.363	4,148.9
1986	769.215	990.430	-221.215	200.228	183.498	16.731	4,406.7
1987	854.353	1,004.082	-149.728	213.402	193.832	19.570	4,654.4
1988	909.303	1,064.455	-155.152	241.491	202.691	38.800	5,011.9
1989	991.190	1,143.646	-152.456	263.666	210.911	52.754	5,401.7
1990	1,031.969	1,253.165	-221.195	281.656	225.065	56.590	5,737.0
1991	1,055.041	1,324.369	-269.328	293.885	241.687	52.198	5,934.2
1992	1,091.279	1,381.655	-290.376	302.426	252.339	50.087	6,240.6
1993	1,154.401	1,409.489	-255.087	311.934	266.587	45.347	6,578.4
1994	1,258.627	1,461877	-203.250	335.026	279.372	55.654	6,964.2
1995	1,351.830	1,515.802	-163.972	351.079	288.664	62.415	7,325.1
1996	1,453.062	1,560.535	-107.473	367.492	300.904	66.588	7,697.4
1997	1,579.292	1,601.250	- 021.958	391.990	310.626	81.364	8,186.6
1998	1,721.798	1,652.585	69.213	415.799	316.604	99.195	8,626.3
1999	1,827.454	1,701.891	125.563	444.468	320.778	123.690	9,127.0
2000	2,025.218	1,788.773	236.445	480.584	330.765	149.819	9,708.4
2001	1,991.194	1,863.770	127.424	507.519	346.838	160.681	10,040.7
2002	1,853.173	2,010.970	-157.797	515.321	355.652	159.659	10,373.4
2003	1,782.342	2,157.637	-375.295	523.842	363.009	160.833	10,828.3
2004****	1,880.279	2,293.006	-412.727	534.745	379.511	155.234	11.546.0
2005****	2,153.859	2,472.205	-318.346	577.476	402.211	175.265	12.290.4

** Social Security Trust Fund*
*** Revenues from the payroll tax*
**** Reflects the decision by Congress to change the fiscal year from July 1 to October 1, 1976*
***** Revised statistics from Historical Tables for Fiscal Year 2007*
Source: Office of Management and Budget – Historical Tables for Fiscal Year 2005

Table 7. Rate of Unemployment vs. Rate of Inflation (percent)

Year	Rate of Unemployment	Rate of Inflation*	Year	Rate of Unemployment	Rate of Inflation*
1948	3.8	8.1	1977	7.1	6.5
1949	5.9	-1.2	1978	6.1	7.6
1950	5.3	1.3	1979	5.8	11.3
1951	3.3	7.9	1980	7.1	13.5
1952	3.0	1.9	1981	7.6	10.3
1953	2.9	0.8	1982	9.7	6.2
1954	5.5	0.7	1983	9.6	3.2
1955	4.4	-0.4	1984	7.5	4.3
1956	4.1	1.5	1985	7.2	3.6
1957	4.3	3.3	1986	7.0	1.9
1958	6.8	2.8	1987	6.2	3.6
1959	5.5	0.7	1988	5.5	4.1
1960	5.5	1.7	1989	5.3	4.8
1961	6.7	1.0	1990	5.6	5.4
1962	5.5	1.0	1991	6.8	4.2
1963	5.7	1.3	1992	7.5	3.0
1964	5.2	1.3	1993	6.9	3.0
1965	4.5	1.6	1994	6.1	2.6
1966	3.8	2.9	1995	5.6	2.8
1967	3.8	3.1	1996	5.5	3.0
1968	3.6	4.2	1997	4.9	2.3
1969	3.5	5.5	1998	4.5	1.6
1970	4.9	5.7	1999	4.2	2.2
1971	5.9	4.4	2000	4.0	3.4
1972	5.6	3.2	2001	4.7	2.8
1973	4.9	6.2	2002	5.8	1.6
1974	5.6	11.0	2003	6.0	2.3
1975	8.5	9.1	2004	5.5	2.7
1976	7.7	5.8	2005	4.9	3.4

** Based on Consumer Price Index*
Source: U.S. Department of Labor, Bureau of Labor Statistics

Recommended Readings

Alter, Jonathan. *Nixon, A Life,* Washington, DC. Regnery Publishing, Inc. 1993..

Ambrose, Stephen E. *Eisenhower Soldier and President*, New York, Simon & Schuster, 1990..

Ambrose, Stephen. *The Triumph of a Politician, 1962-1972,* New York, Simon & Schuster, 1989..

Barnet, Herbert S. *George Bush, the Life of a Lone Star Yankee,* New York, A Lisa Drew Book, Scribner, 1997.

Bordo, Michael D. *The Gold Standard, Bretton Woods and Other Monetary Regimes: an Historical Appraisal: tables and figures* Washington, D.C. National Bureau of Economic Research, 1993.

Bourne, Peter G. *Jimmy Carter,* New York, A Lisa Drew Book , Trademark of Simon & Schuster, 1997.

Brinkley, Douglas. *The Unfinished Presidency, Jimmy Carter,* New York, Viking, 1998.

Burns, James MacGregor. *The Lion and the Fox,* New York, Harcourt Brace & Company, 1956.

Buttinger, Joseph. *Vietnam, a Political History,* New York, Frederick A. Praeger. 1968.

Califano, Joseph A. Jr. *The Triump;h and Tragedy of Lyndon Johnson,* New York, Simon & Schuster, 1991.

Cannon, James. *Gerald Ford's Appointment with History,* New York, Harper Collins Publishers, 1994.

Cannon, Lou. *Governor Reagan, His Rise to Power,* New York, Public Affairs, 2003.

Casserly, John J. *The Ford White House, Diary of a h Speechwriter,* Boulder, Co. Colorado Associated University Press, 1977.

Cummings, Bruce. *Korea's Place in the Sun: a Modern* History, New York, W.W. Norton, 1997.

Dallek, Robert. *An Unfinished Life, John F. Kennedy, 1917-1963,* Boston, Little Brown and Company, 2003.

Dallek, Robert. *Flawed Giant, Lyndon Johsnon and his Times, 1961-1973,* New York, Oxford University Press, 1998.

Davidson, Phillip B. *Vietnam at War, the History, 1946-1978,* Novato, Ca. Presidio Press, 1988.

Davis, Kenneth S. *FDR: The War President, 1940-1943,* New York, Random House, 2000.

Deutscher, L. *A Political Biography,* New York, Oxford University Press, 1949.

Dormani, Armand. *BrettonWoods, Birth of aMmonetary System* New York, Holmes &Meier, 1978.

Dugger, Ronnie. *On Reagan, The Man and his Presidency,* New York, McGraw Hill Book Company, 1983.

Ferrel, Robert H. *Harry S. Truman, A Life,* Columbia, Mo. University of Missouri Press, 1994.

Freidel, Frank. *Franklin D. Roosevelt, A Rendezvous With Destiny,* Boston, Little Brown and Company, 1990.

Goldman, Eric. *The Tragedy of Lyndon Johnson,* New York, Alfred A. Knopf, 1969.

Gorbachev, Mikhail. *On My Country and the World,* New York, Columbia University Press, 2000.

Hersh, Seymour. *The Dark Side of Camelot,* Boston, Little Brown and Company, 1997.

Hoare, James and Pares, Seison. *Korea an Introduction,* Keegan Paul International, London, 1988.

Hornby, Alonzo. *A Man of the People,* New York, Funk & Wagnalls , 1973.

Jordan, Hamilton. *Crisis, The Last Year of the Carter Presidency,* New York, G. P. Putnam's Sons, 1982.

Karsh, Efraim, and Rautsi, Inari. *Saddam Hussein, A Political Biography,* New York, The Free Press, 1991.

Kearns, Doris. *Lyndon Johnson and the American Dream,* New York, Harper & Row, Publishers, 1976.

Khrushchev, Nikita. *Khrushchev Remembers,* Boston, Little Brown and *Company,* 1970.

Kotkin, Stephen. *Armageddon Averted, The Soviet Collapse, 1970-2000,* New York, Oxford University Press, 1989.

Lasky, Victor. *J.F.K. The Man and the Myth, a Critical Biography,* New York, The MacMillan Company, 1963.

Lasky, Victor. *Jimmy Carter The Man and the Myth,* New York, Richard Marek Publishers, 1979.

Lyon, Peter. *Eisenhower, Portrait of the Hero.* Boston, Little Brown and Company, 1974.

Mackay, Sandra. *The Iranianas , Persia, Islam and the Soul of a Nation,* New York, Dutton, 1996.

Marx, Karl. *Das Kapital* 1872.

Marx, Karl and Freidrich Engels. *The Communist Manifesto*, 1848.

Mazo, Earl. *Richard Nixon: A Political and Personal Portrait*, New York, Harper & Brothers Publishers, 1959.

McCullough, David. *Truman*, New York. Simon & Schuster, 1992.

Medvedev, Roy. *Let History Judge, The Origins and Consequences of Stalinism*, New York, Columbia University Press, 1989.

Metz, Helen Chapin (Editor). *Iran, a country study*, Washington, D.C., Federal Research Division, Library of Congress, 1989.

Morris, Roger, *Richard Milhous Nixon, The Rise of an American Politician*, New York, Henry Holt and Company, 1990.

Nutting, Anthony, *Nasser*, New York, E. P. Dutton, 1972.

O'Souza, Dinesh, *How and Ordinary Man Became an Extraordinary Leader*, New York, The Free Press, 1997.

Pemberton William E. *Exit With Honor, The Life and Presidency of Ronald Reagan*, Armonk, N.Y. M. E. Sharpe, 1997.

Perret, Geoffrey. *Eisenhower*, New York, Random House, 1999.

Phillips, Kevin. *American Dynasty, Aristocracy, Fortunes, and the Politics of Deceit in the House of Bush*, New York, Viking, 2004.

Reeves, Richard. *A Ford not a Lincoln*, New York, Harcourt Brace Jovanovich, 1975.

Reeves, Richard. *President Kennedy, Profile in Power*, New York, Simon & Schuster, 1993.

Schweitzer, Peter and Rochelle. *The Bushes, Portrait of a Dynasty*, New York, Doubleday, a division of Random House, 2004.

Simon Seborg Montefiore. *Stalin, the Court of the Red Tsar*, New York, Alfred A. Knopf, 2003.

Simons, Geoff. *From Sumer to Saddam*, New York, St, Martins, 1994.

Stephens, Robert. *Nasser, a Political Biography*, New York, Simon & Schuster, 1971.

terHorst, Jerald F. *Gerald Ford and the Future of his Presidency*, New York, The Third Press, Joseph Opaka Publishing Company, Inc. 1974.

Volkogonov, Dmitri. *Stalin's Triumph and Tragedy*, New York, Grove Weiden, 1988.

Walleson, Peter J. *The Power of Conviction and the Success of his Presidency*, Cambridge, Ma. Westview, a member of Perseus Books Group; 2003.

Wicker, Tom. *George Herbert Walker Bush, A Penguin Life*, New York, A Liffer TM/ Viking Book, 2004.

INDEX

Printed in the United States
.60088LVS00004B/25-54